Florida A&M University, Tallahassee
Florida Atlantic University, Boca Raton
Florida Gulf Coast University, Ft. Myers
Florida International University, Miami
Florida State University, Tallahassee
University of Central Florida, Orlando
University of Florida, Gainesville
University of North Florida, Jacksonville
University of South Florida, Tampa
University of West Florida, Pensacola

RÉPUBLIQUE D'HAITI.

Nº *108*

NOUS, FABRE GEFFRARD,

Président d'Haïti,

Attendu que le sieur *H. B. Williamson* natif de *Maryland* âgé de *Cinquante ans* est habile à devenir haïtien, d'après l'article 6 de la Constitution ;

Attendu qu'il a déclaré devant le juge de paix de *Saint Marc* assisté de son greffier, qu'il est venu en Haïti, avec l'intention de s'y fixer, et qu'il a, en même temps, prêté entre les mains dudit juge de paix, le serment qu'il renonce à toute autre patrie qu'Haïti, ainsi qu'il est constaté par l'acte dressé au susdit tribunal de paix de *Saint Marc* en date du *dix huit novembre mil huit cent soixante et un* enregistré le *vingt-huit même mois*

Délivrons le présent acte de naturalisation conformément à la loi portant modification à l'article 14 du Code civil, au dit sieur *H. B. Williamson*

pour qu'il jouisse des droits attachés à la qualité de citoyen haïtien, et qu'il en supporte les charges.

Donné au Palais national de, *Port au prince*, le *31 Mars* mil huit cent soixante-*dix*, an 59.e de l'indépendance d'Haïti.

Geffrard

Par le

Certificate of Naturalization issued to Harry B. Williamson by the Republic of Haiti, November 18, 1861. Harry B. Williamson Collection, The Schomburg Center for Research in Black Culture. By permission of the New York Public Library, New York, New York.

Haitians and African Americans

A Heritage of Tragedy and Hope

Leon D. Pamphile

Foreword by Richard K. Seckinger

University Press of Florida

Gainesville · Tallahassee · Tampa · Boca Raton
Pensacola · Orlando · Miami · Jacksonville · Ft. Myers

06 05 04 03 02 01 6 5 4 3 2 1

Library of Congress Cataloging-in-Publication Data
Pamphile, Léon Dénius.
Haitians and African Americans : a heritage of tragedy and hope / Leon
D. Pamphile ; foreword by Richard Seckinger.
p. cm.
Includes bibliographical references (p.) and index.
ISBN 0-8130-2119-7 (cloth : alk. paper)
1. African Americans—Relations with Haitians. 2. United States—
Relations—Haiti. 3. Haiti—Relations—United States. 4. United States—
Race relations. 5. Haiti—Race relations. 6. African Americans—Civil
rights—History. 7. Blacks—Civil rights—Haiti—History. 8. Haiti—
Politics and government. 9. African Americans—Relations with
Haitian Americans. 10. African diaspora. I. Title.
E185 .P19 2001
305.896'07294—dc21   2001048077

The University Press of Florida is the scholarly publishing agency
for the State University System of Florida, comprising Florida A&M
University, Florida Atlantic University, Florida Gulf Coast University,
Florida International University, Florida State University, University of
Central Florida, University of Florida, University of North Florida,
University of South Florida, and University of West Florida.

University Press of Florida
15 Northwest 15th Street
Gainesville, FL 32611–2079
http://www.upf.com

This book is dedicated to
my parents, Pastor and Mrs. Devèse Pamphile,
my wife, Rozelle,
my children, Rose Ellen, Martine, and Frantz,
and my adviser and mentor, Dr. Richard Seckinger.

Contents

Foreword

Five centuries ago the African diaspora to the New World began. Men, women, and children were wrenched from their native communities in Africa and shipped in chains across the Atlantic to live out their lives in bondage on plantations in European colonies in the New World. Some ships took them to the Caribbean island of Haiti, while others scattered them along the Atlantic coastline of North America. This is the story of how these displaced Africans, despite formidable barriers of distance, language, and culture, found, within their mutual suffering and struggle for freedom, courage, dignity, and hope.

Europe's special interest in Haiti began when Columbus, on his maiden voyage, heard the exciting news from the natives that gold mines were in operation in the interior of their country. The Spanish and French planters realized, however, that the real wealth lay in Haiti's fertile valleys and plains. With slaves from Africa to provide cheap labor in their fields and merchant ships to transport their products to Europe, they felt confident their future was secure. By the end of the eighteenth century about half a million African slaves worked on Haitian plantations. While the plantation system developed in the English colonies later, the number of Africans held in bondage at this same time was almost as large. Brutal black codes, which legally sanctioned the slave owners' right to use whatever force they deemed necessary to control their enslaved Africans, were drawn up in both Haitian and English colonies. Perhaps the most vicious of these laws were those that made it a crime to teach African slaves to read and write. Floggings and/or fines were the prescribed punishments for those who attempted to spread literacy among these human beings in bondage.

At a time when the future for these African slaves appeared most bleak, European visionaries such as Montesquieu in France and Locke in England were dreaming of societies where liberty and equality were natural rights for their citizens. At last, enslaved Africans throughout the

New World dared hope that one day they too would be free and equal. As the shots for liberty at Lexington and Concord were heard around the world in 1775, so would be the salvos from the guns of the Haitian slaves as they began their battle for freedom in the 1790s. These shock waves even stirred Napoleon to action, but his troops who were dispatched to Haiti were powerless to quell the desire of these slaves to be free. When the slaves established their republic in 1804, Haiti became for the still-enslaved African Americans in the United States their great "sun of hope."

For African American leaders and newspaper publishers, the success of the Haitian slaves in crushing the forces of oppression and creating their own republic demonstrated convincingly that peoples of African ancestry were capable of creating and administering their own national state. Missionaries from the United States traveled to Haiti to establish churches and schools. Some African Americans, wishing to escape from oppression in the United States, emigrated to Haiti but, unprepared to deal with the problems confronting the new republic, returned home rather quickly. Amidst this excitement in the African American community, white Americans, bewildered over the success by the African slaves in Haiti and embroiled in an escalating slavery crisis of their own, refused to recognize the existence of the black republic. Sixty years would pass before Lincoln, in 1862, welcomed Haiti to the family of nations. Following the Civil War, Frederick Douglass, the great champion of equal rights for African Americans, was among the early ambassadors sent to represent the United States in Haiti.

The end of slavery in America coincided with the rapid acceleration of the industrial revolution. As the African slave trade came to an end, the new industrial powers increasingly devoted their energy to the exploitation of Africa's natural resources. In 1915, as the United States was expanding its economic power in the western hemisphere, its marines invaded Haiti, beginning, in the words of our author, "an imbroglio of the politics of race and color within the triangular relationships among Haitians, African Americans, and the United States government." African Americans saw clearly during the nearly two decades of military occupation "the spread of racism to Haiti, and the rape of the independence as an attack on the race."

In the eyes of many Westerners, such forceful intervention was acceptable since it was the "White man's burden" to assist the world's backward peoples. The Social Darwinists' classification of the world's races into five distinct groups offered further justification for Western political and economic dominance over the globe. Children's schoolbooks in the United States were quick to teach their new social philosophy. To the question, "What is known about the White Race?" students were to reply: "The white race is superior to the others and is found chiefly in Europe and North America." As was explained: "The Caucasian is the most intellectual and civilized race, and embraces the leading nations of the earth." The black race, however, was described as "ignorant and degraded," with some who "may be called savages."

When, in the 1920s, Haitians, reacting perhaps to such vicious racial characterizations, set in motion a renaissance in the arts to honor "the black man's unique achievements," African American poets, writers, and intellectuals flocked to Haiti to join in this movement. When Haitians celebrated the 150th anniversary of their independence in 1954, African Americans were also present.

Today, when Haitians seek political asylum in the United States, various African American political, religious, and humanitarian groups rally to help them. Dr. Pamphile's success in marshaling support among African Americans and Haitians for his literacy schools in Haiti is but another indication of the continuing and inspiring vitality of the centuries-old tradition of mutual support among the peoples of African descent in these two nations.

Richard K. Seckinger
Professor Emeritus, University of Pittsburgh

Acknowledgments

I am grateful to all who directly or indirectly provided their generous assistance to me in the course of my research during the last decade. I would like to acknowledge the diligence of Jane Schneider and Anita Johnson at the Pittsburgh Theological Seminary for their help in securing through interlibrary loan many texts that were not available in Pittsburgh. André Elysée assisted me at the Schomburg Research Center in Harlem, New York, in accessing many documents highlighting the linkages between Haitians and African Americans. I also owe a debt of gratitude to the staff of the Archives of the Episcopal Church in Austin, Texas, for access to the papers of James Theodore Holly.

It would have been most difficult to conduct this research without the help of the librarians at the Hillman Library of the University of Pittsburgh: Mary Scipone and Kevin Burell of the microfilm section and Ann Kenderson and Pearl Woolridge of the African American collection. Mary Sommerfield of the Carnegie Library of Pittsburgh, Pennsylvania, was also very helpful for interlibrary service.

I am grateful for the support and suggestions of the late Professor Rollo Turner and Professor Rolland Paulston of the University of Pittsburgh. Professor Lawrence Glasco of the history department of the University of Pittsburgh provided me with great assistance in giving shape to the orientation of the research. Special recognition is due Dr. René Piquion, one of the foremost scholars in the field of Afro-Haitian studies, for making his books available to me. It was, however, the friendship, steadfast encouragement, and untiring support of Dr. Richard Seckinger that brought me through the many years of conducting this research. He served as my adviser and reviewed and edited several versions of this manuscript. May he find here my special expression of gratitude.

I am also indebted to Dr. John Rogers, Mary Vesilich, Margaret Havran, Ronald Winkler, and especially Thomas Forgrave for their patient assistance in editing the manuscript at its various stages of development over the years. I am also grateful to my colleagues George Gensure and Stephen Populo for their assistance in formatting the manuscript.

May my wife of thirty years, Rozelle, my daughter Rose Ellen who took time to find and send me copies of many newspaper and magazine articles from New York, my daughter Françoise Martine and my son Frantz, my mother-in-law, Marie Françoise Joseph, who all have been supportive in their understanding, find here the expression of my deepest gratitude and abiding love.

Chronology

1492   December 6: Columbus lands in Hayti to establish the first Spanish colonial outpost in the New World.

1508   King Ferdinand of Spain sends first official cargo of African slaves to the New World.

1607   First permanent English settlement established in North America.

1619   Twenty African slaves arrive aboard a Dutch vessel in Jamestown, Virginia.

1697   Treaty of Ryswick; Spain recognizes France's claim to western part of the island.

1751   Makandal leads insurrection against the French.

1776   The thirteen English colonies declare their independence from England.

1779   France sends troops from Saint-Domingue to support Americans in War of Independence. Troops fight at Battle of Savannah.

1789   July 14: The Bastille is stormed.
         August 26: Declaration of Rights of Man and the Citizen.

1790   October: Ogé and Chavannes take up arms in the North to claim civil and political rights for freeborn men of color.

1791   August 22: Revolt of slaves marking the beginning of the Haitian Revolution.
         September: Toussaint Louverture joins slave revolt.

1792   French colonists with their slaves begin to emigrate to the United States.

1793   August 29: Sonthonax decrees liberation of slaves.

1797   March: Sonthonax appoints Louverture commander-in-chief of French forces.

1800   Gabriel Prosser, inspired by Toussaint Louverture, leads insurrection in Richmond, Virginia.

1801   Louverture adopts constitution and becomes governor for life of Saint-Domingue.

1802   Louverture betrayed and sent to France, where he dies.

1803   May 18: Haitian flag is adopted at Archaie.
        November 18: Battle of Vertières. French evacuate Cap.

1804   January 1: Haitian independence declared by Dessalines at Gonaives.
        May 20: Dessalines ratifies Haiti's first constitution as a free nation.

1806   October 17: Dessalines ambushed and killed at Pont-Rouge.
        February 17: Christophe proclaimed president of newly created State of Haiti in North.
        March 11: Pétion elected president of republic of Haiti.

1809   Second wave of French colonists settle in Louisiana.

1816   Robert Finley launches American Colonization Society to remove African Americans to Africa.

1818   Boyer becomes president of Haiti.

1822   After seeking help from Boyer, Denmark Vesey plans his insurrection.

1824   Dewey organizes first emigration of African Americans to Haiti.

1825   April 17: France grants independence to Haiti.

1829   Four Haitian women establish the world's first black religious community, the Oblate Sisters of Providence.

1831   Nat Turner rebels in Southampton County, Virginia.

1847   March 1: Soulouque elected president of Haiti.

1848   African American poet George B. Vashon moves to Haiti as correspondent of the *North Star.*

1854   James Theodore Holly, appointed commissioner at National Emigration Convention in Cleveland, meets with Soulouque in Haiti.

1859   January 15: Soulouque abdicates.
        January 18: Geffrard takes oath of office as president.

1860   March 28: Concordat between the Vatican and Haiti signed.

1861   First emigrants of second emigration movement leave for Haiti.
        Civil war over slavery erupts.

1862   United States recognizes Haiti's independence.

1863   William Wells Brown publishes *The Black Man: His Antecedents, His Genius, and His Achievements.*
        President Abraham Lincoln issues Emancipation Proclamation.

1869   Ebenezer Don Carlos Bassett appointed as U.S. minister to Haiti.

1874   Holly consecrated as first African American bishop of the Episcopal Church for Haiti.

1879   Salomon elected president.

1885   Anténor Firmin publishes *De l'égalité des races humaines.*

1889   Frederick Douglass appointed U.S. minister to Haiti.

1904   January 1: Centennial celebration of Haitian independence.

1909   NAACP founded to fight the wrongs of prejudice.

1915   July 28: U.S. Marines land in Port-au-Prince.
        August 11: National Assembly elects Dartiguenave president.
        August 21: Americans take charge of Haitian customs houses.

1919   Death of Charlemagne Péralte. End of Caco war in the North against American occupation.

1920   March: NAACP board of directors sends James Weldon Johnson to investigate reports of brutality by U.S. marines in Haiti.
        November 17: Georges Sylvain revives Union Patriotique as means of resistance to American occupation.

1922   February 11: Russell appointed American high commissioner.

1929   October: Student strike at Damiens followed by general strike.

1930   Vincent elected president.

1934   August 14: End of American occupation.

1937   October: Dominican massacre and deportation of Haitian citizens.

1946   Estimé elected president.

1949   Port-au-Prince International Exposition. Marian Anderson sings.

1950   May 10: Estimé deposed.
        December 6: Magloire inaugurated president.

1951   Walter White makes suggestion to Magloire of a five-year economic and industrialization plan for Haiti.

1954   Haiti celebrates Sesquicentennial Anniversary of Independence.

1956   December 12: Magloire deposed.

1957   October 22: François Duvalier inaugurated as president.

1964   April 1: Duvalier declares himself président-à-vie.

1971   January 22: Duvalier announces Jean-Claude will succeed him.
        April 21: Death of Duvalier.

1975   Drought hits northwest. Edward Brooke requests aid for Haiti.

1979   "Boat people" begin appearing in U.S. waters.

1980   Haitians and African Americans march in Washington to protest U.S. refugee policy.

1986   February 7: Jean-Claude Duvalier goes into exile in France.

1990   April: 50,000 Haitians take over Brooklyn Bridge to protest FDA regulation linking Haitians to AIDS.

December 16: Jean-Bertrand Aristide elected president with 67 percent of vote.

1994   May 8: Clinton appoints Gray to end Haitian crisis.

September 30: Jean-Bertrand Aristide ousted by army coup. Cédras heads junta.

September 18: Jimmy Carter, Colin Powell, and Sam Nunn reach agreement avoiding military conflict.

September 19: U.N.-sponsored invasion begins.

October 15: Aristide returns to Haiti.

1995   René Préval becomes president.

2000   Aristide reelected president.

Introduction

The people of Haiti, by reason of ancestral identity, and kinship, are far more interesting to the colored people of the United States than to all others. For the Negro, like the Jew, can never part with his identity [and] with his race. (1893)

Frederick Douglass, *Frederick Douglass Papers*

The linkages between Haitians and African Americans are rooted in the African motherland. These two peoples are bound by a deep sense of identity stemming from a shared heritage. Both were uprooted against their will from the African continent; both endured the journey across the Atlantic known as the "Middle Passage"; and both were scattered across the plantations of North America and the West Indies where they experienced, adapted to, and participated in developing dissimilar if not conflicting cultures.

This study seeks to demonstrate that, in spite of geographical and linguistic separation, Haitians and African Americans have remained connected throughout the centuries both by oppression and by a common struggle for freedom that make the peoples of the black diaspora what they are today.

The story of the enslavement and the uneven march to freedom of Haitians and African Americans began with Columbus's explorations in the western Atlantic. Though Columbus searched for a trade route to the East, instead he opened a trade route to a continent previously unknown to Europeans.

Columbus landed in Haiti and named it Hispaniola. That opened the door to exploitation of Haiti by the Spanish. As fortune seekers came to exploit the newly found gold mines and to cultivate the land, they enslaved the native Indians, forcing them to work in the mines and plantations. Following a century of forced labor and disease, the Indians of Hispaniola were virtually decimated.[1]

This decimation created a serious manpower shortage not only in the gold mines but also in the burgeoning sugar factories. The Spanish Crown identified the enslavement of African tribesmen as the solution to the labor problem. In 1502, the first slaves were taken from Portuguese Africa to Haiti. By 1540, the number had risen to 30,000 slaves in Hispaniola alone.

Supported by their government, French pirates and buccaneers took control of the island of Tortugas off the northwestern coast of Hispaniola. With the help of Bertrand D'Ogeron, a former pirate hired by the West India Company, they sought to conquer this part of Hispaniola from Spain. By 1697, Spain had tired of the war with the French and yielded the western part of the island in the Treaty of Ryswick.

Seeing that profit could be made on the island, English adventurers tried to break the Spanish and Portuguese monopoly. In 1607, three London Company of Virginia ships established the first permanent English settlement in the New World. In fewer than fifty years, there were more than 60,000 Englishmen in America.

The French and English needed laborers and found them first in indentured servants, people who contracted to work for a period of time in exchange for their passage. Since there were not enough people who wanted to be indentured in this way, the new conquerors turned to Africa for blacks to work in their sugar, coffee, and cotton fields.

As soon as Louis XIII authorized the shipping of human cargo, Atlantic traders flooded the colony with slaves. Displaced Africans would quickly outnumber the French settlers. In 1562, John Hawkins purchased Africans in Guinea and shipped 300 of them to slave owners in Hispaniola, becoming the first Englishman to enter the market for slaves. Soon the British would become the main supplier of slaves to the various European colonies throughout the Americas. Business boomed: In Virginia alone the number of slaves grew from 23,000 in 1725 to more than five times that number (120,000) in 1750, nearly equaling the white population of 173,000.[2]

By the end of the century, the slavery system was well integrated into the fabric of the social and economic life in both Saint-Domingue (Haiti) and the American colonies. In both colonies that system revolved around the sugar, coffee, and cotton plantations, with their attendant mills and factories. In both the American and Haitian (Hispaniolan) settlements, blacks were like chattel to be sold and transferred at the slaveholder's whim.

These barbaric measures only fueled the desire of both Haitians and African Americans to strike back. To seek their revenge, slaves poisoned the slave masters, the children of the slave masters, and the livestock. Slaves even poisoned other slaves just to reduce the available workforce. Evidence of this comes from stories about François MacKandal, a Vodou priest, who developed poisons from plants for use against slave owners. Slaves in New York in 1740 were accused of poisoning the water system, and in 1781, in South Carolina, newspapers warned that slaves had again begun the hellish practice of poisoning.[3]

When conditions became too intolerable, a slave could decide to run away. The threat of severe punishment did not deter the slaves from fleeing. Some of those who escaped established communities in the thickly wooded and mountainous areas of Saint-Domingue, where they grew crops, dug wells, and even built forts. In time, some of the settlements became so strong that colonial authorities negotiated and signed peace treaties with the former slaves.[4]

The struggle for freedom reached its greatest success at Saint-Domingue, where the Haitian Revolution led by Toussaint Louverture resulted in the creation of the first black state of the western hemisphere. This revolution evolved from a chain of sociopolitical events that took place both at the international and local levels. The American Revolution opened up the first crack in this long process as Saint-Domingue colonists beheld the example of American colonists fighting for freedom from a European mother country.

France decided in 1778 to give assistance to the American colonies in their revolution against the British. The following year the French sent a fleet of sixteen ships commanded by Admiral D'Estaing, a former Saint-Domingue governor. D'Estaing took his fleet first to the island for supplies. There he recruited 1,500 freedmen, blacks, and mulattoes to join his military command and arrived in Georgia in August 1779. Haitians fought alongside American revolutionaries against the British.

A decade later, revolutionaries in France announced their Declaration of the Rights of Man and the Citizen, proclaiming that "All men were born free and equal." They brought hope to the blacks of Saint-Domingue. In August 1791, the slaves began a mass rebellion, resisting the repressive laws of the *Code Noir*, attacking oppressors, and burning plantations. Within two months several thousand whites were killed; nearly 200 sugar plantations were destroyed; and most of the thousand coffee, cotton, and indigo settlements were ruined. The rebellious slaves paid a heavy price, as 10,000 slaves died.[5] Toussaint Louverture became both leader and spokesman for the slave insurrection, promising a new social order without slavery and a state controlled and administered by emancipated Africans.

Slave revolts spread fear throughout the French island so much that, beginning in 1792, colonists began fleeing the island.[6] Many took their slaves with them. Comte Laurent Caradeux, a member of the colonial assembly who owned a plantation at Cul de Sac near Port-au-Prince, fled with fifty slaves, settling near Charleston, South Carolina.

Others later went to the French colony of Louisiana where there were merchants in New Orleans who had traded at the Saint-Domingue city of Cap-Français. French émigrés also settled in the Atlantic port cities of New York, Philadelphia, Newark, Wilmington, Baltimore, and Norfolk.

Thomas Jefferson observed, "The situation of the St. Domingo fugitives (aristocrats as they are), calls aloud for pity and charity. Never was so deep a tragedy presented to the feelings of man." While he disapproved of any federal intervention, he thought individual states should provide assistance for those French émigrés. In a letter to Governor Morris, Jefferson said the United States received "the wretched fugitives . . . who escaping from the swords and flames of civil war, threw themselves on us naked and houseless, without food or friends, money or other means, their faculties lost and absorbed in the depth of distresses."[7] In 1794, the U.S. Congress showed compassion when a House of Representatives committee passed a resolution establishing a committee of relief that had funds available to support the oppressed from St. Domingo.

In August 1793, a new era began in Saint-Domingue when Léger Félicité Sonthonax, a member of the commission sent by the French Legislative Assembly to solve the slave crisis, officially declared the abolition of slavery. This declaration, later sanctioned by the assembly, was the turning point. With the way now cleared, Toussaint Louverture used his military insight and political shrewdness to strengthen the foundation of the newly gained freedom.

At the head of the army, Louverture was able to drive out the Spanish. Next, he took on the English, who suffered the severest defeat that had befallen a British expeditionary force between the days of Elizabeth and the Great War.[8] The English retreated to Jamaica.

Louverture then set about consolidating the newfound freedom by turning his attention to the colonial officials committed to the perpetuation of French rule. He removed Laveaux and Sonthonax, sending them back to France to represent the colony in the Council of Five Hundred, the French Chamber of Deputies. He later deported the general T. Hédouville, who had arrived as a French agent. Finally, he expelled Philippe Roume, Hédouville's successor, the last of a long string of French representatives sent out by the Directoire, putting an end to the power of the French in the colony.

Louverture then took on André Rigaud, a mulatto who ruled the southern part of the country and stood ready to assume control of the entire colony. Rigaud's designs on the supreme command interfered with Louverture's own plan. Civil war broke out. As a result of his victory, Louverture became the supreme leader of Saint-Domingue, and in 1801 he enacted a constitution that was a virtual declaration of independence from France, abolishing slavery, granting equal rights to all citizens, and appointing Louverture governor for life.

From the beginning, the United States sided with France. George Washington asked for assistance to help France maintain control over Saint-Domingue. Albert Galatin, who would become Jefferson's secretary of the treasury, described the American fear: "If they [the San Domingans] were left to govern themselves, they might become more troublesome to us, in our commerce to the West Indies, than the Algerines ever were in the Mediterranean; they might also become dangerous neighbors to the southern United States, and an asylum for renegadoes from those parts."[9]

The English were also concerned about the impact of Saint-Domingue on their own slave population. England even joined forces with the United States to counteract any possible transmission of revolutionary ideas, appointing General Thomas Maitland to work out an agreement providing "the measures deemed necessary for the security of the commerce of both nations and the tranquility of our Southern states and of the British West Indies."[10] The result was the Mutual Security Act of 1799. The two slaveholding nations agreed that their vessels would only dock in one or two ports on the island of Saint-Domingue until the situation was more to their liking.

The French and English attempt to keep news of the Saint-Domingue insurrection from their slaves was not successful. In 1795, a conspiracy was formed on the Louisiana plantation of Julien Poydras de Lalande to plan a general slave uprising throughout the parish of Pointe Coupée. Though it failed to materialize, Louisiana authorities tried and executed many slaves for their participation in the plot. A second insurrection broke out in 1811 on the plantation of Colonel Manuel Andry. Several hundred slaves descended on New Orleans, destroying both life and property.[11]

In Virginia, a report circulated that "Since the melancholy affair at Hispaniola, the Inhabitants of the lower country and especially this county have been repeatedly alarmed by some of their Slaves having attempted to raise an Insurrection, which was timely suppressed in this county by executing one of the principal advisors of the Insurrection."[12] The boldness of the slaves in Charleston, South Carolina, frightened the citizens. In 1793, news circulated that "the NEGROES have become very insolent, in so much that the citizens are alarmed, and the militia keep a constant guard. It is said that the St. Domingo negroes have sown these seeds of revolt, and that a magazine has attempted to be broken open."[13]

Though slave owners severely punished those who tried to revolt, the number of serious insurrections only increased, escalating the hysteria among southern whites. In 1800, Gabriel, slave of Thomas H. Prosser of Henricho County, Virginia, lashed out against white oppression. Born in 1776, he became a skilled blacksmith and learned to read and write. Gabriel viewed the events in Saint-Domingue as "a source of inspiration" and the exploits of Toussaint Louverture as proof the insurrectionary path could lead to liberation.[14] Gabriel drew up plans for slaves to take over Richmond, but authorities learned of the plans, and Gabriel and his associates were tried and hanged. Virginia governor James Monroe, in his report to the General Assembly in December 1800, recommended strict measures to prevent further insurrections.

Meanwhile, the Haitian Revolution faced serious threats from France. Napoleon Bonaparte reacted angrily to Louverture's actions. Pressed by émigrés who still dreamed of a prosperous Saint-Domingue with slave labor, Napoleon tried to remove Louverture from power and to reinstate slavery. He mobilized 60,000 soldiers to reconquer the island. The expedition, headed by Général de Division Victor Emmanuel Leclerc, reached Saint-Domingue in January 1802.

French forces captured Louverture. In April 1802, Bonaparte approved a decree to restore slavery in Guadeloupe and Saint-Domingue. The decree backfired when black and mulatto military leaders cooperating with

Leclerc realized that their own freedom was at stake. The imminent threat of reenslavement inflamed and excited the leaders as they joined the freedom fighters, crystallizing "a Haitian national identity."[15]

Under the leadership of Jean-Jacques Dessalines, an alliance of blacks and mulattoes was woven into the new blue and red flag that became the symbol for Haitian independence. Dessalines' army routed Napoleon's troops, who had been weakened by a yellow-fever epidemic. Leclerc, who promised to "wage a war of extermination"[16] to restore slavery, would soon die of yellow fever. His equally determined successor, Donatien Rochambeau, used killer dogs against the freedom fighters. He was unsuccessful.

On January 1, 1804, Haiti formally declared its independence from France. The Haitian constitution abolished slavery, providing that "no slave can be held on the Territory of the Republic."[17] Thus, after three centuries of slavery, Haitians had won their freedom.

1

Haiti: The Sun of Hope, 1800–1865

The negro was . . . a sheep-like creature, having no rights which white men were bound to respect; a docile animal, a kind of ass, capable of bearing burdens and receiving stripes from a white master without resentment or resistance. The mission of Haiti was to dispel this degrading and dangerous delusion and to give to the world a new and true revelation of the black man's character. This mission she has performed and has performed it well. (1893)

Frederick Douglass, *Frederick Douglass Papers*

As Haiti became an independent nation, news of her revolution reached the Caribbean and South America and filtered north through the vast plantations of the United States. Sailors and captains, newspaper reporters, and refugees to America all related the boldness of blacks in conquering slavery and reining in the rule of oppression. Haiti would soon become an icon of liberty on the world map. Loring Dewey, the white abolitionist and emigrationist leader, described the newborn nation as "the sun of hope for all the oppressed of Africa." Foretelling the role the Haitian Revolution would play in the struggle of people of African descent, he further added, "She has now burst the cloud, and will pour the full flood of her brightening influence upon their hard lot. In her liberty, they shall see liberty, and having seen, they will no longer be restrained from enjoying."[1] As African Americans became aware of the Haitian Revolution, its implications began to color their attitude and to shape their behavior as well. They came to perceive Haiti as the guardian of liberty. Thus ensued a crystallization whereby African Americans identified with the Haitians, even emulated them, in their own quest for freedom and self-determination.

The Haitian Revolution and the African American Predicament

African Americans' aspirations to freedom were in no way fulfilled by the American Revolution. African Americans embraced the Declaration of Independence, but the United States did not embrace African Americans. Even as blacks responded to the call of the Continental army and fought honorably on the battlefield under the American flag, their cry for human and civil rights ultimately fell on deaf ears. The American Revolution led to independent nationhood for whites, yet it did not bear the same fruit for African Americans. They were enslaved in the colonies, and those who became free as a result of their enlistment remained second-class citizens. The American victory was bittersweet.

The Fourth of July celebrations with their political speeches, fireworks, and revelry recall America's victory over the British in the Revolutionary War. African Americans found the festivities of Independence Day a harsh irony. In 1830, the Reverend Peter Williams expressed the blacks' sentiments: "While others rejoice in their deliverance from a foreign yoke, they mourn that a yoke a thousand fold more grievous, is fastened upon them. Alas, they are slaves in the midst of freedmen; they are slaves to those, who boast that freedom is the unalienable right of all."[2] Still, African Americans endured in the hope that they would one day share in the liberties promised by the Declaration of Independence. In this spirit, George Vashon expressed this hope from Haiti on July 4, 1848: "The land of Washington and of Franklin will soon be inspired to retrieve the inconsistency of seventy years by breaking every yoke, by loosening every fetter, and by speedily converting into a glorious reality that declaration whose living language, has ever been, in the light of its practice, a high-sounding, empty lie."[3]

By overcoming the contradictions of the American Revolution and extending freedom to all, the Haitian Revolution created a new vista for African Americans. Blacks and mulattoes in Haiti fought and established a state of their own. The status of Haitians was elevated following the Haitian Revolution; the status of African Americans, on the other hand, plunged as the fervor of the American Revolution faded. In the United States, the South held tightly to slavery. By extending the longevity of the slave trade by twenty years, effectively until 1808, the United States Constitution assured the continuation of slavery for southern slaveholders.[4]

For people of African descent, the Haitian Revolution had an even greater significance than either the American or French Revolution. The American Declaration of Independence proclaimed the equality of all men and outlined their inalienable rights, yet the rights of slaves were conspicuously denied. Subsequently, the French Revolution reaffirmed these rights in the Declaration of the Rights of Man and the Citizen in 1789. Even after this declaration, however, the practice of slavery persisted in the French colonies. The Haitian Revolution fulfilled man's universal aspiration to be free by including people of African descent.

Professor T. G. Steward observed in a study of the three revolutions that, while the American Revolution transformed dependent colonies into an independent state, and the French Revolution ended the monarchy and brought Napoleon to power, the Haitian Revolution was unique in that it provoked a "prodigious social cataclysm. . . . The old Saint Domingo [sic] came to a complete end, and a new social as well as political entity came into being with the establishment of a new state." The Haitian Revolution, he reasoned, is the "special heritage of the Negro race."[5]

The newfound independence of Haitians did not go unnoticed by African Americans who drew parallels between the Haitian experience and their own quest for self-determination. Freedmen in the United States fought to make these aspirations of liberty a reality. In the South and Northwest, laws denied blacks the right to vote, serve on juries, or testify against whites, and denied blacks the right of assembly. Conditions were better in the Northeast, though blacks were prohibited from casting ballots in five northeastern states—New Jersey, Connecticut, New York, Rhode Island, and Pennsylvania—between 1807 and 1837.[6] Yet Pennsylvania afforded more liberal protection to blacks, especially in Philadelphia where a black elite arose highlighting "the fears and aspirations of the city's black community," and eventually extending their influence to the national level.[7]

Despite their limited rights, free African Americans prospered economically in both the South and the North. They were able to take advantage of the labor shortage and build up businesses that served both whites and blacks. In Philadelphia, "Sizeable numbers of blacks were carpenters, tailors and dressmakers, brick makers, shoemakers and bootmakers, and cabinet makers."[8] With an improved socioeconomic status and better education than either the free African American or slave populations elsewhere, the Philadelphia elite spearheaded the movement for independence.

The African American political-independence movement did not seek absolute autonomy, but rather a measure of freedom of self-expression and determination so that blacks might build separate institutions within American society. It was the dream of a nation within a nation, "the search for independence on the part of individuals and the effort to forge institutions on the part of groups of persons."[9] Inspiration came from Phyllis Wheatley, who arrived from Africa in 1761 and established herself as one of the best poets in the colonies, and scientist Benjamin Banneker, astronomer, farmer, mathematician, and surveyor and publisher of his *Almanac*, containing weather forecasts and astronomical information.

The quest for independence gave rise to the establishment of mutual-benefit orders and religious institutions for the promotion of self-help. In 1787, Richard Allen and Absalom Jones, ex-slaves who had purchased their freedom, with six others formed the Free African Society for mutual help. The society aimed "without regard to religious tenets . . . to support one another in sickness, and for the benefit of their widows and fatherless children."[10]

Religious practices demonstrated an even greater spirit of independence. The first African American Baptist church was formed in South Carolina during the 1790s. Later Allen founded the African Methodist Church, leading to the creation of various black institutions of higher education, including Wilberforce in Ohio, Allen University in Columbia, South Carolina, Paul Quinn College in Waco, Texas, and Morris Brown College in Atlanta, Georgia. Bishop Daniel Alexander Payne, educator and historian of the African Methodist Episcopal (A.M.E.) Church, affirmed that the foundation of the church "has thrown us upon our own resources and made us tax our own mental powers both for government and support."[11]

That same determination also gave birth to the black press when, in 1827, John B. Russwurm and Samuel Cornish set up the *Freedom's Journal*. The editors expressed their intentions clearly: "We wish to plead our own cause. Too long have others spoken for us."[12]

African Americans sensed the connection between their endeavor for self-determination and the Haitian experience. Bishop Payne, the historian of the A.M.E. Church, described the impact of Haitian independence on the church's own movement: "As the Haytians have completely thrown off the white man's yoke in their national affairs, so have the leaders and members of the A.M.E. Church in ecclesiastical affairs. As the Haytians have been endeavoring to demonstrate the ability of the Negro for self-government during a period of over eighty-four years, so also have the leaders of the A.M.E. Church been endeavoring to demonstrate the ability of the Negro for self-government during a period of seventy-two years."[13]

The first-generation Haitian immigrants from Saint-Domingue made a direct and invaluable contribution to African American freedom in antebellum America. In Philadelphia, the center of Haitian immigrants, Moreau de Saint-Méry, a consummate historian on Saint-Domingue, set up a printing press and a bookstore that would become a meeting point for exiled intellectuals in the city. Political activist Tanguy de la Bossière also settled in Philadelphia, where he continued to publish his *Journal des revolutions de la partie française de Saint-Domingue* for French émigrés. Striving to influence political developments in Saint-Domingue, these refugees founded organizations and sent representatives to France with their requests.[14]

People of color and blacks from Saint-Domingue also formed their own political organization in Philadelphia, the *Citoyens de couleur de Philadelphie*, trying to make their voice heard in France in order to further their cause. The white population feared an imposing group of mulattoes and slaves, whose revolutionary ideas and insurgencies might spread to the American slave population.[15] Whites also believed the group's presence would politicize the city's free blacks, realizing that these refugees would give "Negroes a first hand story of how black men of the West Indies had righted their wrongs."[16]

The 500 slaves brought to Philadelphia with refugees from Saint-Domingue continued to fight for their cause and heightened the awareness of African Americans. They claimed they were entitled to freedom by virtue of the general emancipation decree issued by Sonthonax in Saint-Domingue in August 1793. With support from the Abolition Society, they succeeded in gaining the freedom of 456 San Domingan slaves between 1793 and 1796.[17]

In Baltimore, first-generation Haitian immigrants advanced the African American cause for independence through education. Baltimore lacked public schools for black children until two years after the Civil War. Father Joubert, a French Sulpician priest who had lived in Saint-Domingue, encountered the illiteracy of both Haitian and African American children during catechism instruction. "The class, begun in French thirty years before for literate San Domingo colored people, was by now being conducted in English. But French or English, the descendants of the San Domingo refugees, as well as the American colored children, found it an enigma. Deprived of a chance to learn to read through the absence in Baltimore of schools for their race, they had to learn it by heart from others at home."[18]

Father Joubert established a religious community to correct the lack of educational opportunities for black and colored children. Four courageous Haitian women led the community: Elizabeth Lange, the founder of the religious order, and Marie Magdelene Baas, Marie Rose Boegue, and Marie Therese Duchemin. In 1829, they established the Oblate Sisters of Providence, the world's first black religious community. They also founded and supervised the School for Colored Girls under the direction of the Sisters of Providence, Baltimore, Maryland, to help eliminate illiteracy. The school taught "reading, writing, French, English, arithmetic, all kinds of fine sewing, embroidery, bead work, and gold work, geography, music, and washing and ironing."[19]

In a letter of October 2, 1831, Roman Catholic pope Pius VII commended the community for its efforts. During this period, the school won praise for its work "for the education of the colored people of the District and of the country at large. For many years it was the only colored school within reach of the colored people of the District and it was there that many of the first well-trained colored teachers were educated for their work in the Capital."[20]

Students from other cities, especially Philadelphia and Washington, D.C., attended the Oblates' school. Two women who trained at the Oblate Convent School, Martha Costin and Arabella Jones, later founded successful schools for African American children in the District of Columbia.

The Oblates soon became a national institution, with missions and schools in St. Louis, Missouri, and Charleston, South Carolina. In Kansas City, both boys and girls attended Oblate schools. In 1830 Marie Annie Barclay became the first African American woman to be received into the ranks of the Oblates.

The Haitian presence was particularly strong in Louisiana. Several thousand refugees who had earlier settled in Cuba following the defeat of the French expeditionary forces sailed into New Orleans in 1809 on American ships. The Spanish Crown expelled them from Cuba when Napoleon launched his assault against Spain and forced the abdication of the royal family. The refugees went to Louisiana on account of the French presence there. Governor William Claiborne appealed to Washington in order to admit the slaves brought in by the refugees. Based on the lists of passengers reported at the mayor's office by the captains who came from Cuba, the overall number of refugees stood at 2,731 whites, 3,102 people of color, and 3,226 slaves. These people of color and slaves doubled New Orleans' black population and gave the city the highest percentage of nonwhites in its history.[21]

In New Orleans, first-generation Haitian immigrants contributed significantly toward the ability of African Americans to develop their own institutions. Haitian editors and publishers continued to exercise their profession in Louisiana. San Domingans also had an impact on business and agriculture. They helped revive the lagging agriculture of Louisiana, which, under Spanish rule, had declined to the two main crops of cotton and tobacco. Even the cultivation of sugarcane introduced from Saint-Domingue by Jesuit fathers languished until the migration of the émigrés. Jean Etienne Boré, a man of color from Saint-Domingue, spurred the sugar industry to greater productivity. In 1795 he discovered a successful method for manufacturing sugar by granulating the syrup. Boré led a collective effort, tapping the experiences of both white and black émigrés, that revolutionized the industry.

Emigrés from Haiti prospered in their trades. They amassed fortunes, which they returned to the community through acts of philanthropy. Such was the case of Thomy Lafon, a financier who accumulated extensive properties and contributed to both charitable and patriotic causes. Another example is Julien Déjour, born in Aux Cayes, Haiti, whose success in the slate roofing trade enabled him to give generously to the "white, the black and the yellow."[22]

Perhaps the most distinctive contribution by a San Domingan emigrant was that of John James Audubon, whose work as one of the world's greatest ornithologists benefited the entire nation. Born on May 4, 1780, in Aux Cayes, Haiti, Audubon was the child of French Naval Lt. Jean Audubon and a Creole woman. After his mother was killed in a slave revolt, he spent his boyhood in Nantes, France, and then moved to Pennsylvania to manage his father's estate. It was there that he became fascinated with birds. In 1821, he went to New Orleans as an art instructor. His works include *An Account of the Habits of Birds in the United States* (1826), *Birds of America* (1838), and *Quadrupeds of America* (1846). His work as an ornithological illustrator is unsurpassed.[23] Audubon societies are established in all parts of the United States.

In spite of the limitations on their citizenship, Haitians contributed to the military defense of Louisiana. Under the French, Louisiana enlisted the First Battalion of Free Men of Color who helped fight the Natchez Indians in 1731. In light of the superb performance of black soldiers, General Andrew Jackson formed a second battalion commanded by Joseph Savary, a Saint-Domingue free man of color who was a distinguished officer in the French army. Savary enlisted 256 immigrants on December 19, 1814, to form the Second Battalion of Free Men of Color. Savary, who became Negro Staff Officer for the battalion, "had the unique distinction of being the first Negro man appointed to the rank of second major in the United States Army."[24] Major Savary led the Haitians in the battle of the plains of Chalmette against the English during the war of 1814–15.

When the free Haitian emigrants came to Louisiana, they formed a new social hierarchy that was separate from the slave class of African American blacks. As they reconstructed their lives in Louisiana and other places in America, Haitian immigrants were able to maintain their past social structure. Unlike the rest of the United States, Louisiana had developed a social hierarchy similar to that found in Saint-Domingue. A three-caste system was prevalent there, made up of whites, people of color, and slaves. French was a common language and Catholicism a common religion.[25]

Although they adjusted to their new circumstances, first-generation Haitian immigrants resisted assimilation into American culture, creating their own newspapers and establishing educational institutions where their own language and culture were taught. They also intermarried along caste lines.

Because of their education and more extensive experience with freedom, first-generation immigrants became leaders in the black community. James Pitot, an exile from Saint-Domingue, was the first mayor of American New Orleans. Elsewhere, Haitian immigrants Louis Mirault, Joseph Dubergier, and Andrew Morel all prospered in a Savannah tailoring business. They also owned valuable real estate. In Baltimore, the Chatards provided a line of physicians in their family unbroken since Dr. Francois Pierre Chatard arrived from St. Domingo in 1797.[26]

The Haitian Revolution and African American Self-Esteem

Self-esteem, or the need to achieve, to be competent, and gain approval and recognition, occupies an important place in the scale of human fulfillment. Chattel slavery had adversely affected the self-esteem of both Haitians and African Americans, reducing their place in society to the level of beasts. On the fifteenth anniversary of the Female Benevolent Society of Troy, New York, the Reverend Henry Highland Garnet, a political activist, focused attention on the degradation of his people. He had been born a slave in Maryland, escaping to New York, where he became a Presbyterian minister and a leader in the black community. When he looked at African descendants in America, he saw bartered men and women who were sold and mortgaged; women yoked with the horned cattle to till the soil; young men brutalized in intellect with manly energies chilled by the frosts of slavery.[27] Whites pounded the psyches of African Americans with the myth of their inherent inferiority. They trampled underfoot the African Americans' need to gain approval and recognition.

The Haitian Revolution proved to be a catalyst for raising African Americans' self-esteem. William Watkins, a black abolitionist and editor of the *Frederick Douglass Papers*, made this very point at an 1825 meeting of African Americans in Baltimore. In his view, the Republic of Haiti "assumed a character which, we trust, she will maintain, with that dignity and honour that will furnish an irrefragable argument, to prove to her enemies, that the descendants of Africa never were designed by their Creator to sustain an inferiority, or even a mediocrity, in the chain of beings."[28] The Haitian Revolution helped boost the morale of African Americans during their dark age of slavery. O. L. Holly reiterated the message: "If considered without prejudice, no revolution furnishes so much matter to arrest attention, and compel men to pause and ponder, as that of St. Domingo; and by none has the vigor of human nature . . . been so strikingly exemplified."[29] White abolitionists also recognized that the Haitian Revolution exercised a cathartic influence on the African American psyche. For emigrationist Loring Dewey, "It removed a heavy reproach from the whole, and will compel their oppressors everywhere to feel that they possess the high energies of human nature, of which they have so long attempted to deprive them."[30]

Vermont Aurora likened the Haitian independence movement to principles penetrating where armies cannot—passing "overseas, mountains and deserts, free as the progress of the wind, and extended as the bounds of the horizon." These principles have "thrown the blacks of St. Domingo into notice."[31]

Those African Americans who visited Haiti returned to tell stories of the celebrated island. Robert Douglass Jr., a native of Philadelphia and an antislavery reformer, witnessed the Haitian independence celebration. Douglass described the joy of the Haitian emancipation. "The sight of what these people have arisen to from the most abject servitude, caused in my bosom a feeling of exultation which I could not repress."[32]

The overwhelming impression of the reality of freedom likewise hit home for George Boyer Vashon, correspondent for the *North Star*. He described the experience of his first trip in 1848: "It would be impossible for me to describe the rapture with which I beheld for the first time, this land, unpolluted by the foul stain of slavery, upon which the insults and the cruelties of the tyrant had been washed out in the blood of himself and his children. During almost the entire day, I remained keen in a lent contemplation of those magnificent broad lands—Nature's own bulwarks, thrown up to hurl back the invader from this soil of freedom."[33]

In the eyes of African Americans, Haiti had claimed its rightful place in the world order of the nineteenth century. Haiti had a liberal constitution, and African Americans were gratified that it stood among the first of the free, enlightened, and prosperous republics. As well, they considered Haiti to be a flourishing nation in the arts. The editor of the *Colored American* (1836) commented that, "In morals and in literature, Hayti takes the lead of all the South American Governments and in literature, she will favorably compare with our own, at the same age of independence."[34]

In the United States during this time, though, whites did not share the benefits of the American Revolution with blacks, believing in the myth of Negro inferiority. Whites opposed all attempts to educate African Americans, insisting that blacks lacked the mental capacity to be equipped to function as citizens.[35] With their high academic performance in France, Haitians proved this myth to be a lie and boosted African American self-esteem. Dr. John S. Rock, a medical doctor and lawyer, and the first African American attorney admitted to the bar of the U.S. Supreme Court, witnessed the achievement of the Haitian Mr. Faubert in winning the Sorbonne's highest prize, along with two other Haitians, and was impressed. "Have the brawlers about negro inferiority," he asked, "forgotten that, a few months since, three black gentlemen—Messieurs Faubert, Dupuy, and Delva, from Hayti—took all the prizes at the reunion of the colleges of France?"[36] In his estimation, Haitians compared favorably with the best scholars on the continent of Europe.

Haitians remained conscious of their revolution and shared its advantages with other oppressed peoples. The gates of the country were opened to all people of African descent: "All Africans or Indians and their descendants, are able to become Haytians." Haiti's founding fathers took the necessary steps in the country's constitution to preserve the national territory exclusively for people of African descent: "No white man, whatever be his nationality, shall be permitted to land on the Haytian territory, with the title of master or proprietor, nor shall he be able, in the future, to acquire there either real estate or the rights of a Haytian."[37]

Haiti began the nineteenth century with the conviction that it had rehabilitated the black race. Mark Baker Bird, a Methodist minister in Haiti from 1839 to 1879, noted that the great principle upon which the glory of Haiti was founded made clear that "Independence is the dignity of the black man."[38] Haitian leaders became the defenders of the black race against oppressors. They fulfilled that task in intellectual, diplomatic, and political arenas. When Henri Christophe became king of Haiti, he articulated this policy in a speech on November 29, 1818: "We will confound the calumniators of our race by proving ourselves in no respect inferior in moral and physical powers to the other inhabitants of the Globe, and by showing that we are capable of acquiring and practicing the sciences and the arts and attaining to an equal degree of improvement and civilization with Europeans."[39]

By 1820, Haiti's population was made up of island natives, foreign agents, merchants, and traders. Haiti had become "a place of refuge to all persons of those classes, who either have, or suppose themselves to have, reason to be dissatisfied with their own country; and the capital . . . is the place of principal resort, especially on first emigration," according to Charles Mackenzie, the British consul in the island.[40] Haiti, indeed, had an open door policy that beckoned the oppressed.

Since Haiti had become a symbol of black self-government during the nineteenth century, African Americans wanted to identify with this nation. They expressed their pride in Haiti by giving its name to their own communities. African Americans in Pittsburgh, for example, called a section of their city "Hayti."[41]

African Americans named their children in honor of Haiti. Martin Robinson Delany was a cofounder of the *North Star* with Frederick Douglass and fought in the Civil War. His marriage to Kate H. Richards resulted in eleven children whom he named after prominent individuals, two after Haitian leaders, to instill in his children pride in their race and color. His first son was named Toussaint L'Ouverture, and the fifth was named Faustin Soulouque, after the late Haitian emperor.[42] Likewise, one of James Theodore Holly's sons was named Joseph Geffrard after the Haitian president Geffrard.

Honoring the official abolition of slavery in New York State in 1827, a special service was held in Albany. The Reverend Nathaniel Paul, pastor of the African Baptist Society in Albany, praised the progress of the emancipation movement and anticipated the day when slavery would be abolished forever. This hope was grounded mainly in the "indefatigable exertions of the philanthropists in South America, the catastrophe and exchange of power in the Isle of Hayti."[43] The Haitian offered hope for the liberation of African Americans in the United States.

The Haitian Revolution also helped raise African Americans' self-esteem by shattering the racist myth of black docility. It gave African Americans a hero and a role model with Toussaint Louverture. African American historian William Wells Brown described Louverture as a remarkable man known beyond Saint-Domingue. He asserted, "Without being bred to the science of arms, he became a valiant soldier, and baffled the skill of the most experienced generals that had followed Napoleon . . . He possessed splendid traits of genius, which were developed in the private circle, in the council chamber, and upon the field of battle. His very name became a tower of strength to his friends and a terror to his foes."[44]

Alexander Crummell, a Black Nationalist leader born in New York City and educated at the Free American School, viewed Louverture as a statesman, a general, a hero, and a historical figure. Crummell became a minister in the Episcopal Church, worked as a missionary in Liberia, and embraced abolitionist activities. He described Louverture as "one of the

ablest commanders of the age: a man for whom the highest notes of min-
strelsy have been struck; around whose name and history all the attrac-
tions of romance have hung."[45]

By proclaiming Saint-Domingue's autonomy, Louverture thwarted
Napoleon's grand design of a French empire in the New World, playing a
decisive role in integrating Louisiana into the United States. Newspapers
published accounts of Louverture's military prowess. Antislavery proponents used him as a living example of blacks managing the responsibilities of citizenship. Wendell Phillips, the radical abolitionist leader who
was known as "the modern Demosthenes," compared Louverture to Napoleon, Cromwell, and Washington in his "Eulogy of Toussaint Louverture." In Phillips's view, because of Toussaint Louverture, "the Negro
race, instead of being that object of pity or contempt which we usually
consider it, is entitled, judged by the facts of history, to a place close by
the side of the Saxon."[46] Louverture was the soldier, the statesman, the
martyr, Phillips thought.

African American Defense of the Haitian Revolution

After the 1804 Haitian proclamation of independence, foreign colonialist
powers openly tried to squelch the independence movement, fearing it
might spread. They isolated Haiti from the rest of the world, branding it
a country of outcasts. The French led the offensive against liberty in
Haiti, applying diplomatic pressure to isolate Haiti. In a diplomatic statement in 1805, the French foreign minister, Charles-Maurice de Talley-
rand, urged the American government to stop trading with Haiti: "The
existence of an armed Negro people, occupying places that they have de-
spoiled by the most criminal acts is a horrible spectacle for the white
nations; all of them should feel that, by allowing them to continue in that
state, they are sparing incendiaries and assassins. There is no reason
strong enough for private individuals of a loyal and a generous government to aid brigands who have declared themselves the enemies of all
governments."[47] Complying with the French demand, Congress quickly
passed a law prohibiting Americans from trading with Haiti. This law was
reenacted in 1807 and 1808.

In subsequent years, the United States resumed trade with the island,
yet ignored all pleas for its recognition for over half a century. In 1822,

the editor of the *Colored American* argued for Haitian recognition on the basis of its commercial importance. In 1835, Haiti surpassed many European powers, accounting for $1,815,812 of American exports and $2,347,556 of imports. Italy, in contrast, had $285,941 of exports and $1,457, 977 of imports. Although the Haitians had secured independence, with a constitution and laws modeled after the United States, "We have, at one Session after another, of our National Legislature, taxed our wits, for excuses not to acknowledge Hayti."[48]

To African Americans, the refusal of the United States to recognize Haiti defied all logic. In 1853, the Colored National Convention in Rochester raised the question, "Why does not the American government recognize the independence of Hayti whose trade is only surpassed in value by two other nations, with whom they are connected in commerce?"[49] African Americans persisted in calling for recognition.

Because of Haiti's economic importance, Haitian president Jean-Pierre Boyer echoed these sentiments. Boyer, a mulatto who was educated in France, took part in the war of Haitian independence and became president of Haiti in 1818. He was able to unite the island following the deaths of Pétion and Christophe. After the death of Dessalines, the founding father, Pétion and Christophe had squared off in a civil war over the rights of succession. As a result, the country was divided. Boyer argued that Hayti was of great importance in the scale of commerce. "It is hoped that time and experience, enlightening governments upon their true interests, and destroying all the prejudices founded on trifling and absurd considerations, will produce the reign of a wise and reasonable policy, and will cause the governments to feel the necessity of acknowledging the independence of the Queen of the Antilles."[50]

The fear that Haitians might negatively influence African Americans precluded the possibility of any rapprochement between the United States and Haiti. Senator Thomas Hart Benton of Missouri summed up the American position: "The peace of eleven states will not permit the fruits of a successful negro insurrection to be exhibited among them. It will not permit black ambassadors and consuls to . . . give their fellow Blacks in the United States proof in hand of the honors that await them for a like successful effort on their part."[51] Recognition was denied Haiti even though the United States had granted similar status to the recently liberated Latin American nations of Colombia, Chile, Argentina, and Mexico.

Nineteenth-century African American leaders interpreted the hostility of the American government toward Haiti as a pervasive attitude toward all people of color. When they considered their own dealings, they felt that the United States "has never proved itself anxious or even willing to do us even-handed justice, but to do us all injury and inconvenience in its power." They felt that the same "tyrannical and despotic spirit" energizing the government against their cause extended to Haitians. Explaining his position on this point, the editor of the *Frederick Douglass Papers* asserted that "The Negro hating disposition of the General Government is also seen in its ungenerous dishonorable and despicable conduct toward Liberia and Hayti, both free and independent nations with all the appliances of national existence, and both have an important and valuable commerce. Indeed Hayti is master of a commerce, which the United States can ill afford to lose. Notwithstanding all this, the United States Government has steadily and persistently refused to acknowledge their independence, and bid them an honorable welcome to the family of nations."[52]

In spite of the hostility of their government, African Americans were committed to helping Haiti gain recognition. When King Charles X of France finally took the lead in granting recognition to Haiti (1825), African Americans expressed great satisfaction. In Baltimore, they commemorated the event. "Success to the Republic of Haiti. May her sons ever wear the laurel wreath of virtuous liberty, and her daughters the robes of innocence," affirmed Mr. E. Brown. Echoed H. A. Webb, "Well may Haytiens say: Though surrounding nations look with scorn upon the Tree of Liberty, planted in our isle, yet Heaven protects it, and its branches are gloriously spreading, to overshadow the land."[53] In the same vein, William Watkins addressed a meeting of "colored people" in Baltimore's Camden Street with this statement expressing his interest in and perceptions of Haiti:

Of all that has hitherto been done in favour of the descendants of Africa, I recollect nothing so fraught with momentous importance—so pregnant with interest to millions yet unborn—as the recent acknowledgement of Haytien Independence, by one of the European Powers, under whom the African population of that island had long groaned in the most abject bondage. It is this circumstance, and the consideration of the important consequences likely to result to a people for whom we feel deeply interested, that have produced in our hearts those emotions of gratitude which we now offer as a feeble tribute of praise to Him who is the Sovereign Ruler of the Universe.[54]

Other African American abolitionists also rose to defend the Haitian Revolution. John Browne Russwurn, the second African American college graduate in the United States, discussed the Haitian Revolution during his commencement address at Bowdoin College in Brunswick, Maine, in 1826. Russwurn proclaimed that the "degraded man will rise . . . to claim his right." In his view, Haiti stood as a living example of this vision. He declared, "The Revolution in Hayti holds a conspicuous place. The former political condition of Hayti we all doubtless know. After years of sanguinary struggle for freedom and a political existence, the Haytiens on the auspicious day of January first 1804 declared themselves a free and independent nation. Nothing can ever induce them to recede from this declaration."[55] He praised Haiti's heroes who "showed to the world that though slavery may benumb, it cannot entirely destroy our faculties."[56]

Following his commencement address Russwurn heralded the Haitian example as a motivational force for African Americans. In 1827, he joined abolitionist editor and minister Samuel Cornish in establishing the first black newspaper in the United States. In the inaugural editorial, they emphasized the struggle against slavery and discrimination: "We would not be unmindful of our brethren who are still in the iron fetters of bondage." They said their efforts to break loose from ignorance and degradation were inspired by "the establishment of the Republic of Hayti after years of sanguinary warfare; its subsequent progress in all the arts of civilization."[57]

Russwurn and Cornish had already taken precautions to defend Haiti from false allegations, noting, "We caution the dissatisfied and envious in this country, who are continually forging 'News from Hayti,' to desist from their unmanly attacks upon a brave and hospitable people. Were our readers as well acquainted with their motives for venting their spleen as we are, they would give as little credit to their fabrications."[58] The editors of *Freedom's Journal* pledged to their readers to provide correct information concerning the state of affairs in Haiti.

African American support of the Haitian Revolution had by no means nullified the significant differences between Haitians and African Americans. The conflict is implicit in Molefi Kete Asante's affirmation that "All African people participate in the African Cultural system although it is modified according to specific histories and nations."[59] Divergent geographical settings and contrasting cultural assimilation often resulted in marked dissimilarities between these two peoples. While Haitians adopted Latin culture, African Americans embraced Anglo-Saxon trends; Haitians cultivated their French cultural affiliations, while African Americans valued English culture more.

This conflict explains the ambivalence historian Brenda Plummer, author of several studies on Haiti, described between these two peoples: "Black Americans' sentiments toward Haiti from the nineteenth century through the early years of the occupation thus swung between the poles of expectation, pride, and missionary zeal on the one hand, and embarrassment, despair and irritation on the other."[60]

Dessalines, the founder of the nation, established a military-style regime that prevailed throughout the nineteenth century. He used his unbridled power and all available resources to transform the nation into an armed camp. He put those who were loyal to him in defeating the French expeditionary army in charge of various regions of the country. Because of this policy, militarism became an integral part of Haitian life, as was a propensity for uprisings and political instability. Some African American leaders distanced themselves from the bloody militarism of Haitian life.

African Americans actually disapproved of militarism. During his stay in Haiti, Robert Douglass found that "The military throughout the island hold the superior power." Though he praised the soldiers, he also said he was "too much of a peace man to approve of military government."[61] Other African American leaders who stayed in Haiti also denounced the political turmoil. Benjamin Hunt, a seventeen-year resident of Haiti, identified militarism as "the greatest bar to industry, and therefore to the general progress of Hayti."[62] It instigated factions, destroyed property, and kept the people from their work.

As correspondent for the *North Star*, George Vashon also denounced Haitian militarism, devoting two reports to the June 1848 uprising against the government of Faustin Soulouque. He described how "fierce clouds, freighted with dread elements of civil war, hung lowering over this unhappy country, threatening to deluge its highlands and savannas with fraternal slaughter."[63] Because of this, Vashon changed his mind about becoming a Haitian citizen and wrote, "The unsettled state of that country deterred me from carrying out my intention of becoming a citizen thereof; and I was, in consequence, debarred from the exercise of practicing my profession there."[64]

James McCune Smith, a Scottish-educated, New York–born physician, espoused the Haitian Revolution, but without the bloodshed. He cited the Haitian Revolution, and Toussaint Louverture in particular, as proof that African Americans were not inferior to whites. In 1841, he delivered his *Lecture on Haytien Revolution*, affirming that Louverture overthrew "an error which designing and interested men had craftily instilled into the civilized world, a belief in the natural inferiority of the Negro race." To Smith, the Haitian leader demonstrated that "Even with the worst odds against them, the race is entirely capable of achieving liberty, and self-government."[65] Smith also argued that these revolutions constituted an epoch worthy of the anxious study of every American citizen.

Smith tried to write a balanced account, explaining the horror stories that spread across the United States. Despite the bloody deeds witnessed in Saint-Domingue, blacks were not vicious, he wrote. "I place emphasis on these facts in order to endeavor to disabuse the public mind of an attempt to attribute to emancipation the acts of retaliation resorted to by the Haytians in imitation of what the enlightened French had taught them."[66] Reacting to the white attitude featured in a series of articles entitled "Massacres of St. Domingo," Smith tried to show that blacks handled citizenship with both restraint and responsibility. The action of the Haitians did not equal the atrocities committed on them by the French.

James Theodore Holly, whose life became closely connected with Haiti, had similar reservations. Born in 1829 in a Washington, D.C., that was inhospitable to African Americans, Holly moved with his parents to Brooklyn, where there was a larger black presence. He became a shoemaker while continuing his studies, then became an Episcopalian priest called as rector to a church in New Haven, Connecticut. Holly became both leader and educator in the black community, as well as promoter of emigration to Haiti.

In his 1857 lecture "A Vindication of the Capacity of the Negro Race For Self-Government," Holly defended "an abused race" caught between the downright prejudice and "this woeful distrust of his natural equality, among those who claimed to be his friends."[67] Like Smith, Holly praised Louverture as a leader who, "by the evident superiority of his statesmanship, has left on the pages of the world's statute book, an enduring and irrefutable testimony of the capacity of the Negro for self-government, and the loftiest achievements in national statesmanship."[68] Holly focused on Haitian independence as practiced by Dessalines, as well as the signs of progress, self-government, and stability on the island. He firmly believed Haiti stood at the forefront by making "a name, and fame for us, that is imperishable as the world's history."[69] Holly highlighted the "self-possession of blacks" in the Haitian Revolution as evidence of their ability to govern themselves. He promoted the belief that Haitians and African Americans had the ability to govern themselves.

Holly regarded Haiti as an indispensable element in the struggle for black freedom. He provided the following interpretation of Haiti's role for African Americans: "And if we were to be reduced to the dread alternative, of having her historic fame blotted out of existence, or that celebrity which may have been acquired elsewhere by all the rest of our race combined; we should say preserve the name, the fame, and the sovereign existence of Hayti, though everything else perish . . . Let the names and deeds of our Nat Turners, Denmark Veazeys, Penningtons, Delanys, Douglasses and Smiths be forgotten forever; but never let the self emancipating deeds of the Haytian people be effaced; never let her heroically achieved nationality be brought low; no, never let the names of her Toussaint, her Dessalines, her Rigaud, her Christophe, and her Petion be forgotten, or blotted out from the historic pages of the world's history."[70]

Despite reservations, African American abolitionists invoked the Haitian Revolution in the defense of the "Negro character." Slaveholders and other proponents of slavery wanted to justify slavery as an institution ordained by God. They tried to propagate the theory that blacks were inferior to whites. A congressional committee on colonization suggested that, "To render freedom a blessing, man must be qualified for its enjoyment, that a total revolution in his character cannot be instantaneously wrought by the agency of ordinary moral and physical causes, or by the sudden force of unprepared revolution."[71]

African Americans resisted these stereotypes, as their leaders focused on the Haitian Revolution as proof to the contrary. They also supported the Haitian Revolution in the convention movement between the 1830s and the 1890s. Their basic objectives focused on promoting racial solidarity, self-help and cooperation.[72] African Americans maintained their solidarity with the Haitian Revolution during these conventions. In 1853, the prevailing sentiment in the black community inspired the Committee on Emigration of the Amherstburg Convention: "Every Colored man should feel binding upon himself the duty to sustain the national existence of Hayti, intact against the intervention of any or all powers whatsoever, and should pursue a policy to that end."[73]

Spirits were just as high at the New England Colored Citizens' Convention six years later. The assembled delegates gave Haiti a vote of confidence despite the ongoing revolutions there. The convention adopted a resolution that, "Notwithstanding the studied misrepresentation of the pro-slavery American press with regard to the island of Hayti, we know that the Haytians are the only people who achieved their independence by the sword, unaided by other nations; and that they have maintained it to the present hour, through their various revolutions . . . is full confirmation of their capacity for self-government."[74]

Similar sentiments resounded at the November 1858 Convention of the Colored Men of Ohio, held in Cincinnati. One of the adopted resolutions reaffirmed the importance of Haitian independence: "Resolved, that Hayti sets the colored people of this country an example of proper independence; and that the government is doing more for the up-building of the black race, than all other instrumentalities proposed or controlled by colored men."[75]

The Haitian Revolution and African American Resistance

As the nineteenth century progressed, the behavior of African Americans continued to be shaped by events associated with the Haitian Revolution. Many whites, called abolitionists, also endorsed their cause where they, too, found the inspiration to carry on their demands for the abolition of slavery. Abraham Bishop of Connecticut, one of these white abolitionists, spoke out for the "rights of black men" by attacking the hypocrisy of the American Revolution, whose leaders fought for freedom while keeping slaves. Defending the Haitian Revolution, he urged, "Let us be consistent, Americans, and if we justify our own conduct in the late glorious Revolution, let us justify those, who, in a cause like ours fight with equal bravery."[76]

On December 4, 1833, white abolitionists founded the American Anti-Slavery Society in Boston to galvanize and coordinate the drive against bondage. The abolitionists found in the Haitian Revolution irrefutable proof that blacks were capable of governing themselves. They used this event to correct misconceptions about blacks. "The people have a regular and enlightened government of the republican form—more liberal, perhaps, in its operation than any now existing in Europe . . . The superior branches of science and the most useful of the arts are protected and encouraged. The public offices are filled by native citizens of talents and character—they have their judges and courts, and other establishments like ourselves."[77] The abolitionists believed a closer affiliation with Haiti would weaken prejudice against Africans in general and African Americans in particular.

William Lloyd Garrison emerged as the most radical leader of the abolitionist movement. Born in 1805 in Newburyport, Massachusetts, Garrison was a printer and a writer for the *Herald* and later founded the *Free Press*. In the first edition of this paper Benjamin Lundy, editor of the *Genius of Universal Emancipation*, wrote, "That this abomination of abominations, the system of slavery, must be abolished, is as clear as the shining of the sun at noonday; the very nature of our government forbids its continuance, and the voice of the Eternal hath decreed its annihilation."[78] While Lundy favored gradual emancipation, Garrison insisted on immediate freedom for all slaves. He later edited *The Liberator*, a publication financed by James Forten to crusade against slavery.

Garrison maintained contact with Haitian leaders. In July of 1836, his friend Henry Benson went to Haiti with references to see Haitian president Boyer, Secretary of State General Inginac, and others. Benson returned with news of an antislavery society in Haiti. Garrison said, "I shall be greatly surprised, if, as soon as the fact is published, it do[es] not alarm our southern adversaries, and subject us to the charge of having entered into a 'conspiracy' with the Haytians, to stir up negro rebellion in the United States."[79]

African Americans also joined the abolitionist movement. Frederick Douglass headed this list. Born into slavery on a Maryland plantation as Augustus Bailey Washington, Douglass escaped to New Bedford, Massachusetts. In his *Narrative*, Douglass described how he overcame illiteracy against the wishes of his masters, who claimed, "Learning would spoil the best nigger in the world." Undaunted, Douglass recounted, "Though conscious of the difficulty of learning without a teacher, I set out with high hope, and a fixed purpose, at whatever cost of trouble, to learn how to read."[80]

At this stage of the abolitionist movement, Douglass staunchly condemned the institution of slavery, recognizing "The slave is still in his chains; the galling fetter is still on his limbs; the knotted scourge is still wet with his blood; the red-hot branding iron is yet applied to human flesh."[81] Douglass knew that Haiti was an inspiration to African Americans. He visited Haiti and wrote the manuscript *Around the Island of Santo Domingo*, in which he described the geography and topography of Haiti as well as the history of the Haitian Revolution. He later became a diplomat in Haiti for President Harrison.

In 1843, Henry Highland Garnet delivered his "Address to the Slaves of the United States of America": "Brethren, arise, arise! Strike for your lives and liberties. Now is the day and the hour. Let every slave throughout the land do this, and the days of slavery are numbered."[82] During the speech Garnet drew on a Haitian example, recalling how "Oge, Toussaint La-Ouverture [*sic*], Dessalines, Christophe, Petion, and Boyer, have driven the demon of slavery from that island, and have buried his carcass in the sea."[83]

These abolitionists regarded the Haitian Revolution as their prototype. Dr. John S. Rock, the distinguished African American abolitionist, compared whites and African Americans militarily and was convinced that blacks were not cowards, as was commonly charged. He stressed, "The history of the bloody struggles for freedom in Hayti, in which the blacks whipped the French and the English, and gained their independence, in spite of the perfidy of the villainous First Consul, will be a lasting refutation of the malicious aspersions of our enemies."[84] The myth of black docility was, at this stage, diminishing.

Others called on the slaves to follow the Haitian example, among them David Walker, whose pamphlet *Appeal to the Colored Citizens of the World* was both an indictment of slavery and a call for free northern blacks to join slaves in their fight.[85] Walker characterized the white race as the natural enemy of blacks. He illustrated this view through the history of Haiti, where blacks "were butchered by the whites." Walker also saw Haiti as "the glory of the blacks and the terror of tyrants," condemning the Catholic religion as a scourge. He was confident Haiti would survive: "I hope that she may keep peace within her borders and be united, keeping a strict look out for tyrants, for if they get the least chance to injure her, they will avail themselves of it . . . But one thing which gives me joy is, that they are men who would be cut off to a man, before they

would yield to the combined forces of the whole world."[86] Walker fore-
saw an end to the wretchedness of American blacks. He envisioned the
coming of a black messiah who would lead slaves out of the house of
bondage. "The whites want slaves, and want us for their slaves, but some
of them will curse the day they ever saw us." Some heeded David
Walker's appeal by killing their masters.

A letter received at Jerusalem, Virginia, signed by a man identified
only as Nero, equally showed the Haitian Revolution's impact on the
growing threat of rebellion in America. According to Ira Berlin, who discovered the letter in the Virginia State Library, the writer's purpose was
to describe a plan that would avenge the wrongs and abuses endured by
the slaves. According to Nero, the anticipated leader would be "a native of
Virginia, where he lived a slave till he was almost sixteen years old, when
he found an opportunity to escape to St. Domingo, where his noble soul
became warmed by the spirit of freedom, and where he imbibed a righ-
teous indignation, and an unqualified hatred for the oppressors of his
race."[87] Nero also asserted that members of the military unit included
"about thirty-five chosen ones in Hayti, who are learning the French and
Spanish languages and at the same time are taking lessons from the ven-
erable survivors of the Haytian Revolution ... They will know how to use
the knife, bludgeon, and the torch with effect—may the genius of Toussaint stimulate them to unremitting exertion."[88] The violent tactics that
brought about the liberation of Haiti were endorsed and promoted to
obtain the same results in America to restore the black man's dignity.

There were leaders who would try to put these fierce plans into action.
Denmark Vesey, called the "Intellectual Insurrectionist," had a thorough
knowledge of Haiti's valiant efforts to achieve freedom from colonial slavery and oppression. Born in Africa, Vesey spent many years aboard a
slave-trading ship. Settling in South Carolina, he bought his freedom for
$600. Determined to free the slaves in the state, Vesey planned for the
annihilation of the white population of Charleston, turning to Haiti for
inspiration and help.

Vesey wanted to emulate the success of Haitian leaders. His scribe,
Monday Gell, wrote a letter to Haitian president Boyer, relating the suf-
ferings of the blacks, and soliciting aid. Governor Thomas Bennett of
South Carolina referred to this letter in his report of the rebellion:
"Among the conspirators, the most daring and active was Monday, the
slave of Mr. Gell. He could read and write with facility, and thus attained

an extraordinary and dangerous influence over his fellows . . . This man wrote to Boyer (by his own confession) requesting his aid, and addressed the envelope of his letter to a relative of the person who became the bearer of it, a negro from one of the northern states."[89] One plan called for the takeover of Charleston. If that failed, the insurgents were to decide "either to retire to the swamps or to rob the banks and sail away to San Domingo."[90] When the authorities learned of the conspiracy, Denmark Vesey and his lieutenants were captured, tried, and executed.

The Vesey insurrection rekindled fear and panic in the United States. Authorities reacted by prohibiting free Negroes from entering the harbor on ships, especially those from the West Indies.[91] Local slaves saw their activities and movements drastically restricted.

The rebellion gained momentum again with the insurrection of Nat Turner. In August 1831, in Southampton County, Virginia, Turner plotted an end to slavery. Perhaps believing himself the messiah Walker had predicted, Turner claimed to be a prophet who had seen visions and heard voices bidding him to deliver his people. Obsessed with this idea, Turner mapped out a plan with a small group of confidants. They launched an attack by killing all the members of his master Joseph Travis's family. Joined by others, they spread carnage and destruction by killing sixty-one whites within twenty-four hours. They were overpowered by heavily armed bands of whites who captured and executed everyone but Turner, who managed to escape. He was able to elude authorities for six weeks before he was captured and hanged.

Still, some African Americans believed armed struggle was the only answer. William Wells Brown, noted literary figure, historian, and abolitionist, wrote, "Who knows but that a Toussaint, a Christophe, a Rigaud, a Clerveaux, and a Dessalines, may some day appear in the Southern States of this Union. That they are there, no one will doubt. That their souls are thirsting for liberty, all will admit. The spirit that caused the blacks . . . to shed their blood in the American revolutionary war, is still amongst the slaves of the south; and, if we are not mistaken the day is not far distant when the revolution of St. Domingo will be reenacted in South Carolina and Louisiana."[92] As late as 1861, John C. Bowers, a black community activist in Philadelphia, reinforced this view. He argued, "If it was right for the slaves of St. Domingo to resort to arms to put down the slave powers and regain their liberty . . . then it certainly will be right . . . for the slaves . . . after exhausting all their efforts to obtain a peaceful emancipation, to resort to arms with a determination to be no longer held in bondage, to either die slaves, or live freemen."[93]

Not every African American abolitionist had the same sentiments. Brown's image of shedding "rivers of blood" repulsed many abolitionists. They led their antislavery campaign to achieve both "the liberation of the four millions of American slaves, the enfranchisement of six hundred thousand half freemen, but the preservation of American liberty itself."[94]

J. G. Benjamin was among those abolitionists who believed education rather than violence would help end slavery. "Had these slaves been properly educated as were the domestic slaves, such scenes of inhuman debauchery would have been unheard of." He urged southern slaveholders to use "education and laws" to avoid the violence of St. Domingo.[95]

Others rejected the Haitian example as well. H. Ford Douglass, a leading black lecturer of the period, vowed "uncompromising and untiring effort" in the struggle against slavery, without violence. Though he praised John Brown, he repudiated the call to arms: "I am not an advocate for insurrection; I believe the world must be educated into something better and higher than this before we can have perfect freedom, either for the black man or the white. In the present moral condition of the people, no true liberty can be established, either by fighting slavery down, or by voting it down."[96]

These black abolitionists tried to use the established political system to help free the slaves, even though such a system fell short of the ideal of the Haitian Revolution. Political activist John Mercer Langston tried to explain the "bloody contest of Hayti" as having been carried out by people who, "driven to desperation by inhuman and intolerable oppressions, made one last, mighty effort to throw off their yoke, and gain their manhood and assert and maintain their rights."[97] He favored the tactic of using existing laws to achieve not only the liberation of the 4,000,000 slaves and the enfranchisement of 600,000 half freemen but also "the preservation of the American Government—the preservation of the American Liberty itself."[98] Another abolitionist, J. W. C. Pennington, endorsed a similar position in a speech at Freemason Hall, London, England. Putting into perspective the overall mission of the Convention Movement in the United States, he stated that "These conventions . . . are not and have not, been intended to excite commotion or insurrection, but, on the contrary, by every peaceful means, to improve the moral and intellectual condition of my people."[99] Unfortunately, few paid attention to them.

African Americans did perceive the Haitian Revolution as a ray of hope. The revolution raised their self-esteem by reminding them they could rehabilitate and elevate their race through their own efforts. "Only to think that less than one million of colored people in Hayti have made her in a few years the seventh nation in the world in her exports—they being only a few years ago slaves—I think it entirely useless to look for anything from the whites as a class—they hate us too bad to assist us much."[100]

While the debate over the means of ending slavery raged on, a segment of African American leaders continued to build national institutions that strengthened their autonomy. Another segment supported efforts to remove themselves altogether from the American landscape to improve their conditions. This alternative led to the emigration movement to Haiti and other lands during the antebellum period.

The Quest for an Asylum, 1824–1865

In her Constitution, her President, and her Cabinet, Hayti is one of the most democratic of Republics. Those who seek a home there, are at once placed upon a political equality with the natives. (1861)

William Wells Brown, *Black Abolitionist Papers*

Hezekiah Grice was one of the first African Americans to emigrate to Haiti in search of freedom and economic opportunities. He was born in Baltimore in 1801. In 1817, he apprenticed himself to a man 200 miles off to the southeast. The relationship between the two turned sour and Grice returned to Baltimore. At the age of 23, he was engaged in the summertime in supplying Baltimore with ice from his cart, and in winter in cutting up pork for Ellicots' establishment. Grice also became involved in political activism to advance the cause of his people, helping Bishop Richard Allen organize the first convention of African Americans in Philadelphia at Bethel A.M.E. Church on September 15, 1830. Increasingly dissatisfied with the oppression of blacks in the United States, he moved to Haiti in 1832. Once there, he pursued the crafts of carving and gilding. He was successful and, in 1843, was appointed director of public works in Port-au-Prince.[1]

Like Hezekiah Grice, other freedmen decided to emigrate to Haiti to cast off their "second-class" citizenship. Baptist missionary Thomas Paul encouraged this in the July 3, 1824, issue of the *Columbia Sentinel*. He stressed that Haiti was the right place for them. "Having been a resident for some months in the Island of Hayti, I am fully persuaded that it is the best and most suitable place of residence which Providence has hitherto offered to emancipated people of colour, for the enjoyment of liberty and equality with their attendant blessings."[2] Many African American freedmen considered the option of emigration to Haiti.

The Rise of Emigrationist Ideology

Dissatisfied blacks in the United States contemplated emigration as a means of escaping discrimination and oppression and seeking self-fulfillment. The movement began with New England blacks who wanted to leave behind the limitations on their citizenship status and liberate others in their homeland.

Paul Cuffee, a wealthy African American shipowner and repatriationist entrepreneur, was the first advocate of this view. Cuffee, a New Englander, resolved to use his wealth to campaign for black civil rights. He first tried to repatriate blacks to Africa, promoting "the civilization of the Blacks in their own country with a view to draw them off from the vile habits of life to which they have been accustomed."[3] In 1815, Cuffee paid the transportation costs for thirty-eight black volunteer settlers to Sierra Leone. He wanted to contribute to the Christian regeneration of Africa and to expedite the emancipation of the American slave.[4]

White Americans responded with their own racist agenda. Many considered the presence of freedmen an anomaly and would not tolerate them living in their communities. Historian D. W. Meinig assesses this intolerance: "Their presence constituted the deepest human problem and exposed the worst contradictions in American life: eagerly purchased for their labor but generally despised as people, unwanted as a social presence, feared as a potentially rebellious force."[5] As the black population increased, incidences of racism increased, too.

Sexism was also a factor. The editor of the *Niles' Register* expressed his eagerness to see America relieved of its "colored population" and of "the young free female persons of color." He argued that "By removing a male, we only remove one person—but a female has effect on the future as well as the present population of the country; and if it is really desired to reduce the relative amount of the blacks compared with the whites, it may be surely, yet imperceptably, accomplished by a resort to this measure."[6]

After the Gabriel insurrection of 1800, this proposition gained wider support. The Virginia legislature requested that Governor James Monroe ask President Jefferson to remove blacks from the western territories. Jefferson refused, knowing that neither Virginia nor any other state would ever accept such a colony into the Union. Jefferson believed the West Indies was a "more probable and practicable retreat for them" because of their race and color. "Nature seems to have formed these islands," he suggested, "to become the receptacle of the Blacks transplanted into this hemisphere." Of these islands, San Domingo, "where the Blacks are established into a sovereignty *de facto*, and have organized themselves under regular laws and government,"[7] seemed a particularly good place for freed African Americans. The Virginia legislature, however, rejected Jefferson's proposal to deport blacks to Haiti because they feared these exiles would threaten slavery in the southern states.

The movement gained new support when the Reverend Robert Finley of Basking Ridge, New Jersey, founded the American Colonization Society in 1816. Finley suggested, "Could not the rich and benevolent devise means to form a colony on some part of the coast of Africa . . . which might gradually induce many free blacks to go and settle, devising for them the means of getting there, and of protection and support till they were established?"[8] To skeptics, Finley argued that colonization was "a scheme from God." It would help the "Sons of Africa" to find true freedom and equality in their homeland and save American society from the "intermixture of colours." Above all, the reverend believed that colonization was a means of promoting Western civilization and Christianity in Africa.[9]

Finley chose Washington, D.C., as his base. In his campaign for colonization, he lobbied Congress and the president. Major ecclesiastical organizations—the Methodist General Conference, the General Assembly of the Presbyterian Church, the Baptist General Association, and the General Convention of the Protestant Episcopal Church—endorsed the scheme. Legislatures in Virginia, Maryland, Tennessee, Georgia, and Ohio also pledged support. Positive responses like these encouraged Finley to send emissaries to Africa to identify appropriate colonization sites.

African Americans vigorously opposed the idea. Philadelphia's black elite, led by Richard Allen, James Forten, Absalom Jones, and others, voiced their opposition to the colonization scheme that had overwhelming support among whites. In a January 1817 meeting at the Bethel A.M.E. Church in Philadelphia, freed African Americans resolved, "We never will separate ourselves voluntarily from the slave population in this country; they are our brethren by the ties of consanguinity, of suffering, and of wrongs; and we feel that there is more virtue in suffering privations with them, than fancied advantages for a season."[10] In 1834, Samuel Cornish, pastor of the African Presbyterian Church in New York and one of the founders of *Freedom Journal*, reiterated the message: "In every city and town in our country where the colored people are permitted to assemble, they have always entered their solemn protest against colonization, as a system of proscription and cruelty."[11]

Even as African American leaders adamantly rejected colonization, some left open the option of a black-initiated emigration to Haiti seeking, as Thomas Pauls advised, "the enjoyment of freedom and equality with their attendant blessings." Samuel Cornish, now editor of the newspaper *The Rights of All*, although opposed to colonization, supported the Haitian option. Cornish argued for African Americans' right to stay in America and for the rights of those who wished to leave: "Why not emigrate, either to Canada or the beautiful island of Hayti, where the people are civilized, the laws good and well administered."[12] Cornish felt African Americans could find a home without the assistance of the American Colonization Society.

Abolitionist William Garrison also asserted that African Americans as a whole rejected colonization but held Haiti in high esteem: "They are as unanimously opposed to a removal to Africa, as the Cherokees from the council-fires and graves of their fathers. It is remarkable, too, that they are as united in their respect and esteem for the republic of Hayti."[13] At an anticolonization meeting in Boston, a committee report explained this sentiment: "They know of no better way of expressing their disapprobation of such measures, than to use every exertion to persuade their brethren not to leave the United States upon any consideration whatever; but if there are or should be any exasperated in consequence of abuse from their white countrymen, and who are determined to leave the country, we think it desirable to recommend them to Hayti or Upper Canada, where they will find the laws equal."[14] The attainment of freedom, especially in Haiti, proved to be a compelling emigration force.

In the name of nationalism, Haiti's founding fathers had given impetus to this migratory movement. Insurrections and war had severely reduced the Haitian population and affected the country's ability to withstand potential foreign confrontations. They saw immigration as an avenue for maintaining the independent black nation. Guided by these considerations, Emperor Jean-Jacques Dessalines offered an emigration incentive to "captains of American vessels the sum of forty dollars for each individual native black, or man of colour, whom they should convey back to Hayti."[15]

Recognizing the need for a strong national defense, King Christophe was interested in the immigration of blacks. Thomas Clarkson, the English abolitionist, presented both racial and national-defense arguments to the king to convince him to welcome African Americans to Haiti: "There can be no doubt that such an emigration, if it consisted of persons of character, would very much add to your population, and of course to the security of your Dominions." Clarkson suggested that he should receive them "provided the American Government would purchase the Spanish part of the Island and cede it to you."[16] Clarkson believed incorrectly that Spain could dispose of this part of the island.

Prince Saunders, an African American educator, supported Christophe's efforts. Saunders played a major role in early Haitian history, serving as attorney general in President Jean-Pierre Boyer's government. A teacher at Boston's African School of Thomas Paul, he also founded the Belle Lettres Society. In 1815, Saunders accompanied Paul to England as a delegate of the Masonic Lodge of Africans. On this trip, Saunders met William Wilberforce and Thomas Clarkson, both English philanthropists devoted to the abolition of the slave trade. Under their guidance, Saunders became an advocate of a Haitian emigration policy, a belief he held for the rest of his life. He would become an emissary both for King Christophe and these abolitionists.[17]

When Prince Saunders attended the American Convention for the Abolition of Slavery in Philadelphia in December 1818, he noted, "Among the various projects or plans which have been devised or suggested in relation to emigration, there are none which appear to many persons to wear so much appearance of feasibility, and ultimate successful and practical operation, as the luxuriant, beautiful and extensive island of Hayti."[18]

One of the hurdles impeding widespread emigration to Haiti was the island's reputation for military despotism. Aware of the ongoing rivalry between King Christophe and the newly elected President Boyer, who ruled the western part of the country following the death of Alexandre Pétion, Saunders recognized this hindrance. He was confident that once differences were settled, there would be "many hundreds of the free people in the New England and middle states who would be glad to repair there immediately to settle."[19] By helping to reconcile these differences, Saunders hoped, with the assistance of the American Convention for the Abolition of Slavery, to promote emigration.

After receiving a measure of abolitionist support, Saunders returned to Haiti in the fall of 1820 to continue to promote emigration. Christophe supported Saunders and entrusted him with the responsibility of bringing African Americans from Philadelphia to Haiti. He agreed to provide a ship and $25,000 for expenses. Before the plan was implemented, a mutiny erupted against Christophe in St-Marc, and his regime ended. Despondent over these turns of events, the king took his own life.

Buoyed by its success with the American government and with the legislatures of the fourteen states that passed favorable resolutions, the society sent emissaries to Africa to help identify appropriate colonial sites. In 1820, the first attempt to establish a colony was made at Sherbro Island. The settlement did not come about because negotiations with the natives to buy the land proved unproductive. But in 1822, the society received Cape Mesurado on the Grain Coast, about 225 miles south of Sierra Leone, and the colony was established. The territory was named Liberia, after the Latin *liber*, for freeman.[20]

The 1824 Emigration Movement

During the 1820s, emigration became a popular option for those who felt victimized by both economic and racial inequalities. In Haiti, President Jean-Pierre Boyer promoted the first mass-emigration movement. Boyer was a member of the mulatto faction of Haitian politics. After the deaths of Pétion and Christophe, he ruled the western, Spanish part of the island for twenty-two years. During his tenure, he established a socioeconomic foundation for the upper class. Like the founding fathers of Haiti, he was a staunch defender of Haitian independence, writing to Thomas Clarkson in 1821, "Haitians, in their pride at having raised themselves from the depths of misery to an independent political existence, will never turn back along the path on which their steps were set by the horrible injustice of their oppressors and their own love of liberty."[21]

Like his predecessors, Boyer's immigration focus was based on two fundamental considerations. First, Haiti needed laborers. Like Dessalines and Christophe, Boyer tried to revive the plantation production system that had made Saint-Domingue prosperous in the eighteenth century. He promoted giving large estates to the upper class and tried to force the peasants to work the land. Boyer further used provisions of the *Code Rural* of 1826, a stringent set of agricultural laws, as justification, although workers did not comply.[22] For newly freed men, liberty meant owning their own land, and they would not work on the plantations. Consequently, Boyer sought African Americans as laborers since they already had experience growing cotton, coffee, tobacco, and sugarcane.

Second, Boyer wanted international recognition for Haiti. Like earlier leaders, Boyer was frustrated that other countries continued to snub Haiti. After Boyer set himself up as leader of the entire island, international recognition became even more important to him. He focused on trade with the United States, since that country maintained commercial relations. Efforts to gain Secretary of State John Quincy Adams's support proved fruitless, however, even after Boyer offered concessions on import taxes.[23] Boyer then offered emigration to African Americans to heighten Haiti's recognition and promote American spending in the island.

Since Boyer was aware of the American Colonization Society campaign to remove blacks from America, he decided to capitalize on the race issue. In 1820, he published an appeal in the *Niles' Register*, citing reasons African Americans should come to Haiti: "Our past sufferings, our unexampled efforts to regain our primitive rights, our solemn oath to live free and independent . . . Our wise constitution which insures a free country to Africans and their descendants; all lead us to believe that the hand of Providence has destined Hayti for a land of promise, a secret asylum, where our unfortunate brethren will, in the end, see their wounds healed by the balm of equality and their tears wiped away by the protecting hand of liberty."[24] As a member of the mulatto elite, who rejected African culture, Boyer emphasized that African Americans would enjoy a richer life in Haiti than they would experience in Africa.

Other Haitians independently promoted their own immigration programs. Silvain Simonisse, a mulatto from South Carolina, moved to Haiti in 1818 when he was unable to adjust to American life after returning home from schooling in England. With Secretary General Balthazar Inginac's support, Simonisse joined the group *La société philanthropique d'Haiti*, working to establish the settlement of free American blacks in Haiti. Members of the society paid a membership fee that was used to defray emigration costs for agricultural workers and artisans.[25]

Loring Dewey, a Presbyterian minister, rekindled interest in Haitian emigration when he became president of the fading New York chapter of the American Colonization Society. In March 1824, Dewey wrote Boyer to inform him that good men were "looking for asylum for the injured Sons of Africa in some other country." He told Boyer that African Americans preferred to go to Haiti rather than return to Africa. Dewey also said he was gathering information "on every point that looks like affording benefit to my unhappy coloured countrymen."[26] Finally, he asked President Boyer to defray the cost of the voyage, assign the colonists land to cultivate, and offer incentives to mechanics and merchants. To help sell his story in the United States, Dewey also asked for information about religious tolerance and the Haitian school system.

Boyer welcomed this proposal. Boyer told Dewey Haitians "cannot see with indifference the calamities which afflict their brethren."[27] He promised that Haiti would provide financial assistance and land to those African Americans who relocated. With the additional guarantee of the freedom to worship, he said he would accept 6,000 agricultural workers in the first year from Dewey. They would be relocated throughout the island.

To assure the project's success, Boyer asked prominent people for help. To Charles Collins, a merchant and philanthropist, Boyer said he could expect to ship "fifty thousand weights of coffee to be sold to facilitate the emigration of such individuals of the African race, who, groaning in the United States, under the weight of prejudice and misery, should be disposed to come to Hayti and partake with our citizens the benefits of a liberal constitution and paternal government."[28]

In June 1824, Secretary General Balthazar Inginac asked Thomas Paul, the founder of the Black Baptist Church in Boston, for twelve men to work his coffee plantation, to join the five African Americans he had already received. Paul had spent time in Haiti as a missionary and had promoted the emigration of free blacks to Haiti. With this request, the secretary general reiterated President Boyer's offer to the "descendants of Africans, who groan in the United States in misery and humiliation, an asylum, where they will have the means of enjoying the invaluable rights of equal laws and citizenship."[29]

Other African American leaders endorsed emigration on ideological grounds. Black abolitionist William Watkins explained he would not compare the Haitian emigration movement to African colonization since emigration was a "movement emanating from a branch of our own people who cannot but have the welfare of the whole race at heart."[30] The emigration concept conformed to African American nationalist aspirations whereas African colonization was believed to be a scheme to remove African Americans from the American landscape. Emigration was something African Americans saw as a means of improving their economic situation. Prior to the American Civil War, freedmen had hoped for wealth and prosperity, but Philadelphia, center of the black middle class, was in a recession. That made the promise of economic opportunity in Haiti more attractive. Blacks saw Haiti as a land that offered them positions of leadership away from the social and political constraints of the United States.[31] They held up Prince Saunders as an example of one who had climbed the ladder of Haitian politics.

To coordinate emigration, Boyer sent Jonathas Granville to the United States as special agent to help persuade freedmen to move to Haiti. Granville was born in northern Haiti in 1785. He joined the French armed forces after graduation from a French school, returning to Haiti in 1816 where he held various administrative posts under both Pétion and Boyer.

Granville launched his mission in June 1824, beginning in Philadelphia. The black leadership there supported him and welcomed him into their community. In Baltimore, another bastion of Haitian immigrants, R. Cowley, a reporter for the *Genius of Universal Emancipation*, described him as "the profound scholar, polite gentleman, and benevolent man." Cowley said that because of these qualities, the "shafts of calumny fall harmless at his feet."[32]

Granville met with Loring Dewey and was discouraged early on to learn that Dewey was acting independently of the American Colonization Society. Actually, the managers did not endorse colonization to Haiti because of the "apprehension of danger" by southern slaveholders. At a New York meeting on the issue, one account reported, "The National Colonization Society was decidedly opposed to sending any of our black population to Hayti, that place being considered too near for the safety of our Southern brethren, whose numerous slave population might then become more dangerous than at present."[33]

Conflicts threatened to kill the project. Since the managers disapproved the policy of sending blacks to Haiti, Dewey created a separate agency, The Society for Promoting the Emigration of Free Persons of Colour to Haiti. Quaker groups who did not embrace the American Colonization Society's agenda contributed to the Haitian project.[34] Other white groups welcomed the opportunity to promote their own cause, an expulsion of all African Americans from the United States. The Manumission Society of North Carolina declared that "Emigration to Hayti ought to be encouraged to a reasonable extent; that is, all free Negroes, capable of earning a livelihood, should be advised to emigrate; and masters should be encouraged to liberate, and prepare their slaves for emigrating."[35] Dewey's society believed that Haiti, with an area of about 50,000,000 acres and a population of less than 1,000,000, could admit the whole population of 2,000,000 African Americans.

The emigration movement reached its height when Granville met with Bishop Richard Allen. The bishop called a meeting with black community leaders at Bethel A.M.E. Church to review emigration proposals. The Haytian Emigration Society was born out of that meeting, with Allen becoming its first president. The society adopted a resolution that "We do approve of the proposals of President Boyer, also, heartily concur with him in the belief that the emigration to the island of Hayti will be more advantageous to us than to the colony in Africa."[36]

Emigration groups emerged in Baltimore and New York, and as far west as Cincinnati, Ohio, with a goal to "ascertain correct intelligence in regard to the soil and climate of the island."[37] The Baltimore Emigration Society endorsed Granville's plan, resolving "that this Board approve of the object of the mission of Citizen Granville; and recommend to the coloured people of Baltimore to accept of the liberal offers now made to them through him, by the Government of Hayti."[38]

In speeches that Granville gave to emigration societies as Haiti's emissary, he minimized the linguistic and religious differences between Haitians and African Americans. In an address at the church on Elm Street, New York, he observed that "Your habits, though somewhat different from ours, have nothing in them at variance with our institutions, and we shall find nothing in them as an accusation against you. Your religion differs in some points from ours, but we all worship the same God."[39] Privately, Granville painted a less optimistic picture, revealing the cultural gap between the two peoples. He wrote to Boyer, "The colored people here are, whatever they say, in such a state of abjection that each time I am with them I feel that their degradation reflect on me."[40] Yet Granville, ever the diplomat, continued to recruit, promising fertile land and noninterference in their domestic lives and religious beliefs.

Haiti became the land of hope for thousands of African American freedmen. On August 23, 1824, thirty families were the first to sail from Philadelphia to their new home. More followed, and, it was reported, "Nine or ten vessels filled with passengers have just sailed or [are] about to depart from Philadelphia, Port Elizabeth, Baltimore; and it is calculated that between 3 and 4,000 will migrate within a few days."[41] Granville ended his campaign in December, leaving Philadelphia with seventy emigrants for Samana, in the Spanish section of the island under Haitian rule.

Benjamin Lundy, editor of the *Genius of Universal Emancipation* and a fervent proponent of emigration, estimated that Granville motivated "between four and five thousand coloured persons" to move to Haiti. In light of Granville's success, Lundy called for the implementation of a plan to establish agencies to "facilitate the transportation of the people of colour . . . in every State and Territory, where any considerable portion of this class exists, to be under the control of the Legislatures thereof, or Societies formed for the purpose of promoting the emigration of such as might be at liberty to go."[42] Lundy was convinced that America possessed sufficient means to reduce the rapidly increasing African American population. Other whites took a different view of Granville's crusade. They accused Granville of removing their servants to another land and of making Haiti a staging area for attacks on the South.[43]

Ultimately, emigration programs did not result in a mass exodus. Garrison noted that, though a great highway "has been opened to the Haytien republic . . . only here and there a traveler is seen to enter upon the road."[44] Some 13,000 African Americans made the journey to Haiti between 1824 and 1827.[45] Although the promise of political freedom was enticing, Haiti did not prove to be a "promised land." Cultural differences between Haitians and African Americans proved to be overwhelming. This was corroborated by an anonymous American commercial agent at Port-au-Prince who reported to his superiors that "Religion, laws, manners, habits, and in fact everything is so totally different from what they have been accustomed to that they cannot feel so happy or so comfortable as in a country where the difference of soil or climate was the only change they had to encounter."[46]

Complicating matters, the Haitian government had a different role in mind for the immigrants. One of President Boyer's primary goals for these immigrants—to use them as agriculturists—was scarcely realized. "for most of the new settlers were barbers, shoemakers, and scrapers etc.

in the United States, who did not want to leave the Haitian cities to settle in the plains and mountains to embrace the noble labor of agriculture."[47] Boyer's hope for American diplomatic recognition was unfulfilled. The editor of the *National Gazette* warned, "The question of colonizing in Saint Domingo, to which must be added the recognition by this government of the independence of Hayti, is connected . . . to the prosperity, nay, to the very existence of our southern States. The naked example of a flourishing black empire established through a bloody but successful revolt of slaves on the very confines of our Union is in itself of terrible import to those whose misfortune it is to be slaveholders; but if this example is rendered more striking and familiar by the intercourse and communication which, in the event of colonizing in Hayti, must necessarily subsist between these colonists who shall go and their connections left behind in this country, it may add fearfully to the apprehended danger."[48]

General Robert Harper of the American Colonization Society concurred, stating that "A still more immediate and formidable objection to blending the two schemes arises from the alarms and apprehensions of the Southern States, to which attention must be paid and which would be excited in the highest degree by seeing the negro population of the islands in their neighborhood thus increased."[49] Since Boyer was unsuccessful in recruiting enough agriculturists and in securing American recognition, he stopped subsidizing the immigrants after June 1825.

Most African Americans returned to the United States. Those who stayed, though, adjusted well to the Haitian environment. They were mulattoes accepted by the Haitian elite, which was also predominantly made up of mulattoes. The primary reason for their success was their easy assimilation into the Haitian class and color structure. Emigrationist Benjamin Hunt observed, "I can call to mind but thirteen Americans of African blood, who have been what I might be called 'successful' in that country, and several of this number were moderately so . . . and all were men of color or mulattoes."[50] Since six of the thirteen came from French-speaking New Orleans, the transition was easier.

Some favorable reports reached America. John Summersett of Philadelphia, for example, described in a letter to Bishop Allen the kind of treatment fellow immigrants received in Haiti. "When we landed," he wrote, "the inhabitants, generally, received us more like brothers than strangers, their houses were opened to accommodate us, and everything possible to make us happy and content, was done . . . We are confident that no African of candid or industrious habits can deny this being the happy land of African liberty."[51] John C. Allen, one of Bishop Allen's sons, also made the trip and informed his father that he was quite satisfied with Haiti as well as with his hosts. He further related that he was expecting his brother to emigrate and that someday he was anticipating the emigration of the bishop as well.[52]

Just as the experience among the ranks of emigrants varied, so too do historians' analyses of the enterprise differ. Mark B. Bird, a Methodist pastor who served in Haiti during this time, thought the first emigration movement was mismanaged: "It would appear that . . . this difficult undertaking, although well meant and commenced in all good faith on the part of the Boyer Government, upon the whole, was not well managed, for, notwithstanding many respectable people came, with ample means, who were of great use to the country, it must be admitted that many came who were a perfect misfortune to themselves and the community which they had come to join."[53]

Others felt the Haitian government made every effort to facilitate the integration of emigrants into Haitian society. Haitian historian Rulx Léon reported that on August 7, 1824, President Boyer instructed the commandants of eastern *arrondissements* not only to give land to the 300 expected immigrants but also to treat them with "all possible goodwill."[54]

The 1859 Emigration Movement

During the 1840s, nationalism was the predominant ideology for African Americans. Historian Howard Bell said blacks developed the consciousness that they "must shoulder the full burden of their own self-betterment; that they must exercise their political potential by developing a government independent of the white man's supervision."[55] By establishing "national" institutions, the foundations of a black nationality that began earlier in the century greatly accelerated.

Underlying this resurgence of nationalism was a growing disillusionment among African Americans with existing social and economic conditions. Despite an active abolition movement, blacks remained trapped in the shackles of slavery. Discrimination in employment and encroachment on their basic rights was still prevalent as states moved for stricter enforcement of the Fugitive Slave Law. In 1829, for example, the trustees of Cincinnati, Ohio, threatened to fine or jail residents who employed, harbored, or concealed a Negro or mulatto person without a certificate of freedom. This posed a significant threat to African Americans, for Ohio was considered by them to be a tolerant state.

In the same vein, Martin Robinson Delany painted a bleak picture of freedman conditions, noting that free blacks shared the same status as enslaved African Americans. Delany, who was an essayist and the first black to reach the rank of major in the U.S. Army, observed that the bondman "is denied all civil, religious, and social privileges . . . and so are we. They have no part nor lot in the government of the country, neither have we. They are ruled and governed without representation, . . . and so are we."[56] He was disappointed when he compared the promises made by antislavery proponents with the existing poverty of blacks. In an honest though futile attempt to atone for past mistakes, opponents promised bondmen a great deal more than they could ever be able half to fulfill.

Response to the continued oppression of blacks varied. Some called for rebellion. The Reverend Henry Highland Garnet, in his "Address to the Slaves of the United States of America," and pamphleteer David Walker, in his *Appeal*, urged blacks to rebel against the system. The speech earned Garnet the title of "revolutionary nationalist."[57] Others, like Delany, advocated self-improvement reforms. In his view, any elevation of the black race "must be the result of self-efforts, and work of our own hands. No other human power can accomplish it."[58] Emigration once again became a popular notion, and Delany eventually joined those who endorsed it as a means of self-determination and ultimate change.

The prime question facing African American leaders at this stage was where they should emigrate. The first National Convention of Colored Citizens, meeting in Philadelphia on September 20, 1830, endorsed considering "the propriety of forming a settlement in the province of Upper Canada, in order to afford a place of refuge to those who may be obliged to leave their homes, as well as to others inclined to emigrate with the view of improving their condition."[59]

The Reverend Lewis Woodson suggested blacks settle in rural areas as well as emigrate to the West Indies and Canada. Woodson, the son of Virginia slaves, lived in Pittsburgh, Pennsylvania, where he was called as a minister and operated a school for black children during the day and adults at night. As Woodson considered the African American situation, he wrote, "I had rather be a living freedman, even in one of these places, than a 'dead nigger' in the United States."[60] Many African Americans did move to Canada in their search for a haven from oppression. Delany, who had advocated emigration to Central America, finally decided that Africa was the most acceptable refuge. Still, Haiti, a symbol for black identity, ranked high on proponents' lists.

In the early 1850s, James Theodore Holly favored emigration to Canada. After working with Henry Bibb as an associate editor of the Canadian *Voice of the Fugitive,* Holly concluded that if blacks were to achieve complete freedom, they had to move to Haiti and away from white domination. He announced this change in belief at the 1853 Coloured National Convention in Rochester, New York.

At the 1854 National Emigration Convention in Cleveland, discussions centered on the African American desire to leave the United States. African American leaders resolved that blacks should form a nation of their own, emigrating to somewhere in the western hemisphere. Holly was appointed a commissioner and sent to Haiti with a mission to devise ways to encourage African Americans to emigrate to Haiti. After meeting with Haitian head of state Faustin Soulouque in 1855, Holly returned with a favorable report for the board at the 1856 convention.

Some African American leaders wanted to make Haiti the center of black nationality. These black abolitionists viewed the struggle in the western hemisphere in racial terms: the Caucasian versus the colored races. Since the economic and political power of Caucasians was strongly established, abolitionists urged the colored races to take steps toward reaching similar goals.

A number of these abolitionists saw Haiti's geographical location as an ideal refuge against slavery. George Lawrence Jr. strongly supported this theory: "We can make of Hayti the nucleus of a power that shall be to the black, what England has been to the white races, the hope of progress and the guarantee of permanent civilization. Look at her position; she is the centre of a circle in whose plane lie Cuba, Central America, and the Southern Slave States. From that centre let but the fire of Freedom radiate until it shall enkindle, in the whole of that vast area, the sacred flame of Liberty upon the altar of every black man's heart, and you effect at once the abolition of slavery and the regeneration of the race."[61]

Emigration also served as an antislavery tactic. By gaining popularity, a nationality could eventually lead to the abolition of slavery. Freedom would be guaranteed, for "A Negro government in the Gulf of Mexico at the very portals of slavery . . . shall be the Gibraltar of the black man's hopes,"[62] said H. Douglass Ford. It would keep in check the greedy desire of some whites to acquire more territories in which to plant the curse of bondage. Others, like historian William Wells Brown, suggested people of color take over not just Haiti but all of the West Indian Islands. He wrote that, "While our representative men are opposing emigration and are living in drudgery, the Anglo-Saxon is going to the uttermost parts of the earth, gaining wealth, power, and influence. The West Indian Islands are eventually to fall in the hands of the sons and daughters of Africa, and the sooner we take possessions of them and develop their resources the better it will be for ourselves, our children, and for humanity."[63] According to Brown, African Americans needed to leave their menial jobs behind them to develop a strong and great nationality.

William Watkins agreed: "Let solid men, who will help Hayti as well as themselves, go thither to develop the resources of the country, and thus conduce to its prosperity."[64] The cultivation of a cotton crop was encouraged as the economic backbone of the country and as a means of fighting slavery. Holly suggested that the development of solid cultural institutions would lead to the eventual greatness of that black nationality. He urged his fellow African Americans to "go and identify our destiny with our heroic brethren in that independent isle of the Caribbean Sea, carrying with us such of the arts, sciences, and genius of modern civilization . . . in order to add to Haytian advancement, rather than to indolently remain here, asking for political rights."[65]

Antiemigrationists disagreed, recalling past emigration projects like the 1824 fiasco. They realized that, beyond race and ethnicity, African Americans and Haitians differed on almost every part of their culture. A. P. Smith, a columnist for the *Weekly Anglo-African*, warned that the emigrants could not possibly succeed in Haiti because they differed "widely from the natives in habits, manners, religion, ignorant of the language of the country."[66] He predicted their eventual failure because of conflicting business, social, and religious elements. He added that the extreme climatic differences between Haiti and the United States would also contribute to the failure of emigration.

Whether from the point of view of black emigrationists who crafted the dream of national security or the dissenters who predicted disaster, the most significant factor affecting emigration was the militaristic heritage of Haitian life. Political developments also contributed to bad feelings about the emigration movement. Faustin Soulouque, the emperor who controlled the national destiny of Haiti, faced mounting internal political unrest. Negotiations between Soulouque and Holly, aimed at stabilizing the political environment, proved fruitless when Soulouque's regime was overthrown in January 1859.

Holly was not the only African American emissary talking to Soulouque about emigration. Haitian American historian and political activist Rodolphe Lucien Desdunes, describing the Louisiana Creoles' life during the 1850s, recounted several stringent laws, including a ban on civil marriage between a person of color and a white, as well as a requirement that people of color must be represented by white attorneys. He reported on other outrageous laws of the time: "A free person of color was forbidden to walk the streets without a permit; a black visitor to the city could not remain in New Orleans without the guarantee or protection of a white person; a black man could not defend his honor nor that of his family with any assurance of justice."[67]

These constraints prompted Creoles to escape, and Haiti seemed to be a natural destination. Emile Desdunes, a Haitian American from Louisiana who was established in Haiti, served as intermediary between Soulouque and the Creole community. Soulouque asked Desdunes to "arrange the expatriation of all Créoles of color who wished to leave the city" and to look "into the condition and opinion of all people of Haitian descent."[68] Like Holly, Desdunes' plan failed when Soulouque was overruled.

Fabre Nicolas Geffrard, a mulatto, became the new president of Haiti and endorsed Holly's emigration project. Emigrationists praised Geffrard as one who could return stability to the government. Geffrard was able to promote progress in Haiti. During his regime, he established a fleet of steamboats to improve Haitian commerce with other nations, commissioned the construction of waterworks for the capital, created a national foundry, and installed gas lighting on the streets of Port-au-Prince. He also overhauled the educational system, opening schools throughout the land.

Like his predecessor, Geffrard planned to enlist the help of African Americans to work the fields. Geffrard invited African Americans to Haiti and promised they would find a land where they could enjoy freedom. With the new labor force, Geffrard hoped to see completion of his development projects and creation of a prosperous Haiti. For those who would come, he offered the right to buy, either on private or public estates, fertile land at a reasonable price.

James Redpath, a friend of John Brown who attacked Harper's Ferry, became Geffrard's official intermediary charged with mobilizing this second emigration movement. A Scottish abolitionist who traveled to Haiti for historical and political research, Redpath became active in black advancement and helped recruit African American laborers. This movement was similar to the first emigration undertaking. Like Dewey, Redpath required specific guarantees from the Haitian government. From these negotiations, he emerged as a kind of emigration czar, becoming general agent for the Haytian Bureau of Emigration. He became a partner with James Theodore Holly in implementing emigration plans.

Two factors contributed to the rekindled interest in emigration: the vocal support of both African American emigrationists and white leaders in the United States and the support offered by the Haitian government. In January 1858, Francis Preston Blair, a Missouri congressman, proposed to colonize free blacks in Central and South America under the protection and patronage of the United States. Many African American leaders agreed with Blair's proposal. Holly wrote Blair to inquire about his plan. Holly assured the congressman that "Thousands can be readily enrolled as emigrants to the intertropical regions of our continent with the slightest effort."[69]

J. M. Whitfield, editor of the *African-American Repository* in Buffalo, New York, agreed that "While there are hundreds—yes, thousands—of enterprising and industrious colored men, ready and anxious to embark immediately in any feasible movement of emigration to either of the places named, the means to commence such a movement properly are not attainable among them."[70] Whitfield believed that many African Americans were ready to leave the temperate regions of the western hemisphere and move on to the tropics. Another strong endorsement came from George B. Vashon, a former resident of Haiti, who wrote, "More than ten years ago, I spent two years and a half in Hayti, as an educator; and although the country was then far more unhappily situated than it is now, I became deeply attached to it, so much so, that I came at length to regard it as 'the country of my soul.' And, although my hopes in reference to the destiny of the descendants of the African in this Western

World, are not confined by its narrow limits, but embrace the 'whole boundless continent,' still I have always regarded Hayti as the germinating point of their fortunes."[71]

Vashon extended hearty support for this emigration plan. Frederick Douglass, the foremost African American leader of the period and long-time opponent of emigration, added his support as well. Earlier, Douglass had advocated that "The place for the free colored people is the land where their brothers and sisters are held in slavery, and where circumstances might some day enable them to contribute an important part to their liberation." His views had changed by the beginning of 1861 when he said, "While we have never favored any plan of emigration, and have never been willing to concede that this is a doomed country, and that we are a doomed race in it, we can raise no objection to the present movement towards Hayti."[72] Douglass was even invited to go to Haiti for a six-month visit, but he changed his plans when the American Civil War broke out.

A second factor that contributed to the emigration momentum involved the Haitian government itself. In response to Redpath, President Geffrard and his cabinet provided firm guarantees to emigrants. Elie Dubois, Haiti's minister of education, made this appeal: "Men of our race dispersed in the United States! Your fate, your social position, instead of ameliorating, daily becomes worse. The chains of those who are slaves are riveted; and prejudice, more implacable, perhaps, than servitude, pursues and crushes down the free: Come, then, to us! The doors of Hayti are open to you."[73] The Haitian government promised to grant "new citizens" the right to create their own schools or to attend existing ones at a very low cost. It exempted them from military service and guaranteed them freedom of worship. It also surveyed unoccupied lands and established immigration offices in St-Marc, Cap-Haitien, Port-au-Prince, Gonaives, and Cayes. Emigrationists welcomed these measures. Douglass praised the effort: "The good of the country, and the good of the emigrant, are equally consulted in the arrangement proposed."[74]

The political climate in Haiti became refreshingly stable, ushering in an era of "light, labor, enterprize, order, and all the arts of an advanced civilization."[75] Under Geffrard, Haitians not only developed the country but also supported African Americans, as shown in their reaction to John Brown's raid on Harper's Ferry in 1859. An African American wrote from Haiti, "The Hayti papers are so full of John Brown that they have little room for anything else. The country appears to be quiet, and the government is vigorously pursuing its measures of improvement and amelioration."[76] On January 20, 1860, Catholics in Haiti held a high mass for the repose of Brown's soul. William Newman, a Baptist clergyman involved in the antislavery movement in Ohio, attended that mass. Newman reported, "There were many things to interest and affect me as they could, perhaps, no one else present, because of my personal acquaintance with Captain Brown, and our many consultations for the liberty and welfare of my afflicted people."[77] In subsequent letters, Newman added his support: "I am doing all I can for those who wish to come to this country. I have organized an Emigration Society here to aid in the work of fixing them who wish to emigrate."[78]

Incentives to emigrate to Haiti at this period appeared irresistible to many American blacks who were searching for freedom and better economic conditions. To take advantage of the turn of events, Redpath opened the Haytian Bureau of Emigration in Boston. Frederick Douglass strongly endorsed Redpath as "a man of ability [who] has twice visited Hayti, has done much towards enlightening the public mind here as to the character and qualifications of those who administer the affairs of that country, and is zealous and faithful, we believe, in the prosecution of his work."[79]

Redpath published *Guide Book to Haiti* to promote the beautiful landscape and important events in Haitian history. He described Haiti as the only country in the Western world where "the Black and the man of color are undisputed lords; where the White is indebted for the liberty to live to the race which with us is enslaved; where neither laws, nor prejudices, nor historical memories, press cruelly on persons of African descent; where the people whom America degrades and drives from her are rulers, judges, and generals; men of extended commercial relations, authors, artists, and legislators."[80] Many nationally known African American leaders worked with Redpath, too. Holly headed that list, taking charge of the campaign in Pennsylvania and New Jersey. Henry Highland Garnet, a prominent New York clergyman, directed recruiting efforts in that state. Dennis J. Harris led the drive in Ohio. Harris wrote *A Summer on the Borders of the Caribbean Sea* as a record of his travels to Haiti. Haitian American Alexander Tate, along with William J. Watkins, toured Canada West, the African American colony just across from Detroit, Michigan, to gather converts for emigration.

Lectures and speeches delivered by these activists, and a full-page advertisement carried in *Douglass' Monthly* during 1861 and 1862, kept the emigration issue alive. Advertisements conveyed President Geffrard's invitation to the "black and yellow brethren," reminding them that Haiti was "the common country of the black race" bought by the blood of their ancestors for all descendants of Africa.[81]

Finally, former African American residents in Haiti reinforced interest in emigration. Benjamin Hunt provided a firsthand account of the living conditions on the island. Trades such as shoemaking, tailoring, and cabinetmaking were popular among the emigrants, he said. The best tailoring establishment in Port-au-Prince was conducted by two young men of color from one of the southern states, while one of the most prosperous bakers in Port-au-Prince came from New Orleans.[82]

Not every African American leader agreed with emigration to Haiti. Martin Robinson Delany saw no potential in Haiti since the island was small and had no prospects for acquiring more land. He continued to favor a return to Africa and deeply resented the leadership of Redpath, a white man. He wrote, "I am surprised that in the face of the intelligent black men who favor it . . . the government would appoint over them, to encourage black emigration, a white man, thereby acknowledging negro inferiority."[83] Delany believed the black man could act and provide for himself just as the white man could.

Though a staunch defender of Haitian independence and a supporter of the antislavery movement in the United States, James McCune Smith opposed emigration as well. Smith criticized Henry Highland Garnet for his involvement in the emigration movement. Smith offered this explanation to Garnet on why he did not want to emigrate "either to Abbeokuta or Hayti": "More than a quarter of a century ago, you and others, among whom I was the humblest, pledged yourselves to devote life and energies to the elevation and affranchisement of the free colored people on this, the soil which gave them birth, and through their affranchisement, the emancipation of the slaves of the South. This may be called old-fashioned doctrine; but it is none the less sound, and our pledges are none the less binding on that account."[84]

The conflicts continued; one of the most serious threats came from a former proponent of the movement, William Newman. In his clarion call "To the People of African Origin," Newman listed three factors he felt undermined the Haitian emigration process: "1st—its military system of government; 2nd—white ministers of the national religion; and 3rd—the public lands not being put into the market at a definite price."[85]

However, in a letter to the *Weekly Anglo-African*, J. B. Smith denounced Newman as "a very nervous, excitable and impulsive man" whose judgment could not be trusted. Smith encouraged emigration to those "whose spirit of enterprise and progress is prompting them to abandon their cramped condition, and the enervating circumstances to which they are subjected in this country, and journey to a land of brighter and greater promise."[86] The same attitude prevailed in Canada West where emigration preparations proceeded at full speed. George Cary, an organizer of an emigration society in Chatham, Massachusetts, also rejected Newman's criticism. Blacks from Canada West wanted to emigrate because of "the damning prejudice to contend against," Cary wrote. Newman "used every means to set the people against the Haytians . . . I'm happy to say that his temperament is too well known here to effect anything with any one in this neighborhood who entertained any serious notion of emigrating."[87]

Despite these conflicts, emigration proved popular, and the first emigrants of the second movement left for Haiti in early 1861. By the next summer, emigration requests were so great that Redpath kept busy processing them all. James Theodore Holly, a tireless worker for the Haitian cause, sailed from New York with the New Haven Company of 111 emigrants to pick up an additional 52 in Boston. They arrived at Port-au-Prince on June 1, 1861. The following statistics on those who departed for Haiti were compiled from *The Pine and Palm*, the official publication of the movement: "In May and June 140 blacks from four different ships disembarked at Port-au-Prince. Another 757 emigrants were reported to have sailed during the remainder of the year . . . Prospective emigrants from as far west as Kansas were applying to Redpath's agency in Boston for berths."[88]

Arguments from dissenters proved to be self-fulfilling prophecies. The same problems that plagued the emigration movement of 1824 haunted the second wave of newcomers. Once again, word of discontent reached the United States. Some emigrants complained that the Haitian government did not deliver on the promised-land allotments. Others found the heat of the tropical sun too harsh. Ultimately, it was sickness and death from "lack of cleanliness, excesses in eating and drinking, and a smallpox epidemic which had been introduced by one of the emigrant parties" that hurt the cause.[89]

Cultural differences proved to be a tremendous obstacle hindering the assimilation of African Americans into the Haitian way of life. Many simply could not endure such a drastic change. Most were relegated to the countryside, where they did not have the same standard of living they had left behind. One emigrant complained, "It was a common thing to see the Haytian women washing their clothes, men and boys bathing, and horses being washed, in the very stream we drank from. This alone was enough to create sickness."[90] Others complained about the customs and habits of Haitians: "The natives, male and female, generally go half clad, bordering on nudity. The women wear turbans on their heads and do not seem to have any use for hats. The men always go armed."[91]

The immigrants longed for the political stability of the United States and resented the military despotism prevalent in Haiti. As civil strife escalated, able-bodied men were drafted into the Haitian army, including African Americans who would cloak themselves with the American flag to avoid military service. The American consul in Port-au-Prince confirmed this: "Among the American immigrants who arrived here some five or six years ago, a great many have constantly refused to renounce their allegiance to the United States. Nevertheless an attempt is being made by the civil and the military authorities of this consular district to have these individuals from their family and from their peaceful occupation, and to compel them to serve in the armies and labor upon the public roads."[92] These individuals appealed to the American consul for protection from the Haitian civil disruptions.

These factors explain why many who participated in the second emigration movement returned home disillusioned and dissatisfied. One Pennsylvania emigrant wrote, "Hayti is not the place for a colored American, unless he is a capitalist, and it is utter folly for a poor man to go there and expect to make money or even procure as decent a living as can be easily obtained here."[93] As Haitian emigration fell into disrepute, so did the heroes of the movement. Educator and women's rights advocate Mary Ann Shadd asked, "Who . . . is this James Redpath, in the hollow of whose hand lies trembling the destiny of our people? This man, who by a species of moral jugglery, beyond my stupid comprehension, has succeeded in throwing glamour over the optics of all our friends, and who has made the bitter pill of colonization sophistry long since discarded by them, a sweet morsel of hundreds of devotees of the god 'Palm.'"[94]

Returnees tried not only to denounce Redpath but also to destroy the entire emigration plan. In Bishop Holly's hometown of New Haven, Theodore Griffin, a young man just returned from Haiti, described the miserable conditions there in a meeting with concerned townsfolk. The meeting concluded with a resolution condemning Holly and "all persons connected with this infamous scheme, be they commissioners, agents, sub-Agents or whatever named."[95] These lectures throughout the country contributed to the end of Haitian emigration. Another returnee, Joseph E. Williams, called it "the mischievous enterprise." Listeners agreed that the scheme was a "perfect humbug inducing our best citizens to leave their homes, led on by the accomplished deceiver, the notorious Jim Redpath, who cares nothing about the colored people of this country no farther than self-interest goes."[96]

By the end of 1862, Alexander Crummel, an Episcopalian minister from New York and an advocate of recolonization to Africa, wrote the epitaph on Haitian emigration: "Emigration to Hayti, which has been in progress for a year or two with very fair success, is interrupted, if not wholly suspended."[97] He explained that the Haitian government was unwilling to adopt measures deemed essential to the success of the emigration movement. Redpath resigned under pressure, and his *Pine and Palm*, the paper advocating emigration, stopped publication.

Despite others' feelings of bitterness and betrayal, some immigrants survived and adjusted to their new home. On April 15, 1862, a group from the St-Marc area wrote to dissociate themselves from the dissatisfaction of others, saying that Haitian government officials had fulfilled their pledge. In spite of disease and death, they strongly believed that "No people ever rose sooner from the inferior positions accorded to us a few months ago in the United States and Canada, to the respected position which . . . we occupy today in Hayti."[98] Many chose the naturalization path, demonstrating some level of union between African Americans and Haitians. A. B. Williamson was one of them, as attested by his naturalization certificate.

Equality Liberty
REPUBLIC OF HAITI
WE, FABRE GEFFRARD, PRESIDENT OF HAITI

Considering that Mr. A. B. Williamson, born in Maryland, fifty years old, is qualified to become Haitian, according to article 6 of the Constitution;

Considering that he has stated before the justice of the peace of Saint Marc assisted by his recorder, that he came to Haiti, with the intention to reside, and that he has, at the same time, sworn in the presence of the said judge, that he renounces any other nation but Haiti, as indicated by the certificate written at the justice of the peace on the eighteenth of November eighteen hundred sixty one and recorded that same month,

Deliver the present act of naturalization in accordance with the law modified by article of the Civil Code, to the above mentioned Mr. A. B. Williamson that he may enjoy the rights attached to privilege of Haitian citizenship, and carry out the duties as well.

Given at the National Palace of Port-au-Prince on March 31, eighteen hundred sixty two, the 59th year of the independence of Haiti.

signed: President Geffrard.[99]

The prospect of emigration persisted as the federal government contemplated the colonization of blacks in foreign lands. President Abraham Lincoln, a confirmed colonizationist, asked Congress to remove "the large numbers of negroes made dependent on the government by the fortunes of war."[100] Bernard Kock, a freelance capitalist from New Orleans, convinced Lincoln that he could colonize blacks on the Ile-à-Vache, a small island off the southern coast of Haiti, an island ceded to the United States by the Haitian government. Secretary Steward asked the Haitian diplomatic representative to investigate the plan since Kock promised "homes, employment, subsistence and wages"[101] to 5,000 emigrants he would relocate. Unfortunately Kock was discovered to be an impostor with no reliable resources. In another scheme, more than 400 blacks emigrated to the island with the help of the New York firm Forbes and Tuckerman, but the project resulted in the deaths of many emigrants.

Immigration and emigration were closely intertwined with the struggle of both Haitians and African Americans. While Haitians fought to consolidate their own independence, African Americans searched for a nation of their own. Neither of the two resettlement projects was completely successful due to the disparities, both cultural and political, that distanced Haitians from African Americans. The testimonies of the emigrants suggest that something more than the commonality of race and ethnicity was necessary for an effective emigration campaign; when it came to fulfilling the dream of securing a unified black nationality, the cultural and linguistic disparities proved to be a great divide.

Religion as a Weapon, 1824–1900

Let me come to speak more particularly of what should be the character-
istic of Haytian emigration. The leading motive and the actuating spirit
of this emigration movement should be that of religion, as in the case of
the pilgrim settlers of New England. (1859)

James Theodore Holly, *Anglo-African Magazine*

Even though African Americans viewed Haiti as the land of liberty, their
definition of liberty was different than that practiced in Haiti, especially
in matters of religion. A.M.E. Bishop Payne, the historian of the church,
noted that adherents of the Haitian religion kept many of the vices practiced by their former masters, similar to the Jews who retained many
Egyptian practices: "Added to the vicious habits of their Spanish and
French masters were fetishism and cannibalism, heightened and intensi-
fied by Romish superstition, and combined with all these evils, there
were the envy and jealousy already existing between the men of mixed
blood and the blacks, and thus we see abundant reasons for the evils
which have broken the unity and distracted the peace of the Haytians,
and which have also damaged their commerce and weakened their political strength and power."[1]

James Theodore Holly felt that Haiti was living under severe disabilities. "The dissemination of sound religious morality as the basis of public
virtue, and the cultivation of Literature, the Arts and Sciences, as the
sources of national prosperity, are inseparable concomitants of political
sovereignty in making up true national greatness. These things Hayti
does not and could not possess; and in this destitution we have the sum of
her disabilities."[2]

African Americans believed they could remedy these weaknesses by
rejuvenating Haiti with a potent dose of sound and pure Protestant
Christianity, unlike the tenets taught by their former masters.

Religion and Liberation

African Americans endeavored to enlighten and advance Haitians. As anthropologist George Simpson notes, "On the whole, Afro-American religions have tended to reinforce the social and political status quo, but nearly everywhere some religious groups have sought to change existing structures."[3]

The mixing of religion and politics had a long tradition in Africa. John Mbiti, a scholar on African religions, describes this way of life: "Religion is found in all areas of human life. It has dominated the thinking of African peoples to such an extent that it has shaped their cultures, their social life, their political organizations and economic activities."[4]

African priests were active in both secular and sacred affairs. Mbiti claims that "The duties of the priest are chiefly religious, but since Africans do not dissociate religion from other departments of life, he has or may have other functions. The priests are the depositories of national customs, knowledge, taboos, theology, and oral history. This wide knowledge qualifies them to act as political heads, judges, and ritual experts."[5]

At the end of the eighteenth century religion was a concern of the revolutionary movements in Haiti. Slaves returned to their African gods for their faith. According to Professor Leonard Barrett, the emergence of "redemption cults" was the result of the hostility slaves encountered. "In their struggle against oppression they invoked their African gods, especially the war gods, Ogun and Shango and others. They resorted to their own culturally approved techniques of resistance by practicing deception, and by reinterpreting their native folklore," Barrett writes.[6] Traditional African religion thrived with new cults: Cumina in Jamaica, Shango in Trinidad, Santeria in Cuba, Vodou in Haiti, and Candomblé in Brazil.

Vodou, an African religious term for "spirit" or "god," has roots in the old Dahomey kingdom, now Benin in West Africa, and is the primary source of Haitian cultural traits. Once they arrived in Saint-Domingue, slaves relied on ancestral gods for "spiritual comfort, protection from misfortune and cures for . . . ills."[7] Vodou emerged as rituals of various African tribes who commingled when their quality of life failed to improve. Vodou cult practices appealed to the masses who were faced with poverty, illiteracy, and a lack of health care.

Haitians have modified and enriched the Vodou rites and symbols. Haitian slaves found Catholicism to be an ideal venue for their Vodou practices. In the religious acculturation of the slaves, there emerged a syncretism, "the recombinations of cultural elements from different societies into new wholes."[8] Catholic prayers and songs are often used in Vodou services. Catholic saints became "incorporated in the repertoire of their supernatural beings."[9] The deities, called *lwas*, are analogous to Catholic saints. They come to life by incarnating themselves in the faithful through the phenomenon known as possession, that is, when the devotee becomes both the mouthpiece and the instrument of the god.

Vodou became a politico-religious movement that allowed slave leaders to marshal their energies for their revolution against institutional slavery. According to Haitian historian Dantès Bellegarde, "The slaves found in Vodou the ideal stimulus for their energy—since Vodou had become less a religion than a political association . . . dedicated to the destruction of the whites and the deliverance of the negroes."[10] Guided by priests who kept African beliefs and rites alive, slaves used the liturgy of the cults as a weapon against their oppressors. When gathered for worship, "Chants of revolt and prayers invoking the aid of the Voodoo deities against the white man were heard in the nocturnal gatherings."[11] Their songs manifested their awareness of the system of exploitation they endured.

Vodou served as a unifying force in the struggle against this servitude. Black leaders drew on their religious authority to help influence the masses in insurrections and, more commonly, in destructive raids on plantations. The revolutionary role of the Haitian priest and priestess is best shown in the life of François Makandal, traditionally thought of as the forerunner for Haitian independence. A slave from the African coast of Guinea, Makandal used his religious power to instigate a guerrilla war against colonial rule. He established himself as a prophet inspired by the higher African divinities and as one possessed with the mission to chase the whites out of the colony and make Saint-Domingue a kingdom for the blacks. Makandal also persuaded his fellow slaves that he was invulnerable. Even when the colonists seized him and burned him alive, he remained a prominent figure with his followers. They believed he used his magical powers to escape the flames and fade out of sight. Figures like Makandal managed to link Vodou to the revolutionary fervor of the time.

Vodou had its critics. Founding fathers Toussaint-Louverture and Jean Jacques Dessalines publicly abhorred it. Others, like Emperor Faustin Soulouque and François Duvalier, embraced it. Pioneer African American missionaries who were critical of the heathen influence in Haiti used Protestant Christianity as a force for political regeneration. Others were more critical of the cult. E. L. Blackshear, from Prairie View State Normal and Industrial College in Texas, alerted the Secretary of State in Washington: "As a colored citizen of the United States interested in the welfare of my race in all parts of the world, I wish to enter a protest against the conditions in Hayti. These conditions, including not only political anarchy that gets nowhere, but a horrible religion known as Vaudaux or Voodooism, a degrading mixture of sensualism, snake-worship and cannibalism. Hayti is the worst spot on the globe. Its condition is very worse than savagery. Nowhere else is the human so low, so degraded. Hayti is a blot on the human race."[12]

Blackshear rejected Vodou, even suggesting an American occupation of Haiti to eliminate it. He neglected to consider the strength of the cult, even in the United States. Vodou was a folk religion in Louisiana. Like the slaves in Haiti, Louisiana's blacks based their beliefs and customs on those of their West African forebears. These slaves created their own version of Vodou that colonial authorities tried to suppress.

Vodou was especially popular in Louisiana during the black exodus from Saint-Domingue from 1791 to 1809. Vodou was openly practiced as an organized religion with many new converts. In Congo Square, where city officials allowed slaves to perform, blacks danced the *Calinda* as they did in the bushes of colonial Haiti.[13]

Marie Laveau was a legendary figure of Louisiana's Vodou practice. She was a free woman of color, a descendant of Haitians who migrated to New Orleans. There she married Jacques Paris, a native of Jeremie, Saint-Domingue. After her husband died, Laveau lived with another San Domingan, Captain Louis Christophe Duminy de Glapion, a member of a black battalion. Laveau used her talents to spread Vodou, transforming it into a business. She invited to her religious meetings "the press, the police, the sporting world and any thrill-seekers ready to donate a fee for admission."[14] Laveau became the "Voodoo queen" who was sought by politicians, business leaders, and admirers of her magical powers to place and remove curses and to tell fortunes.

As in Haiti, the African priests used their influence over American plantation slaves to stage their insurrections. American educator W. E. B. Du Bois wrote that these men served as the "interpreter of the supernatural, the comforter of the sorrowing, and as the one who expressed

. . . the longing and disappointment and resentment of a stolen people."[15] In the early days, the priests officiated in a church that still practiced "heathen rights" despite their Christianization.

One of these priests was Gullah Jack, a conjurer, or witch doctor. Just as Makandal did in Haiti, Jack, an African native, claimed to be invulnerable. An able lieutenant in the Vesey rebellion, he urged recruits, in the words of Professor Robert Starobin, to use "African religious symbols to guarantee victory," and encouraged superstitious slaves to seek freedom.[16] As these slaves retained their African customs and practices, they also kept and practiced the art of conjure—the practice of healing work, which continued in colonial America. Conjure was also known as "hoodoo" (linguistically connected with the voodoo practiced in colonial Saint-Domingue).

There remained a fundamental religious difference between the Latin and Anglo-Saxon systems of slavery. In Saint-Domingue, Catholicism was practiced exclusively under Spanish and French control; in the North American colonies, there were many religious denominations. Both the United States and France required the baptism of slaves into the Christian faith. While the French religious establishment had an elaborate baptismal ceremony, the process of indoctrination was more complex in the North. Because of this more advanced religious practice, slaveholders feared the education required of their slaves for baptism would eventually lead to a plea for freedom. These slaveholders deeply resented this baptismal ritual. That is why the Anglican Church made little progress in converting blacks, even though the Society for the Propagation of the Gospel in Foreign Parts of the Church of England later devoted more attention to both blacks and Indians. Anglicanism failed to reach African Americans in particular because of the difference in worldviews. Historian Mechal Sobel describes this difference: "In the African world view, most matter is permeated or penetrated by the holy. In the Anglican, the holy has been reduced to a moral-ethical dimension . . . It does not penetrate every aspect of daily life in a dramatic fashion but is highly segregated."[17]

Evangelization of the slaves began when the Baptists and the Methodists made direct personal appeals to the masses. During what is called the Great Awakenings (1720–40 and 1790–1815), "Enthusiasm ran high for reaching blacks with the gospel, and large numbers of Negroes were converted."[18] Blacks responded to their call because they thought they could incorporate African religious elements into the Baptist and Methodist tradition of camp meetings.[19] In 1780, when the General Conference of the Methodist Church in America declared slavery to be "contrary to the laws of God, man and nature, and hurtful to society," blacks converting to the Baptist and Methodist faith increased considerably.[20]

The history of American black Christianity began with what is now called the "invisible institution." There were a limited number of religious options open to African Americans, so they created their own style of worship using the African ethos as their model. This invisible institution evolved without ordained ministers, membership rolls, or even meeting places. Though forbidden, it was celebrated in the woods at night. It brought African Americans together as a community and fulfilled their needs for comfort and relief from their daily servitude and bondage. That invisible institution incorporated its own preaching styles and songs, which were the spirituals that translated the feelings and aspirations of the slaves.[21]

The invisible church was finally practiced openly as African Americans gained their freedom. When the once forbidden evangelization became popular, African Americans found interracial worship a stumbling block, leaving the predominantly white churches in which they felt marginalized and treated as wards. In 1794, Richard Allen established the Bethel Church, which later merged with others to become the African Methodist Episcopal Church. Allen, associated with St. George Episcopal Church in Philadelphia, left in protest when white clergymen forced him to occupy the rear section of the building during prayer. That was the section reserved for blacks. Absalom Jones, who left St. George with Allen over the same incident, also organized his own church in 1793, the Church of St. Thomas, affiliated with the Episcopal faith.

African American Baptists also established themselves independently from whites, setting up the first black Baptist church in Williamsburg, Virginia, in 1776. Others followed in 1788, in Savannah, and in 1790, in Augusta, Georgia. Several other black Baptist congregations were planted in northern cities as well.

Haitian emigrants added a new dimension to African American religious institutions in the United States. The Haitians were largely Catholic and made an impact in the various cities where they settled across the nation. In Philadelphia, their presence gave rise to biracial congregations at the city's three Catholic churches, especially St. Joseph. In Savannah, most Haitian emigrants attended Saint John the Baptist Catholic Church.[22]

In New York, Pierre Toussaint, a Haitian emigrant, made a lasting impression on the Catholic Church beyond his local parish. He was a slave who came to the city with his master Monsieur Jean Bérard in 1787 and learned the hairdressing business, becoming quite successful. Toussaint was not an activist. His memoir reveals him as a man who "was observant of all the forms of the Roman Catholic Church; through winter and summer he missed no matin prayers, but his heart was never narrowed by any feeling as to sect or color."[23] Toussaint never felt degraded by being black or a slave. In fact, he was able to earn money and bought his sister's freedom while he remained a slave himself. When his master died, Toussaint took care of his master's wife, Marie Elizabeth Bérard-Nicolas. She finally freed him on her deathbed as a token of her gratitude. He gave his money to the Catholic Orphan School for white children and to bring up "colored boys one after another, sending them to school, and, after they were old enough, teaching them some useful business." Toussaint supported all Catholic institutions. His selflessness and faithfulness earned him the privilege of being scrutinized for canonization.[24]

In Baltimore, religion strengthened the communion between Haitians and African Americans. The chapel of St. Mary's Seminary was segregated, with white immigrants worshiping on the upper floor and people of color using the basement, or *chapelle basse*. The French Sulpicians provided spiritual leadership for the Baltimore Catholics, both white and black. Under the spiritual guidance of Father Joubert, the Oblate Sisters created a thriving religious community with branches in various cities. In 1836, the Oblate Sisters helped to found a church, later named St. Francis Xavier's, especially for black worshipers. This chapel was described as "the first building in Baltimore, and, of course in the United States, destined to be used for worship by colored Catholics. The lower chapel of St. Mary's had been used by them and the Jesuits later erected the very first parish church for the colored but this new chapel of St. Frances, was not only the chapel for the Convent of the Oblate Sisters but a chapel of ease for colored Catholics, where they might bring their babies to be baptized, their children to have them make their First Communion and receive Confirmation, where they might be married themselves and might be buried."[25]

St. Mary's also joined the network called "St. Frances Institutions," an organization established by the Oblate Sisters and made up of the convent school, the free school, and the orphan asylum. Both the church and the institutions carried out activities linking the Haitian and African American communities. The sisters held fund-raisers attended by both Haitians and African Americans.[26]

The network of churches became a powerful liberation instrument with slaves, confirming the worst fears of slaveholders. Religious meetings provided an easy way to indoctrinate slaves about the injustice of the slave masters. The "keepers of established order" tried to monitor these religious activities. As early as 1800, South Carolina adopted a law prohibiting free slaves from meeting and assembling "for the purpose of mental instruction or religious worship, either before the rising of the sun or after the going down of the same."[27]

Despite the vigilance of whites, religion continued to undermine oppression. As with any good propaganda machine, the slave leaders interpreted the Bible to suit their immediate interest in liberation. They taught that the God of the Old Testament defended the oppressed. Their unshakable belief in the power of God explains why the three largest insurrections—those led by Gabriel Prosser, Denmark Vesey, and Nat Turner—in the antebellum South had religious underpinnings. Gabriel plotted to free his fellow slaves after reading the Old Testament. Likewise, Vesey used stories of the Israelite liberation as proof that his fight for freedom was sanctioned by God. Finally, Nat Turner, the prophet and visionary, put his religious conviction into action to attain his revolutionary objectives when he led a slave rebellion in Southampton County, Virginia, in 1831.

Spirituals also reinforce the view that religion was a vehicle for liberation. Songs such as "Go Down, Moses," in which God sent Moses "way down in Egypt's land, to tell Ole Pharaoh, let my people go," created a parallel understanding of the life of slaves in the United States.[28] They believed that deliverance from slavery in America would also come about through divine intervention.

When African American religious leaders such as Bishop Richard Allen and Absalom Jones, as well as several Baptists, established their own churches, they could control religious activities of other African Americans. This control created another dimension of black nationalism, that of religious nationalism. This ideology maintains that "Within the Christian fold blacks should establish and control churches of their own, that God, or Jesus, or both were black, and that Afro-Americans are the Chosen People."[29] Religion became not just a weapon against slavery but also an instrument of true enlightenment. Blacks were interested in spreading the Gospel to the former homeland and throughout the world. Baptist minister Lott Carey and Williams Crane, a deacon of the First Baptist Church of Richmond, organized the Richmond African Baptist Missionary Society in 1815. Carey also served as a missionary in Liberia where he established a colony. The Baptist Missionary Society of Massachusetts commissioned Thomas Paul, another pioneering black missionary, to work in Haiti.

African Americans and Protestant Christianity in Haiti

The 1824 and 1859 emigration movements failed to increase the population of Haiti. Many emigrants returned to the United States or died from illnesses. Those who remained, however, joined an emerging independent church movement of Protestant Christianity on the island.

Until 1824, when the first immigrants arrived, Haiti was almost exclusively Catholic. The Catholic faith thrived unchallenged during the Spanish and French colonial periods. Even after independence, Catholicism remained the primary religion on the island.

The Catholic Church could not fulfill the religious and social needs of the people of Haiti for many reasons. From 1805 to 1860, the church was subject to the state. In the early years of Haitian independence, a period marked by a scarcity of priests, Emperor Dessalines acted as head of the church. Upon Dessalines' assassination, when the country was divided, there were only two priests in Pétion's republic and three in Christophe's kingdom. The Haitian church evolved independently and was not recognized by the pope.

Christophe was the only Haitian leader to deviate from the Latin tradition to experiment with the Anglican Church. The *Niles' Register* reported, "It started to be the intention of Christophe to change the religion of his kingdom from the Roman Catholic to the Episcopal communion; and Prince Saunders, who has the superintendence of an academy there, is adopting measures for carrying out his design into execution."[30] Christophe introduced Protestantism to his kingdom when he asked three Anglican ministers to direct his undeveloped school system. His intention was to replace Catholicism with Anglicanism since he felt Anglican clergy were more enlightened and more honest than the Roman Catholic clergy. He viewed the Anglican Church as a weapon he could use in his struggle against the French. To further implement this policy, "He ordered that the children should be instructed in the English language, with a view to prevent the intrigues of the French to recover the country, against whom he expressed the most determined opposition."[31]

At the same time, Pétion invited two Wesleyan Methodist ministers, John Brown and James Catts, from England in 1816. They were to introduce the Methodist denomination to the country. After the deaths of Pétion and Christophe, President Boyer sought to return Roman Catholicism to Haiti. He felt that recognition from the Church of Rome would reduce Haiti's isolation. This proved to be a difficult task. Although Boyer had power over both civil and ecclesiastical jurisdictions, the few colonial priests in the country were known for their misconduct and debauchery. Victor Schoelcher, the French abolitionist and author of a biography on Toussaint-Louverture, observed that "Far from enlightening the people they keep them fixed in the silliest superstitions."[32] These priests were entrepreneurs who sold their religion to the masses; they performed various rites for money, earning a lucrative living at the expense of their flock.

Competition from Protestantism forced the pope to devote more attention to Haiti. To regain the Church's dominance in ecclesiastical affairs, Rome signed a concordat in 1860 that made Roman Catholicism the official religion of Haiti and gave special privileges to its clergy. The church also received financial support from the state. In return, the pope recognized the independence of Haiti. Because of their French heritage, the elite wholeheartedly embraced Roman Catholicism. The French language and cultural values were already deeply embedded, if not cherished. With Roman Catholicism firmly established, cultural supremacy continued for the French.

With their Catholic stronghold and a highly rated school system, French cultural influence dominated the Haitian upper class. Spencer St. John, the British consul, observed that the *Petit Séminaire*, run by the Holy Ghost Fathers *(Pères Spiritains)*, was "the best school in the country."[33] In 1883, this school had an enrollment of 300 students. In 1894, when a host of French Brothers and Sisters arrived to open new schools, the Catholic educational system was further strengthened.

Despite its educational advantage, the Catholic Church failed to make the welfare of the general public in Haiti its primary concern. Instead it devoted its full attention to the elite, seeking to perpetuate the French language and culture and to promote immediate French interests. St. John verified that "The Catholic priests are also comparatively few in number, dislike heartily the life in the interior, and are paid by the State."[34] To fill the void, the masses remained attached to Vodou and their African traditions.

Adherents of Protestantism reached out to the masses of the cities and of the countryside. They offered a sound alternative to the superstitions and magic of Vodou and served as a refuge from malevolent spirits known as *lwas* or spirits associated with the Vodou cult. People converted in order to be cured of the illnesses caused by angry spirits and, at the same time, to escape the punitive action of these spirits.[35] Unlike the syncretism of Catholicism and Vodou, Protestantism promoted a vigorous and complete break with the cult.

Inevitably, rivalry erupted between Catholics and Protestants. Haitian nationalists watched as the power of the Catholic Church grew, in both sacred and secular affairs. To counteract its influence, nationalists denounced Catholicism as an infringement on national independence. To maintain control, the Haitian government promoted religious freedom as guaranteed in Article 26 of the Constitution of 1879. As St. John describes, "Although the Roman Catholic religion is that of the State, all others are tolerated, and many Haytian Ministers have felt inclined to encourage the Protestants, not only to counterbalance any political influence of the priests, but with the object of creating a rivalry in the performance of missionary duties."[36]

Following the lead of Christophe, these nationalists preferred Protestantism, believing it was better at "providing an ideology and an incentive for capitalist development."[37] Louis Joseph Janvier, a Haitian publicist, promoted the spread of Protestantism in the country and led the attack against Roman Catholicism. Janvier, a Wesleyan Methodist, supported Protestantism as the better religion for progress and tolerance in Haiti: "The more Haiti will draw near to Protestantism and free thinking, the better she will be."[38]

Until the 1824 arrival of the African American immigrants, Protestants faced stern opposition in Haiti. Anti-Protestant pressure forced the two English Wesleyan missionaries brought in by Pétion, John Brown and James Catts, out of the country. President Boyer eased the enmity against Protestants in order to support the emigration project. By granting emigrants the freedom to practice their faith, Boyer was forced to expand this freedom to Haitians as well.

African Americans arriving in Haiti established churches and religious societies throughout the island. Methodist minister Mark Baker Bird noted, "At Port-au-Prince a neat little edifice was raised by the American colored immigrants which would accommodate some two hundred hearers."[39] Immigrants brought with them the singing, dancing, and convulsing practices of their camp meetings. Their religious services caused a great deal of excitement for the native population.

Immigrants established mostly Protestant churches. They quite naturally felt the need to continue their religious practices as soon as they arrived. Those of the Baptist faith founded the first Baptist church in Haiti, and the board of managers of the Baptist General Convention of the United States appointed Reverend William Monroe as missionary. He served three years at that post before returning to the United States.

Others originally affiliated with the Bethel African Methodist Episcopal Church in Philadelphia set up an A.M.E. church in Port-au-Prince, naming it after St. Peter. Among them was Henri Allen, the son of Bishop Richard Allen. They asked the A.M.E. headquarters for an ordained missionary to tend to the moral and spiritual well-being of their followers. Bishop Allen was interested in establishing a new church in a foreign land and hoped to strengthen Haitian independence.

Bishop Payne described a vision in which the church would

make the Haytian nationality and government strong, powerful and commanding among the nations of the earth: When we consider the truth that no race of men can establish and perpetuate a strong government upon political principles which are nothing more than an embodiment of human selfishness, we are led to the opinion that to make a government strong and stable, and the nation it represents powerful and truly great, and to perpetuate its power and greatness, the divine approbation, shield and blessing must be obtained and secured. But by conformity to the divine will as it is expressed in the Decalogue and Beatitudes. In view of which we believe it is a dictate of Christian wisdom and benevolence that the African Episcopal Church ought to concentrate her moneys and men upon Hayti until her missions shall be developed into a separate and independent ecclesiastical body like that given to Sierra Leone by the Church of England.[40]

American diplomats emphasized the need for emigration to regenerate Haitian society. B. F. Sanford, U.S. consul in Haiti, was discouraged by what he called the "bestial sin of the world, excess of indulgence in sexual intercourse, and promiscuous embracings of the sexes." As a remedy, he suggested "the emigration to Hayti of the religious moral and industrious colored people that are in our midst. There are in our country a large number of colored people, possessing characters worthy of high respect, who have no field to rise in keeping with their aspirations."[41] Stanford embraced the concept of exploiting religion to serve a moral purpose. Conversely, Bishop Allen saw Christianity as an instrument to strengthen the Haitian government. He "viewed missions in political and social, or cultural terms."[42] As in Africa, religion and politics remained intertwined.

James Theodore Holly held the same view as Bishop Allen, explaining, "The Christian Religion is the salt of the earth; it is necessary to the national preservation of any people; and if this element is not soon strongly infused into the Haytian Commonwealth, beyond anything now at work, looking to that end, it will be impossible to ward off the internal corruption of revolutionary parties in that country, or to delay the ultimate decay and annihilation of its political sovereignty."[43] Holly implemented this agenda during a half century of ministry in Haiti that spanned from 1861 to his death in 1911.

With religion as the cornerstone, a new era had begun for the A.M.E. Church. After a meeting of local leaders and preachers, the A.M.E. Conference appointed Thomas Robertson as missionary to Haiti. Robertson reneged on his appointment for health reasons, and Scipio Beanes of the Baltimore Conference accepted the call. In 1826, the A.M.E. Church commissioned Beanes to serve as the first worker in a foreign missionary field in the West Indies. This also marked the first foreign mission of the A.M.E. Church. In spite of his poor health, Beanes worked tirelessly and was successful in his mission until he died in 1835.

For a while, due to a lack of men and money, the national headquarters of the A.M.E. Church in the United States neglected the churches in Haiti. However, local ministers carried on until the arrival of the Reverend Charles Mossell from the United States in the spring of 1879.

Mossell, a graduate of Lincoln University, gave a tremendous boost to the church. He left St. Peter's because of internal strife among the leadership there and founded the St. Paul A.M.E. Church, which remains an active religious institution in Haiti to this day. He also established a French and English language school at the church.

Ever the scholar, Mossell wrote about heroic Haitian deeds, especially those of Toussaint Louverture. Mossell wrote about these achievements in his book *Toussaint L'Ouverture, or Hayti's Struggle*. John Mercer Langston, an American minister to Haiti, wrote in the introduction, "How can one better serve his race than in making known the virtues of a brave people, whose examples in deeds and sacrifices to advance individual and popular welfare, furnishes a light by which the conduct of others who struggle for freedom, for just recognition, may be guided?"[44]

Through Mossell's A.M.E. church, closer ties developed between African Americans and Haitians. With the help of President Félicité Salomon, Reverend Mossell raised enough money to send five native Haitians to the United States to attend Wilberforce University. One of them, Salomon Dorcé, returned to work in the Haitian church after graduation from the Theological Department of Wilberforce. But Dorcé returned to the United States after one year, married an American, and remained with the A.M.E. Church in the United States.

Reverend John Hurst, a descendant of American immigrants, rose to prominence through the A.M.E. Church. Like Dorcé, Hurst graduated in theology from Wilberforce College with financial help from Charles Mossell. After serving in Haiti, he moved to the United States and was elevated to bishop on May 11, 1912. He served in Florida and North Carolina. Between 1912 and 1922, Bishop Hurst presided over the Board of Trustees of Edward Waters College in Florida and was a well-known figure in diplomatic affairs and in civil rights. Appointed as secretary of the Haitian delegation in Washington, D.C., he also became vice president of the NAACP.[45]

Another missionary scholar, T. G. Steward, also began in the A.M.E. Church. Steward, who had written a book on the Haitian Revolution, strongly believed that the church could improve the conditions of life in Haiti. When he returned to the United States, he sought to impress on the A.M.E. hierarchy the urgent need for help.

Still, African Americans and Haitians stayed apart; African Americans saw Haitians as "heathens" or "semiheathens" whom they wanted to convert, and Haitians saw African Americans as outsiders. Regardless of their relationship with one another, missionary efforts often failed because of the political unrest in Haiti.

Mossell went to Haiti with the mission to "assist in making the Haytians a great nation by making them truly and earnestly Christians."[46] This objective melted in the hot sun of Haitian political chaos. In 1884, because of Boyer Bazelais's revolt against President Salomon, Mossell's property was destroyed and his life was so severely affected that it warranted the intervention of American minister John Mercer Langston. His wife and daughter suffered violence. When Langston interceded, Mossell "was directed to and did make demand of the Haytian government, not only in full payment for his property destroyed but in settlement by payment of a large sum of money as damages for the insults and abuses of himself and his family."[47]

The Protestant Episcopal Church

The commitment to spread Protestant Christianity to Haiti was particularly strong with the Protestant Episcopal Church, from the very beginnings when the church was established during the emigration of 1859. James Theodore Holly was at the forefront of the emigration movement and a prominent member of the antebellum northern black leadership. When he immigrated to Haiti, he believed he was called to enlighten Haitians through the Episcopal Church.

In 1855, Holly traveled to Haiti and was thinking about emigrating there. He studied the country for missionary opportunities. In a report submitted to the foreign secretary of the Board of Missions of the Protestant Episcopal Church, Samuel Denison, he noted the "splendid opportunity" for an Episcopal mission in Haiti. He proposed that he and one other missionary be sent to Haiti. He expected support from the Soulouque administration: "This government accords toleration emphatically to Protestants [sic] missionaries. The emperor is said to be secretly in favor of the success of Protestantism, and grants more liberty to the missionaries who are here than to the Romish priests."[48]

Holly also hoped for support from other Haitian missionaries, especially from the American Methodist emigrants who had settled in the country. "The idea of commencing an Episcopal mission from the United States was cordially received by them also."[49] Although Holly's church rejected his proposal, he continued to work toward his mission.

Holly viewed emigration as a way African Americans could achieve self-reliance through political regeneration and development of Haiti's natural resources. He published his ideas in six installments in "Thoughts on Hayti" in the *Anglo-African Magazine*. Holly closely associated Haiti with the destiny of the black race. As he explains, "If Haitian independence shall cease to exist, the sky of Negro destiny shall be hung in impenetrable blackness."[50] Holly identified Haiti as an ideal location for a strong black nationality. Guided by these objectives, Holly screened prospective immigrants to select those who best personified the qualities of self-reliance and industriousness.

Holly believed religion would play a vital role in promoting progress in Haiti. Even though he knew that the country had severe disabilities, he would not forget that the nation had a history of rule by tyrants, from Dessalines to Soulouque. Because of the instability, he felt Haiti's future must include both sound religious and moral teachings as well as the cultivation of literature, arts, and sciences. He called this theory the "two arms of all national well-being."[51]

Holly thought Catholicism failed to address the nation's problems. David Walker, the abolitionist author, agreed. In Walker's *Appeal*, he denounced the Catholic Church in Haiti as "the scourge of nations."[52] According to Holly, Catholicism burdened the people with the "most distorted and exaggerated features of Christianity." Protestant Christianity, on the other hand, could effect change by providing "the enlightening influences of the pure Religion of Jesus."[53]

Religion not only enlightened the masses but also curbed political instability. It provided the element needed to "be infused in the Haitian commonwealth to ward off the internal corruption of revolutionary parties," precluding the ultimate demise of its political sovereignty. Holly envisioned an emigration movement that would "assume the shape of well-organized religious communities, headed by an educated ministry, and backed and [be] sustained by learned laymen in sufficient numbers to open up the way for, and lead on, the progressive wants of civilized settlements."[54]

Holly's actions demonstrated his conviction. He took responsibility for leading the Madeira shipload of emigrants to Haiti. He required pilgrims to sign and commit themselves to his "Madeira Compact," pledging, among other things, to "seek less to advance our temporal interest than to labor for the establishment of the Kingdom of God in Haiti."[55]

Holly's New Haven colony settled at Drouillard, a government estate about three miles outside of Port-au-Prince. Soon, the colony was plagued by disease and death. Holly lost his wife, Charlotte, his daughter, Cora, and his infant son, Joseph Geffrard. Nevertheless, he held to his dream of developing a self-governing national church in the republic.

When he arrived in 1861, Holly conducted services at Drouillard, attracting many Haitians. He returned to the United States to appeal for financial help from the Protestant Episcopal Church. While in the United States, he married Sarah Henley of New Haven and returned to Port-au-Prince and the survivors of his colony. In 1863, he formally consecrated Holy Trinity, the first Protestant Episcopal church in Haiti.[56]

Holly and his family had some financial setbacks. He opened a shoe-making shop just to make ends meet. Then, in 1863, fire destroyed a newly built church building and the adjoining parsonage and school. Revolutions continued to add to his despair. In 1868, Holly described the situation: "Haiti has been passing through a terrible ordeal since the first of May last. Civil war of the worst kind has unchained the passions of the contending parties, upturned society and is now spreading death and devastation everywhere in its tracks. This result was foreseen by us last year as the inevitable consequence of the radical revolution then accomplished which thoroughly shook and unsettled the foundations of social order in its delirious infatuation."[57] Here Holly referred to the civil strife that followed President Geffrard's overthrow.

Revolution continued in Haiti, and in 1879 Holly wrote, "Civil war in various quarters of the Republic, by attempts at political revolution (the chronic state of Haitian society), has added its burdens to all these and carried our privation to the last point of endurance. At the moment in which I write . . . civil war is raging around me, in the very heart of the capital, and has been for the last four days, with the prospect of several days more of continuance. Many have fallen victims, and many more are like(ly) to succumb to the horrors of internecine strife."[58]

Political instability was a cause of friction between Holly and the elite of his adoptive country, highlighting in his mind the differing viewpoints of the Latin and Anglo-Saxon cultures. Holly believed political strife in Haiti was rooted in the French culture, the very foundation of the French education the elite received. Holly complained of "the blasphemous effronteries of infidelity that the educated men among those people imbibed from France, which was atheistically infidel by the deliberate act of that whole nation at the very moment the Haitiens conceived the idea of struggling for their liberty and independence towards the close of the last century."[59] Though Holly concluded his thesis in theological terms, his primary contention was that French education predisposed Haitians to revolution.

The message came across quite clearly in this condemnation: "It is remarkable that it is only the better educated and wealthier classes of the cities, and therefore, those who ought to be the better behaved, that take part in those conspiracies. The lower classes of the cities, with few exceptions, and the masses of the rural population, remain perfectly tranquil ... Only the few whose brains have been penetrated with the infidel ideas that the French Revolution of 93 imbibed along with the smattering of an education that they have received, are thus corrupt. The masses in their blissful ignorance are yet uncontaminated."[60]

French education gave rise to political institutions that were equally detrimental to the country's stability. Holly referred to the Haitian constitutions, which, he wrote, failed to respect "the true spirit of laws and political constitutions," like those of France. "Constitutions are the slow growth of ages and are not made to order by 'constituent conventions' called together by a revolutionary mob. France nor Haiti have learned this fact yet. Hence the numerous constitutions the one has had made to order in a gust of passion since 1789 and the other by political sprees since 1804. We have just had one made here last year. Hence, we can refer now to the Haitien constitutions of 1804, 1806, 1808, 1816, 1843, 1846, 1849."[61]

Holly prescribed a dose of Anglo-Saxonism for Haiti as a cure against the ineffectiveness of French institutions. He credited the stability of England with gradually developed political constitutions: "No other race but the Saxon race seems yet to fully understand that a political constitution should be the outgrowth of necessities of a people, the expression of their experience and the index of their social, intellectual and other civilized attainments. All other races seem to commit the sad blunder of drawing up constitutions on some ideal theory—from the wild chimeras of their imaginations—without taking into consideration the question of practical adaptation to the condition of the people for whom they legislate."[62] Holly was grateful that French culture did not spoil the spirit of religious tolerance. "The Haitien people, unlike these foreign clerical adventurers from France, are not intolerant ... The African mind is generally disposed to be tolerant in religious matters."[63]

Holly's deep dissatisfaction did not hinder his efforts to continue his mission. His attitude confirms that, in spite of being removed from the American shores, "Emigrationists continued to find American values and ideals attractive, as evidenced by their emphasis on Western notions of civilizing and Christianizing the host people and society."[64] Though Holly left the United States because of its undemocratic policies and became a Haitian citizen, he found American political institutions useful for the advancement of his adopted country. He continued to admire the stability of political constitutions and to revere law and order.

Holly remained faithful to Haiti and his work, despite the disturbances of life in his adopted country, relying on the "quickening influence of the Holy Ghost" to manage the responsibilities of daily life. Work still went forward at Holy Trinity. Holly managed to turn his dream into reality step by step. In 1874, the Protestant Episcopal Church recognized the church in Haiti as an independent national church holding fraternal relations with the American body. This recognition was a substantial victory for Holly, who had long fought in favor of a church under the leadership of black people. He translated the vocation of the church in these terms:

The church in Haiti feels conscious of being called to be the church of the Haitien people. This conviction becomes the more striking from the fact that it is the only ecclesiastical organization in this republic that steadily pursues the fixed design of raising up from among these people a national clergy, flesh of their flesh, and bone of their bone, to minister among them in sacred things. And at this moment the church, though but of 16 years duration in this island, numbers 11 native clergymen, whilst the Roman Catholic Church which dates back near four centuries from its foundation has but two native priests out of 93 that form at the present time its clerical staff in the island; and the Wesleyans who date back their operations in Haiti to 60 years have but one ordained native minister.[65]

To honor him, the mother church elected Holly bishop of Haiti, and he was consecrated at Grace Church in New York City in 1874 as the first African American Episcopal Bishop.

Holly established mission stations and built parish schools in the Haitian countryside. He supported the work of the Methodist Church in securing industrial missionary settlements along the Congo Valley and the

West Coast of Africa, where improved methods of agriculture were introduced. He recommended that Haiti be included in the American Missionary Association. That association built a sawmill as part of its commitment to the people of Jamaica. Holly believed "Such a thing is much needed among the mountaineers of Haiti, and would be of incalculable service in promoting home comforts, and improving the condition of the family."[66] He launched schools for teaching of the classics, agricultural schools, and a medical clinic. By 1874, the church was made up of "14 clergymen, 15 mission stations and schools with a population of 274 students."[67] The Haitian government formally congratulated Holly for his contribution.[68]

Holly's children continued in their father's footsteps, dedicating themselves to the betterment of Haiti. They worked in the ministry, in education, and in publishing, producing studies about Haiti. Arthur Cleveland Coxe Holly, awarded a medical degree from the University of Boston, wrote on education, medicine, and religion in Haiti. A second son, Alonzo Potter Burgess Holly, was consul of Haiti to the Bahamas. In one of Alonzo's reports, he defended religious tolerance in Haiti: "Haiti has a God-given mission to fulfill, and that is the uplifting and rehabilitation of the Negro Race. Few indeed are disposed to gainsay the providential element which attended the events which ushered her birth among the Nations of the Earth."[69]

African Americans saw Haiti as a nation with severe problems both socially and politically, and they tried to correct these problems. Charles Romain, a Haitian scholar who undertook the latest survey on this subject, described Protestantism's increasing popularity: "Until 1920, there was about 1 Protestant for 200 inhabitants. In 1930, the ratio increased to 3 for 200, and since then the Protestant offensive has been growing. In 1968, Protestantism constituted 15% of the Haitian population and 20% by the end of the 70s."[70]

Despite Protestantism's rapid advances, Haiti remains a politically unstable land with a complex social and political framework that continues to defy all diagnoses for change.

4

Partners in Defending the Race, 1869–1915

The African race today contains too many outstanding men, both in
terms of intelligence and moral uprightness, to continue to exist in the
same state of prostration, under the burden of a scorn as outrageous as it
is unjustified. Scholars, in order to calm the conscience of pro-slavery
Europe, proclaimed in times past the dogma of the innate inferiority of
Blacks; we appeal from this sentence to modern science, more impartial
and better informed. (1900)

Benito Sylvain on Pan African Conference of 1900

George Washington Carver was born a slave around 1864 on Moses
Carver's plantation near Diamond Grove, Missouri. He grew up in the
post–Civil War period when three constitutional amendments guaranteed fundamental rights to African Americans. The Thirteenth Amendment abolished slavery, the Fourteenth Amendment ratified blacks as
citizens, and the Fifteenth Amendment removed race as a basis for re-
stricting the rights of citizens. Despite these advances, blacks were still
relegated to the bottom layers of the American classification of peoples.[1]
Carver learned that the hard way. After graduating from Fort Scott High
School in Kansas, he was accepted to Highland College in Iowa. He was
not allowed to enroll when he arrived because "The college did not admit
Negroes."[2] Segregation emerged as a legally enforced system in many
aspects of public life in the United States and severely restricted the
rights of African Americans.

Haitians had to deal with another kind of racism, not white man
against black man, but rather white nations against the black nation. As a
result, both Haitians and African American intellectuals devised strategies to combat racism. They resorted to historical, sociological, and anthropological evidence to promote the rehabilitation of the race. Haitians
and African Americans also used education in both societies to elevate
their status.

On the Diplomatic Front

Diplomatic relations between the United States and Haiti at this time opened a channel for African American diplomats to defend Haitian independence. During the first half of the nineteenth century, the United States resisted recognizing Haitian independence because of racial prejudice. Mounting mercantile pressure and the desire to gain both security and investments in Haiti required the United States to modify its policy. On February 4, 1862, Senator Charles Sumner of Massachusetts, a supporter of the black cause, introduced a bill authorizing President Abraham Lincoln to appoint diplomatic representatives to Haiti and Liberia. In spite of opposition from the antiblack lobby, the bill was adopted and signed into law on June 2, 1862. A treaty between the two nations followed in 1864.

Early in American relations with Haiti, only whites were chosen as diplomats to Haiti. In 1862, the first representative was Benjamin F. Whidden of New Hampshire, who became U.S. commissioner and consul general. In 1864, Everard Peck, a white educator and abolitionist from New York, succeeded him. Following Peck's death from yellow fever in Port-au-Prince, Connecticut lawyer Hiram Hollister was appointed in 1868.

The new political environment following the Civil War placed African Americans in a stronger position to compete for political promotion. Granted suffrage, blacks became politically involved in the newly created Republican Party. Those who worked toward the election of Ulysses S. Grant were rewarded.[3]

Ebenezer Don Carlos Bassett, the first African American foreign diplomat, was appointed minister to Haiti. Black communities applauded Bassett's appointment, and historian George W. Williams interpreted this appointment as the beginning of a new era for African Americans. He noted "The republic that Mr. Bassett went to had won diplomatic relations with all the civilized powers of the earth through the matchless valor and splendid statesmanship of Toussaint L'Ouverture. This was a black republic that had a history and a name among all the peoples of the world."[4]

The assignment of African American diplomats to Haiti continued until the First World War. Some of these diplomats defended American interests in Haiti, contributing to American influence, while others used their service to strengthen the bonds between Haitians and African Americans. William F. Powell (1897–1905) fought the discriminating taxes levied against foreign merchants, while Henry W. Furness (1905–1913) made a priority of gaining concessions for American merchants regarding tariffs and customs duties.[5]

Throughout Bassett's nine-year term, he demonstrated exceptional fairness in protecting both American and Haitian interests. The son of a mulatto father and American Indian mother, Bassett was a grammar school principal in New Haven before President Ulysses S. Grant appointed him to the Haitian post. While Haitian minister, Bassett developed close ties with the Haitian leaders. His study of French at Yale, perfected in Haiti, and his acquisition of Creole helped establish a deep understanding of the country and its people.[6] He became a trusted friend of Boisrond Canal, whose life he saved when he granted him asylum for five months at the American mission, sheltering him from his political foe, President Michel Domingue. When Bassett was replaced in 1877, he reluctantly left Haiti, lamenting that he would never again see his many friends and "this beautiful Hayti in whose soil and among whose people I have passed so many happy days."[7]

After leaving the post, Bassett remained active. President Lysius Félicité Salomon appointed him consul general of Haiti in New York City in 1879. Later, Bassett succeeded Stephen Preston, the Haitian minister for many years in Washington, when Preston was sent on a special mission to Europe in 1885.

While a Haitian diplomat, Bassett pleaded the cause of his adopted country, defending President Salomon and his policies. His diplomatic correspondences with General Brutus Saint-Victor, the minister of foreign relations, suggested Bassett was concerned with Haiti's internal and external problems and not just in events and issues that impinged on relations between the United States and the island.

As an example of his concern, Bassett tried to restore political stability during an armed confrontation between Salomon, representing blacks and the National Party, and Boyer Bazelais, the grandson of former president Boyer and leader of the mulattoes and the Liberal Party. Differences between the two were leading to a civil war.[8] During this political unrest, Bassett was disturbed by the false charges that the Haitian government was victimizing American citizens living in Haiti. As Salomon's foreign-relations adviser, Bassett complained, "They had a thousand times overly abused the generosity and weakness of Haiti." For the sake of justice and equality, Bassett asked the Haitian government to stand firm against such oppressors.

The next minister, John Mercer Langston, also tried to strengthen relations between Haitians and African Americans. Langston was a law graduate from Oberlin College, who held several bureaucratic jobs before becoming the first black congressman. Langston discovered when he arrived in Haiti that blacks had an elevated status, higher than the nominal freedoms granted to blacks in the United States. He wrote that Haitian blacks were the "owner of a great country, the founder and builder of a great government, with a national sovereignty and power respected and honored by all the great Christian civilized powers of the earth."[9]

Langston encouraged trade between the two countries, but preoccupation with political unrest in the country monopolized his time. As he observed, Haiti "is often disturbed by revolutions threatening its very existence, involving and working too frequently immense destruction of property and life and at times the property and lives of citizens of other governments residing therein."[10] While his predecessors did little to defuse the Haitian political unrest, Langston refused shelter and protection to the defeated factions.[11] He criticized Haitians for neglecting the trade and commerce of their country while favoring political maneuvering and creating unrest. Langston's approach to solving Haiti's problem was to narrow the cultural gap between Haitians and African Americans. According to Episcopal bishop James Theodore Holly, Langston tried to help "onward and upward the progress of this people in the way of constitutional self-government and Christian civilization."[12]

Relations between Haitians and African Americans further improved during the tenure of Frederick Douglass, one of the most prominent political figures of the nineteenth century. As an orator and editor of the *North Star* and the *Frederick Douglass' Monthly,* he was an outspoken voice against slavery. The Emancipation Proclamation was a political document, freeing only those slaves in the Confederacy. Douglass became a civil-rights leader to ensure that slaves would be freed throughout the land. Once the American Civil War was over, Douglass stood as a great advocate of Haiti, first as a diplomat, then as its commissioner at the World's Fair in Chicago in 1893. Douglass had been to Haiti before so he was acquainted with its topography and its people. Acknowledging his association with the Haitian revolutionary cause, Douglass said, "Mine has been a long and eventful life identified with the maintenance of principles illustrated in the example of Haiti."[13] He further added, "Let us go back 100 years and look at Hayti, and we find it surrounded by slavery and the whole Caribbean Sea reddened by the curse. The Negro was a slave everywhere, under every nation in the islands of the West Indies. But in the midst of that slavery, in the midst of that doom and despair, they had the manhood to rise from the dust and shake off the fetters and drive out the men who tyrannized them"[14] Douglass admired Haitians for maintaining their independence under such great adversity.

Republican Benjamin Harrison defeated incumbent president Grover Cleveland in 1888 with strong backing from black voters. Harrison recognized this, especially the help he received from Douglass. Because of this, Douglass was named minister resident and consul general to Haiti in 1889.

Douglass's appointment was as sensitive an issue as the emigration movement, primarily because of the attitude Haitians had about African American officials in Haiti. Newspapers like the *Chicago Herald* and *Philadelphia Enquirer* charged that Haiti was reluctant to accept Douglass as the American minister. The *Enquirer* suggested Haitians "have always held the view that the government of the United States showed them disrespect in sending a colored minister to Port-au-Prince, while every other nation was represented at the Haitian capital by a white man."[15] Douglass disregarded this grumbling over his appointment because he held Haiti in such high regard, viewing his assignment as an honor and challenge.

When Douglass presented his credentials to Haitian president Mondestin Florvil Hyppolite in November 1889, he said, "My country has conferred upon me many marks of its favor, but in view of the heroic devotion to liberty and independence exemplified by your brave countrymen in the darkest hour of their history, I can say, in all sincerity, that I have received at the hands of my government no honor that I prize more highly than the honor of my appointment as minister resident and consul general to the Republic of Haiti."[16]

In spite of the uproar reported in the American press over the nomination, President Florvil Hyppolite welcomed Douglass as an abolitionist and as a defender of the black race. Anténor Firmin, the Haitian minister of foreign affairs, described Douglass as "the most remarkable specimen of Afro-Americans." A. P. Holly, son of emigrationist James T. Holly, added that "Haytians hail the nomination of so lofty-minded and liberal a man as the Hon. Frederick Douglass as Minister to their country. In him, we see not an annexationist . . . but a gentle man, who, remembering the depths of disgrace and injustice to which he, as a bondsman, was driven, from which he rose, though painfully, to honor and fame, will be better able to appreciate the heroic efforts of a nation whose past history influenced to no mean degree, his own career."[17] President Hyppolite praised Douglass without reservation: "Your reputation is known in the two hemispheres. You are the incarnation of the idea which Haiti is following—the moral and intellectual development of men of the African race by professional effort and mental culture."[18]

Douglass spent most of his time in Haiti handling Americans' claims of personal and property damages. Yet he resisted blindly serving American business interests. William P. Clyde and Company of New York tried to obtain a subsidy of one-half million dollars from the Haitian government to finance a steamer line between Haiti and New York. Clyde also wanted to reduce the tonnage and the port duties on American vessels. When the Haitian government objected to the concession, Clyde's agent asked Douglass to press for a favorable compromise. Since Douglass was inclined to characterize the American government and U.S. business interests as imperialistic, he did not cooperate, a decision that brought sharp criticism from the American press. Douglass became "a Haitian by heart and by sentiment."[19]

In 1891, Douglass faced a more complex diplomatic crisis when the United States tried to secure the Môle St-Nicolas coaling station from the Haitian government for the U.S. Navy. Secretary of State James Blaine, called the "plumed knight of American diplomacy," considered the acquisition of the Môle part of the fulfillment of Manifest Destiny, that is, the belief developed in the nineteenth century that the United States should "overspread the continent allotted by providence for the free development of our yearly expanding millions."[20]

Blaine did not involve Douglass but entrusted the negotiations to Admiral Bancroft Gherardi, the commander of the Atlantic fleet, appointed as special commissioner. As minister, Douglass abided by the will of his government and supported the admiral's efforts. Gherardi bargained for three months with Haitian negotiators led by Anténor Firmin, minister of foreign relations. Gherardi could not reach a deal and the Haitian government denied his request. Douglass was blamed for the admiral's fiasco. Douglass defended his view: "I am charged with sympathy for Haiti. I am not ashamed of that charge; but no man can say with truth that sympathy with Haiti stood between me and any honorable duty that I owed to the United States or to any citizen of the United States."[21]

Whether intentionally or not, Douglass resisted American imperialism and tried to keep foreigners off Haitian soil. Professor Martin Sears suggests that Douglass "was intoxicated by the hearty welcome he received in Haiti as an exemplar of what the black man can accomplish. Correspondingly, he would feel a painful jealousy of any white man who should encroach upon his just preserves."[22]

In 1891, Douglass took a leave of absence and, to the dismay of the Haitians, never returned as minister. Douglass had transmitted the first cable message opening the communications between Haiti and the United States in December 1890. He shone in Haitian society as a social success, blending his common sense with their views and goals. He also developed a close relationship with President Hyppolite, whom Douglass defended as a man who endeavored to lead his countrymen on the path of civilization, peace, prosperity, and glory. Hyppolite praised the American minister as "the illustrious champion of all men sprung from the African race, himself one of the most remarkable products of that race which we represent with pride on the American continent."[23] Four decades later, highlighting Douglass's significant role as American minister to Haiti, Dantès Bellegarde observed that, "Although he filled the duties of his office with loyalty . . ., Haitians give him credit for having practiced towards Haiti a policy of friendship and goodwill, respectful of the rights and of the independence of this little nation."[24]

Even after his resignation as American minister, Douglass continued to defend Haiti's independence. He sharply refuted those who viewed the island population as uncivilized and superstitious. Speaking at an abolitionist reunion in Boston on September 22, 1890, Douglass commented, "We are not to judge her by the height which the Anglo-Saxon has reached. We are to judge her by the depths from which she has come. We are to look at the relation she sustained to the outside world, and the outside world sustained to her. One hundred years ago every civilized nation had slave-holding. Yet these negroes, ignorant, downtrodden, had the manhood to arise and drive off their masters and assert their liberty. Her government is not so unsteady as we think."[25]

On March 16, 1892, in Boston, Douglass lectured on Haiti to a large audience, denouncing as a curse the revolutionary spirit that was undermining the political stability of Haiti. While acknowledgingthe power of Haitian superstitions, he pointed out that there were many in America who, as he did, preferred to have the first sight of the moon over their right shoulder, and did not like to be one of thirteen guests at a table. This recognition of a shared mentality shows that Douglass had a steadfast commitment to defend Haiti. Above all, he had great hope for the future of Haiti, believing that "whatever may happen of peace or war, Haiti will remain in the firmament of nations, and, like the star of the North, will shine on, and shine on for ever."[26]

Douglass even defended Haiti on the grounds of her Latin connection. While James Theodore Holly criticized the Latin inclinations of the Haitians, Douglass said, "If, as is alleged, Haiti is more cordial to France than to the United States, it is partly because Haiti is herself French. Her language is French; her literature is French, her manners are and fashions are French; her ambitions and aspirations are French; her laws and methods of Government are French; her priesthood and her education are French; her children are sent to school in France and their minds are filled with French ideas and French glory."[27] He charged that it was racism that kept Haitians away from American shores.

When Haiti was asked to participate in the Chicago World's Fair of 1892 in honor of the 400th anniversary of the discovery of America by Christopher Columbus, President Hyppolite chose Douglass as his representative. The Haitians saw the fair as an opportunity to show off their natural resources and achievements in industry and in the liberal arts. Above all, they saw it as an opportunity to represent the black race.

Douglass became commissioner, accepting the honor as a vote of confidence from Haitians. He was especially thankful that black America would be represented at the exposition, but African Americans were outraged because there was nothing depicting the black contribution to American life. They aired their grievances in an 81-page pamphlet, *The Reason Why the Colored Man Is Not Represented at the World's Columbian Exposition*. Their protests forced exposition managers to designate August 25, 1893, as "Colored American Day," celebrated by allowing the participation of African American artists.

The Haitian pavilion opened January 2, 1893, in honor of Haitian independence. Douglass proudly represented Haiti at the fair and used the occasion to strongly defend Haiti: "The heroic chief of Hayti, in the year

1803, declared her independence and she has made good that declaration down to 1893. Her presence here today in the grounds of this World's Columbian Exposition, at the end of the 400th anniversary of the discovery of the American continent, is a re-affirmation of her existence and her independence as a nation and of her place among the sisterhood of nations."[28] Exposition Director General Davis praised Douglass who, "though a citizen of the United States, knows well and sympathizes so deeply not only with [Haiti's] struggles for political independence, but also with her aspirations for industrial growth and intellectual development."[29]

Douglass's role as Haitian commissioner at the World's Fair marked the high point of his final years. When he died in February 1895, the Haitian government paid him one final homage. While Douglass's body lay in state in the Metropolitan A.M.E. Church, the largest African American church in Washington, D.C., beside stood Hayti's coat of arms, in palms, roses, lilies, and orchids,[30] presented by the Haitian minister. That symbolic gesture celebrated a long relationship between Douglass and the island republic he had so steadfastly loved and defended.

Although Douglass devoted his career to the defense of Haiti, he found the political chaos difficult to endure, realizing it hurt the cause of African Americans. Douglass voiced this frustration when he wrote in his *Lecture on Haiti*, "This revolutionary spirit is her curse, her crime, her greatest calamity and the explanation of the limited condition of her civilization. It makes her an object of distress to her friends at home and abroad. It reflects upon the colored race every where. Many who would gladly have believed in her ability to govern herself wisely and successfully are compelled at times to bow their heads in doubt and despair."[31]

Beyond diplomatic circles, other leaders of the African American community were concerned over the Haitian political turmoil. They perceived that Haiti's political disturbances hampered African Americans in their quest for political validation in the United States. The editor of the *Voice of the Negro* charged, "We are struggling in this country to be recognized as a class who ought to be allowed to participate in the affairs of the Government. If the confusion continues in Haiti and San Domingo where Negroes have full control of the government, this very condition of things will further prejudice the world against our cause. If we want to count on the moral support of civilization in our efforts to secure evenhanded justice, we must not have the bad example of this little Negro Republic flaunted before the face of the world."[32]

The next edition of *Voice of the Negro* reiterated the same theme. T. Thomas Fortune, editor of *New York Age*, declared that incessant revolutions in Haiti contributed to "the poverty of the Haytian people and their treasury and for the deterioration of the character of their leaders."[33] Fortune suggested that immediate steps be taken to develop the republic. He encouraged the building of roads and a national system of agriculture and public schools.

Rehabilitating the Race

During the nineteenth century, race equality was a popular though volatile topic. Sociologist George Fitzhugh took the traditional white supremacist view, asserting that "The Negro is but a grown up child, and must be governed as a child. . . No one will differ with us who thinks as we do of the negro's capacity, and we might argue till dooms-day in vain, with those who have a high opinion of the negro's moral and intellectual capacity."[34] President Lincoln resisted enlisting African Americans into the Civil War, believing they lacked the ability and courage to face white men.

Nowhere was American racism demonstrated more graphically than in a *New York Times* editorial eulogizing Frederick Douglass. The editor claimed that "his white blood may have had something to do with the remarkable energy he displayed and the superior intelligence he manifested. Indeed, it might not be altogether unreasonable to ask whether with more white blood, he would have been an even better and greater man than he was, and whether the fact that he had any black blood at all may not have cost the world a genius, and be, in consequence, a cause for lamentation instead of a source of lyrical enthusiasm over African possibilities."[35] Whites believed only white blood could produce intelligence—and preferred the Anglo-Saxon Nordic race above all others. Eugenics advocates and Social Darwinists urged the adoption of sterilization laws in fifteen states to eliminate what they called "defects."[36]

Even France, the birthplace of the Declaration of the Rights of Man, increasingly practiced racism against people of African descent. French diplomat Comte Joseph Arthur de Gobineau hailed the superiority of

Europeans in *De l'inégalité des races humaines* (About the Inequality of the Human Races) (1853), claiming that people of African descent were incapable of becoming civilized.

Haiti was a prime target for criticism. Travelers and journalists returned to describe their observations of Vodou, even fabricating tales to discredit the effectiveness of black autonomy.[37] Former British minister Spencer St. John in his *Haiti or the Black Republic* (1884) epitomized this prejudice: "I know that the black man is, and I have no hesitation in declaring that he is incapable of the art of government, and to entrust him with framing and working the laws of our islands is to condemn them to inevitable ruin. What the Negro may become after centuries of civilized education I cannot tell, but what I know that he is not fit to govern now."[38] St. John devoted his study to "Vaudoux-Worship and Cannibalism" as proof of the barbarism of Haitians.

White charges of an inherent intellectual inferiority of Africans should be evaluated in the context of the imperialistic offensive of European powers as they tried to colonize Africa. Over the two previous centuries, travelers, missionaries, adventurers, and sea captains had penetrated Africa's hinterlands. These wanderers set the stage for the exploration and occupation of Africa. At the Congress of Berlin, held from November 1884 to February 1885, France, Germany, and the United Kingdom set the guidelines for the partitioning of Africa's coasts.[39] They needed theories of racial superiority to justify their actions.

Haitians and African Americans, while continuing to uphold European civilization as a standard, set up a campaign to counter the attacks in St. John's book. Black intellectuals based their arguments of equality on the achievements of those blacks who conformed to the European standard.[40]

Haitian scholars tried to dispel the inferiority stigma. Haitian statesman Anténor Firmin wrote *De l'égalité des races humaines* (About the Equality of Human Races) (1885), as the antithesis of Gobineau's work on European superiority. Firmin was a member of the Society of Anthropology of Paris and the American Academy of Political and Social Science. He rejected "the dogmatic affirmation of the inequality of human races and the innate inferiority of the black race" and trusted that Haiti would show "the entire world that all men, black and white, are equal in quality as they are in rights."[41] Frank Rudolph Steward joined other African Americans in praising this book. He described it in *Voice of the*

Negro as "a thoroughly scientific vindication of the inherent equality of the blacks."[42] Firmin sharply criticized the brutal prejudice of southern whites who believed that "some men are naturally inferior to others, independently of all contingency."[43]

Haitian diplomat Louis Joseph Janvier agreed. In Paris, he earned degrees in medicine and political science, and a law degree in Lille. He later served as Haitian representative in Berne, Switzerland, and as chargé d'affaires and resident minister in London.

Janvier's brilliance was accepted in Europe. According to Marie Edouard Lenoir, a contemporary French observer, Janvier contradicted the common stereotypes about people of African descent. "We have pretended," she wrote, "that the men of Ethiopian race were absolutely incapable of any intellectual work, abstract and philosophical thought, that they are indolent and lazy; here is a twenty-nine year old brain, who proves victoriously the contrary."[44] Janvier was a prolific writer. He produced some 2,000 pages of political writings on the theme of "the defense of the black race and its rehabilitation by the Republic of Haiti."[45]

With *L'égalité des races* (Equality of Races), Janvier rejected Ernest Renan's statement in his *Dialogues philosophiques* that "Men are not equal, the races are not equal . . . The Negro, for instance, is made to serve the great things wanted and conceived by whites."[46] Janvier argued that the black race, which had just recently won its freedom, produced such great figures as Toussaint Louverture in Haiti and Frederick Douglass in the United States. He cited accomplishments of other African Americans and Haitians in the political, literary, economic, and scientific fields.[47]

Hannibal Price, Haitian minister to the United States, addressed this race issue in his *On the Rehabilitation of the Black Race by the Republic of Haiti* (1900). This posthumously published study rebuked those who wrote "sensational stories rather than researching and setting forth historical and ethnological truths." More specifically, Price targeted St. John who, he insisted, presented the "Republic of Haiti in such an odious way."[48]

Price also aimed to enlighten African Americans who were misinformed about Haiti: "I found in the United States millions of men of my race, fighting energetically to rise by their intelligence and morality to the height of the powerful civilization surrounding them, Negroes who are eager to take their place in medicine, law, sciences, letters, arts, and all the fields of human knowledge and strive to insure their welfare and dignity. Well, I see coming to me every day some of the most distinguished of these men, searching for the truth on Haiti, on the state of shameful savagery which, it is said, she would have fallen."[49]

Issues of race and race relations constituted an immediate threat to African Americans exposed to daily racism and disturbed by mob violence. African American novelist and abolitionist William Wells Brown cited historical arguments to combat racial superiority. In *The Black Man: His Antecedents, His Genius, and His Achievements* (1863), Brown traced the achievements of Africans. Brown refuted the misrepresentations of those who had done African Americans "the greatest injury, by being instrumental in their enslavement and subsequent degradation" and aimed to enlighten those who were "ignorant of the characteristics of the race."[50] Brown profiled those who, "by their own genius, capacity, and intellectual development, have surmounted the many obstacles which slavery and prejudice have thrown in their way, and raised themselves to position of honor and influence."[51]

Benjamin Benneker headed the list for his contributions to science and to liberty. In Brown's estimation, Benneker dedicated himself to the emancipation and elevation of the slaves. His *Almanacs* caused his name to be referred to in academic circles in the United States and Europe to "prove the equality of the races."[52]

Brown further demonstrated his thesis of the capacity of blacks by highlighting the literary achievements of the "great colored author" Alexandre Dumas, the celebrated French writer who published more novels, plays, and historical sketches than any other man of his time. For Brown, Dumas was "undeniably a man of great genius, endowed with true fertility of imagination, and masterly power of expression."[53]

Brown included others for their military talents and courage on the battlefield. He spotlighted Toussaint Louverture as a general who devoted himself to the welfare and freedom of his race. Brown compared Louverture with George Washington in their military genius. But, Brown wrote, "Toussaint's government made liberty its watchword, incorporated it in its constitution, abolished the slave trade, and made freedom universal amongst the people. Washington's government incorporated slavery and the slave trade, and enacted laws by which chains were fastened upon the limbs of millions of people."[54]

W. E. B. Du Bois stands as a great crusader for the rehabilitation of the race. He began fighting racism while a student at Fisk, Berlin, and Harvard. Whereas Haitian scholars like Firmin and Janvier focused on the issue of equality, Du Bois in his early writings recognized the *differences* in races. In the pamphlet *The Conservation of Races,* he characterized the existence of eight races in the world by physical distinctions. He suggested that "The deeper differences are spiritual, psychical, differences— undoubtedly based on the physical, but infinitely transcending them."[55] Despite this characterization, he rejected any theory concerned with racial superiority. He encouraged a spirit of understanding and cooperation between the races, affirming that "One ought to combat the irreconcilable contention prevalent among the various groups of mankind that their customs, their civilization, and their physique are superior to those of other groups."[56]

Each race must make a contribution to civilization, Du Bois reasoned. Black artists made a first step in that direction with the Paris Exposition of 1900 where African American exhibits featured photographs, models, industrial work, and illustrations reflecting their history. Du Bois praised this effort. "The most unique and striking exhibit is that of American Negro literature" that included "a bibliography made by the Library of Congress containing 1,400 titles of works written by Negroes . . . 150 periodicals, mostly weekly papers."[57]

In the political arena, second-generation Haitian Americans fought for black political participation during Reconstruction. In Charleston, Robert Carlos Delarge and Alonzo J. Ransier served as the first black congressmen following the Civil War. Delarge was born a slave in 1842 in Aiken, South Carolina. After completing high school, he became a tailor, farmer, and agent of the Freedmen's Bureau. He later emerged as an organizer of the South Carolina branch of the Republican Party and rose to become a prominent politician in the party. At the 1865 Colored People's Convention, Delarge chaired the credentials committee and two years later chaired the platform committee at the state convention. After serving in the lower house of the South Carolina legislature and as land commissioner, he was elected to Congress in 1870.[58]

Delarge is remembered during his brief tenure in Congress for his April 6, 1871, speech in which he advocated establishment of public schools and abolition of capital punishment. In February 1873, the House unseated Delarge when a House investigation proved that fraud pervaded the election in which he defeated Christopher Bowen.

Another Haitian American, Alonzo J. Ransier, succeeded Delarge.

Born in Charleston on January 3, 1834, Ransier was a registrar of the first post–Civil War elections, then became chairman of the Republican state central committee, a presidential elector, and delegate to the 1868 state constitutional convention. In July 1870, he was elected South Carolina's first black lieutenant governor along with Governor Robert Scott.[59]

Ransier fought for a civil rights bill that would ban discrimination in schools, transportation, theaters, and hotels. On June 9, 1874, he joined African American congressman James Thomas Rapier of Alabama in the debate on the civil rights bill. Rapier described the anomalous and absurd status of African Americans who could enjoy political rights while being denied civil rights: "Just think that the law recognizes my right upon this floor as a law-maker, but that there is no law to secure me any accommodations whatever while traveling here to discharge my duties as a Representative of a large and wealthy constituency."[60] Ransier argued, "I ask for the passage of the civil rights bill before we shall adjourn. We ask it as a measure of justice to those people who have been true to the nation and to the party in power. We ask it at the hands of President Grant and the republican party. We ask it . . . as a matter of sound policy in the interest of the republican party and of the country."[61]

In Louisiana, Haitian Americans distinguished themselves as political leaders and civil-rights activists. In 1890, Lucien Rodolphe Desdunes launched the *Comité des citoyens* (Citizens' Committee) to "protest the adoption and enforcement of the statutes that established the unjust and humiliating discrimination against the black race in Louisiana."[62] Arthur Esteves, a Haiti-born Louisiana educator was president; Firmin Joseph, secretary; and Paul Bonseigneur, treasurer. Antoine Caesar Carpentier, one of three African Americans to have served as lieutenant governor of Louisiana, was vice president. Esteves and the committee fought Act 11 of 1890 that established separate accommodations for whites and blacks in trains. They brought the famous case of *Plessy v. Ferguson* to the courts.

Homer Adolph Plessy was a man of mixed blood, reportedly with a proportion of seven-eighths white and one-eighth black. He was engaged by the committee to take the first step in the legal battle against the law forbidding the mixing of races in public conveyances traveling from one place to another within Louisiana. Plessy bought a first-class ticket on the "East" train and took a vacant seat in a coach reserved for white passengers. When ordered to occupy a seat in a coach reserved for blacks, Plessy refused. A police officer ejected him and took him to the parish jail of New Orleans where he was charged with criminal violation of the law. The committee brought the case to the Louisiana courts and ultimately to the U.S. Supreme Court, which upheld the Louisiana law. Justice Henry Brown delivered the majority opinion holding that the Louisiana statute did not violate the Thirteenth and Fourteenth Amendments of the United States Constitution.[63] Judge John Marshall dissented: "The arbitrary separation of citizens on the basis of race while they are on a public highway, is a badge of servitude inconsistent with the civil freedom and the equality before the law established by the Constitution. It cannot be justified upon any legal grounds."[64]

The committee attacked the law forbidding marriage between the races. Though the committee failed to reverse these statutes, members were credited for their assertive stand against discrimination. Desdunes supported the committee's work: "We think that it is more noble and dignified to fight, no matter what, than to show a passive attitude of resignation."

The struggle to gain civil rights continued with the Niagara Movement in 1905. Under the leadership of Du Bois, twenty-nine intellectuals from sixteen states met to launch the movement as an aggressive response to the racial philosophy of the Supreme Court's "separate but equal" doctrine and to Washington's policies of accommodation to segregation.[65] Leaders of the movement proclaimed, "We claim for ourselves every single right that belongs to a freeborn American, political, civil and social; and until we get these rights we will never cease to protest and assail the ears of America."[66]

The Niagara Movement organized annual national conferences until 1908. Though it was disbanded in 1910, its elements were integrated into the larger framework of the National Association for the Advancement of Colored People (NAACP) founded on February 12, 1909, to "fight the wrong of prejudice." A group of whites were involved in the early stages of the organization. They included William English Walling, a wealthy southerner; Mary Ovington, a socialist and abolitionist; and Dr. Henry Moskowitz, a New York social worker. Du Bois was the most prominent African American involved. He became director of research and editor of The Crisis, the voice of the organization.[67]

The rehabilitation of the race was one of the most frustrating issues facing black leaders in the nineteenth century. It led to the 1900 Pan-

African Conference in London convened by Trinidad barrister Henry Sylvester Williams. The conference originated when Benito Sylvain, a Haitian diplomat and activist defending black people, told Williams of a plan to hold an international forum in Paris during the World's Fair. In a letter to Firmin, Sylvain described his plan of gathering qualified people to try to save the world from the "execrable theory of inferior and superior races . . . a moral monstrosity which is based, whatever one might say, solely on the idea of the exploitation of man by man."[68] When this project failed to materialize, Williams continued with Sylvain's dream. Sylvain was a representative at the London Pan-African Conference.

Sylvain helped organize the conference. He told delegates, "The problem of the twentieth century is the problem of the color-line, the question as to how far differences of race . . . will hereafter be made the basis of denying to over half the world the right of sharing to their utmost ability the opportunities and privileges of modern civilization."[69] The delegates believed that blacks would make positive contributions when given the opportunity for education and self-development. Du Bois organized other congresses, too, promoting solidarity and cooperation of blacks to combat not just racism but also imperialism.

Elevating the Race

Another concern for nineteenth-century Haitians and African Americans was education and self-development for people of African origin. As slavery left them in degradation, black intellectuals in both countries applied their energies and resources to reverse the deplorable condition of blacks through education, thus elevating the status of the race.

During the post–Civil War era, a new climate for African Americans helped realize this educational aspiration. The Reconstruction Congress established the Freedmen's Bureau, which, in spite of opposition from racist southerners, promoted the enlightenment of blacks. The bureau was to provide basic health and educational services for freedmen and displaced whites in areas occupied by the federal forces. Beside the Freedmen's Bureau, religious organizations, private philanthropic agencies, and humanitarian groups joined the fight for true equality. Their efforts produced thousands of day and night schools throughout the South.

Haitian Americans, too, continued their antebellum educational involvement. In Baltimore, the war "had thrown a large number of children on the community, orphans, children of slaves made free and now able to place their children in school," but they had "no schools to turn to in this emergency."[70] With the support of Jesuit priest Father Miller, their spiritual leader, the Oblate Sisters raised money through fairs, concerts, and entertainment "to better the condition of the colored child, to care for it when homeless, give it schooling, bring schools for the colored up to the standard of white schools."[71]

The Oblates expanded beyond the city limits of Baltimore. In 1880, Mother Louise Noel and Sisters Dominica Thomas, Mary Gertrude Smallwood, and Mary Evangelist Livingston took charge of a school for freedmen in the diocese of St. Louis. They set up a mission and worked with the orphans there. In 1888, Sisters Victoria Messonier, Genevieve, Gabriel, and Michael established a mission in Kansas where they took over the "Guardian Angels' Home." These Sisters were credited with "building the foundations for future leaders and teachers among the colored Catholics" of the region of Kansas.[72]

Education for African Americans was not equal to that for whites. Freedmen's Bureau commissioners and missionary schoolteachers pushed industrial education as a means of teaching blacks the "values of thrift, industry, and morality."[73] Emphasizing self-help and economic and moral development, Booker T. Washington, one of the most renowned of the freed slaves, used these values as the cornerstone of his social and educational philosophy.

Born to slavery in April 1856, Washington became highly regarded in America as a teacher, educator, reformer, and author. General Samuel Armstrong, who promoted industrial education as particularly suitable for backward people, became Washington's mentor at Hampton Institute. As the head of Tuskegee Institute, which he founded in 1881, Washington became a national spokesman for the plight of African Americans. He agreed with Armstrong, promoting vocational education and industrial training. After being freed, blacks were still ostracized in mainstream America. Washington carefully formulated a plan aimed at making his people self-sufficient. As described in a speech at the opening of the Atlanta International Exposition in 1885, Washington urged blacks to develop skills in agriculture, mechanics, domestic service, and the professions.

Washington's concern for Haiti, Liberia, and Santo Domingo paralleled his social philosophy and racial strategy. In his writings and lectures to Tuskegee students, he talked about the "discouraging condition" in these countries and reasoned that the cause was a lack of agricultural development. He maintained that "Nature has given the inhabitants of these countries immensely rich territories," but believed "these people have not turned their brains to the cultivation of the soil. They have not put their brains into the construction of the agricultural implements and machinery which go toward laying the foundation of a race."[74]

Washington praised Haiti for her high rate of literary education. However, Washington said, "practically none [of the Haitians] has been trained along industrial and scientific lines. Whenever the government of Hayti wants an engineer for her men-of-war, it sends to England or the United States; or for an engineer to build the bridges and other work requiring technical knowledge and skill."[75] While Haitians ranked high scholastically, he regretted they did not take advantage of "the excellent training which is given here in the colleges of physical sciences, agriculture, mechanics, and domestic sciences. They would then be in a position to return home and assist in developing the agricultural and mineral resources of their native land."[76]

Other African Americans criticized the lack of material development in Haiti. As Haitians celebrated their independence centennial, black scholar and bibliophile Arthur Schomburg asked, "Is Haiti decadent?" The ongoing warfare, the lack of industry, and the meager existence of agriculture continued to plague the nation. Schomburg wrote, "You may look over and over the field and you will not be able to find anything coming from Hayti that can bear the trade mark 'Made in Hayti.'" He suggested that Haitians work for the "welfare of the race" by something other than warfare implements to instill in the people that wealth depends on successful agriculture rather than internal squabbling.

Many Haitian social scientists agreed with Washington's criticism that Haiti lacked material production. In 1908, several reports in Le Matin, a Port-au-Prince daily, concurred. Auguste Magloire collected these reports and published them in a book, Etude sur le tempérament haitien (Studies of the Haitian Temperament). Magloire suggested that by inheriting the French temperament, Haitians imitated an educational system that emphasized intellectual knowledge. "Most coveted positions, in France are the bureaucratic and administrative posts, generally available through the State."[77] While this education efficiently served France's socioeconomic problems, it was poorly suited to Haitians' needs. This heritage proved disastrous and was responsible for "all our troubles, almost without exception. It has created in our country debasement of characters, contempt for work, a scandalous democracy . . . , discredit of manual labor, lagging in primitive ignorance, removal from rural life and finally this fatal disposition left in us by the bad habit of ever looking at things with only French feeling and never with our own."[78] To remedy this, Magloire suggested a change to Anglo-Saxon ideals that praised initiative and individual spontaneity in its system of education. Anglo-Saxons also emphasized practical, agricultural, and vocational education.

Other Haitian educators agreed and tried to reduce the French influence on Haitian education. Educational historian Fleury Féquière praised Washington's views and work, describing him as the man who helped change opinions on the intellectual ability of blacks and whose work at the Tuskegee Institute helped black Americans better themselves. Féquière believed Haitians should have "some real interest in knowing America, not only because blacks live in America, but so that they could mostly see in full expansion the strong education designed to make them trained men for the whole struggle of existence."[79]

Jean Price-Mars, the famous anthropologist and educator, endorsed the techniques and methods practiced at Hampton Institute and Tuskegee Institute as relevant for the Haitian masses. As inspector of public instruction during the period 1912–13, Price-Mars favored "the setting up in each of the geographical departments of arts and trade schools with agricultural branches properly equipped with laboratories and experimental gardens."[80]

Washington's views did not receive unanimous approval. Anthropologist and statesman Anténor Firmin, though dissatisfied with the Haitian educational system, rejected Anglo-Saxonism. In his view, the "Haitian mentality," which is French, "has nothing to lose but has everything to gain by following French discipline."[81] He concluded that France offered the highest example of sound economic, financial, scientific, and literary performance in the nineteenth century. Others who shared Firmin's view argued, "It is by our high intellectual knowledge that we will prove to the world the equality of races and wipe out the prejudice entertained against the unfitness of the negro brain.[82]

The elite remained attached to the French system by sending their children to France for their education. Even Haitians who were interested in technical education turned to France, primarily due to overt policies against blacks in the United States. Haitians were reluctant to import American cultural and educational theories. Historian and diplomat Bellegarde was highly committed to French ideals and would advise, "If we want to have good skilled workers, good agriculturists, good foremen, let us direct them without fear to the French schools where they will be welcomed, with open arms, and where they will not be exposed, because of their color, to the hazing and despising invectives of their little mates."[83]

Washington's philosophy and policies brought about a dichotomy in African American thought. The black leadership, divided into conservative and radical camps, where conservatives "put greatest emphasis on moral and economic improvement, while the radicals stressed agitation, political action, and civil rights."[84] Du Bois emerged most likely the staunchest critic of Washington's educational program. The two men frequently disagreed. Their differences were probably the result of their dissimilar backgrounds. Washington was a graduate from Hampton, where he thoroughly absorbed the value of practical education under General Armstrong. Du Bois studied in Berlin and received a Ph.D. from Harvard University. In his book *The Souls of Black Folks*, he denounced Washington's educational program as unnecessarily narrow. With honest and earnest criticism, he asserted, "This is an age of unusual economic development, and Mr. Washington's programme naturally takes an economic cast, becoming a gospel of Work and Money to such an extent as apparently almost completely to overshadow the higher aims of life."[85] He favored an education that develops a self-actuated man. "Above our modern socialism, and out of the worship of the mass, must persist and evolve that higher individualism which the centres of culture protect; there must come a loftier respect for the sovereign human soul that seeks to know itself and the world about it; that seeks a freedom for expansion and self-development."[86] Du Bois promoted familiarization and communion with Shakespeare, Balzac, and Dumas, with Aristotle and Aurelius.

Du Bois' position was probably best described as elitist. He pictured the emergence of a "talented tenth" of college-trained blacks as leaders who would devise a solution for racial improvement and would promote the cultural and economic advancement of the masses. Du Bois said this "Negro intelligentsia would be able to lift the Negro mass upward as a largely self-contained social unit, with a minimum of labor exploitation and a maximum of uplifting progress."[87] Haitian class hierarchy was very similar with its elite set. But the Haitian "talented tenth" failed to use their leadership for any advancement of the masses. Firmin demonstrated his utter discontent with that elite when he charged that "The ideal of the ruling class seems to preserve skillfully the ignorance of the masses in order to use them as stepping-stones and to realize at their expense sordid and selfish profits."[88] From Firmin's perspective, the talented tenth left much to be desired in Haiti. Du Bois realized this, too, when he acknowledged that "Talented Negroes like other human beings are going to produce a large number of selfish and self-seeking persons, who will not work for the best interests of the masses of the people."[89]

Du Bois disagreed with Washington's concession to whites regarding African American political and civil status. Du Bois denounced not only Washington's program of industrial education but also his visible efforts at "conciliation of the South, and submission and silence as to civil and political rights."[90] Du Bois favored physical freedom, political power, the training of brains, and the training of hands.

It is clear that both Haitians and African Americans maintained a vigorous battle for the defense and elevation of the race. Some of the era's greatest minds, representing both peoples, used scientific and historical reasoning to refute the half-truths and so-called data about the inferiority of people of African descent. Though they were certainly divided, they encouraged the promotion of education as a key solution for the betterment and elevation of the race.

5

The Struggle Against a Racist Occupation, 1915–1934

The United States has violated the independence of a sister state. With
absolutely no adequate excuse she has made a white American Admiral
sole and irresponsible dictator of Hayti . . . The lynching and murder in
Port-au-Prince is no worse than, if as bad as, the lynching in Georgia.
Hayti can, and will work out her destiny and is more civilized today than
Texas. (October 10, 1915)

W. E. B. Du Bois, *The Crisis*

Throughout the nineteenth century, African Americans viewed Haiti as
the keeper of liberty in the New World. Though they were disenchanted
with Haiti's political instability, they defended its right to be free. As
Episcopal bishop of Haiti James Theodore Holly explained, "If Haytian
independence shall cease to exist, the sky of negro-destiny shall be hung
in impenetrable blackness."[1] Early in the twentieth century, Ebenezer
Bassett, sensing Haiti's impending fall, reaffirmed, "Let Haiti alone; let
her alone to work out her mission for the children of Africa in the New
World and to fulfill her destiny among the Nations of the Earth.[2]

In 1915, the U.S. Marines landed in Haiti in what the Wilson administration originally billed a "mission of peace." But America's intervention
was really the result of a struggle to gain influence in Haiti between the
United States and European foreign powers, specifically France and Germany. For the next two decades, Haiti evolved under full-scale American
control.

Two consequences of the American occupation are important for consideration. First, the occupation rekindled racial nationalism in Haiti by
reuniting blacks and mulattoes for national defense. Second, the occupation led to racial unity among African American leaders that might not

have occurred otherwise. Together, these consequences resulted in a direct communication link between Haitians and African Americans.

Early Reaction

Once the Marines had occupied Haiti, the Wilson administration defended the invasion as necessary "for the protection of foreign lives and property . . . and to preserve order." Secretary of State Robert Lansing reassured the Haitian people that the United States had no objectives other than to "insure, establish, and help maintain Haitian independence and to establish a stable and firm government."[3] Military officers, who wanted to establish a Haitian leader who was sympathetic, bypassed the formalities of a standard presidential election. Sensing that Americans sought a leader who would bow to Yankee pressure, possible leaders like Solon Ménos, Tertulien Guilbaud and Jacques Nicolas Léger turned down American offers to become president because they would not compromise the national interests. Sudre Dartiguenave, president of the Haitian Senate, could be bought and became president because American officials discovered in him a man who "realizes that Haiti must agree to the terms laid by the United States" and who "will use his influence with the Haitian Congress to have such terms agreed upon by Haiti."[4]

African Americans did not agree with this approach. Two distinct groups—those who rallied for confrontation and those who opted for accommodation—formed. African American leaders opposed the occupation, believing the military action would lead to more racism in Haiti and loss of independence for that country. Haitian American bishop John Hurst said, "It is but the Negro question in a new form. After one hundred and more years of struggle to fulfill a mission that Providence had entrusted to them, namely to assist in the rehabilitation of the Negro race, the Haitian people find themselves violently arrested, the work of their fathers pulled down, their traditions shattered and now at the mercy of those whose only right to manage their affairs is that they are strong."[5]

The occupation of Haiti coincided with the rise of black nationalism in America, a period of self-assessment. The NAACP organized a massive campaign against black oppression in the United States. James Weldon Johnson recognized the importance of this issue when he became leader of the NAACP. Like Bishop Hurst, Johnson was convinced that racism was not confined to the U.S. borders but was rooted in American policy. For Johnson the occupation of Haiti was American imperialism pure and simple.[6]

Early in the occupation, W. E. B. Du Bois, editor in chief of *The Crisis*, used the publication to rally African American sentiment against the intervention. Du Bois was proud of his Haitian roots and defended Haiti's independence throughout his life. His grandfather migrated to Haiti, accepting Boyer's offer to African Americans in the 1820s of freedom and land. His nephew, François Elie Dubois, served ably as minister of education during the administration of President Geffrard. In response to a letter from W. A. Domingo regarding the ancestry of Marcus Garvey, Du Bois identified himself with Haiti and its heroic past: "American Negroes, to a much larger extent than they realize, are not only blood relatives to the West Indies but under deep obligations to them for many things. For instance without the Haitian Revolt, there would have been no emancipation in America as early as 1863. I, myself, am of West Indian descent and am proud of the fact."[7] He condemned the occupation and denounced the United States for violating "the independence of a sister state. With absolutely no adequate excuse she has made a white American Admiral sole and irresponsible dictator of Hayti. The anarchy in Hayti is no worse than the anarchy in the United States at the time of our Civil War, and not as great as the anarchy today in Europe. The lynching and murder in Port-au-Prince is no worse than, if as bad as, the lynching in Georgia."[8] A man of action, Du Bois asked the 10,000,000 African Americans of his time to take a stand by writing President Wilson and voicing their outrage.

On August 3, 1915, Du Bois protested Wilson's policy by writing, Haiti "is almost the sole modern representative of a great race of men among the nations. It is not only our privilege as a nation to rescue her from her worst self, but this would be in a sense a solemn act of reparation on our part for the great wrongs inflicted by this land on the Negro race."[9] He asked the president to organize a commission to assure the Haitian people that the United States did not wish to interfere with internal Haitian affairs or infringe upon their integrity as a nation and would cooperate in the establishment of permanent peace and order.

Other African Americans vied for a policy of accommodation with the United States. They saw intervention as an opportunity to elevate Haiti and promote their own interests as well. Booker T. Washington was one of those. In Washington's estimation, the American occupation was justified to avoid European intervention. For that reason, he wrote, the Government of the United States "found it necessary to take a hand in the affairs of Haiti. It was absolutely necessary for the United States to do this or permit others to do so."[10] He advised the United States to send the right class of white men to Haiti who could work in a black man's country with people who were proud of their independence.

Washington headed those who saw the occupation as a chance to advance education in Haiti. Consistent with his views, Washington suggested the United States give the Haitian people "an up-to-date system of common school, agricultural, and industrial education." Washington recommended that "Some of the young colored people of this country, well trained in the best American school methods, might go to help their Haitian fellows; while some of the most promising Haitian students might be sent to schools in the United States."[11] Had it been implemented, this would have been a model for the Peace Corps.

The Negro Educational Association of Richmond, Virginia, went one step further, reviving the idea of emigration to Haiti. During the 1915–20 period, African Americans migrated in great numbers to the industrial centers of the North in search of job opportunities, eager to escape poverty and discrimination. The association called then for a commission of "colored" men sympathetic to the Wilson administration to "inquire into the industrial, social and commercial conditions of Haiti without in any way interfering with any treaty with, or any violation of any domestic or other rights of Haiti and its people, and to determine its stability as a place of emigration for the elevation and uplift of the Negro race."[12]

The Hannibal Club and Forum of Brooklyn, New York, shared that view. The club called on Wilson to send a commission to investigate the industrial and commercial conditions of Haiti for possible emigration. As they described their cause, "The vast opportunity open to the American Negro in Haiti to engage in industrial and mercantile pursuits, has attracted the attention of many of our citizens with the thought of settling in Haiti for a period to better their fortunes."[13]

Some whites joined in, thinking the movement would persuade African Americans to move to Haiti. Garrison Villard, publisher of the *New York Evening Post* and grandson of abolitionist William Lloyd Garrison, tried to influence Washington policy makers to appoint African Americans to the "minor offices" in Haiti. He felt, for instance, that "Colored officers might be employed advantageously in connection with the organization of a constabulary in Haiti."[14]

While African Americans sought a limited emigration for economic opportunities, racist whites hoped for a full-scale exodus of southern blacks. Essayist Frantz Fanon suggested in *Black Skin, White Masks* that sex might have been the reason for this black-white hatred. Fanon believed that the Jew is feared because of his greed, and the black male is feared because of his sexual power. "Our women are at the mercy of the Negroes. For the sexual potency of the Negro is hallucinating."[15] While his theory is without scientific merit, it emerged as the fundamental reason motivating B. Barringer of Charlottesville, Virginia, to ask the Wilson administration for a mass emigration of Negroes. He wrote, "In the past thirty years there has been a great improvement in the rural South in educational, agricultural, financial conditions, and in practically every line, with one ominous exception. There is no improvement in the safety of the white woman of the rural sections." He suggested that shipping blacks to Haiti would protect white women from sexual assault; "The very children amongst the coming generation of Negroes are now yielding to this sexual obsession."[16]

Senator John Sharp Williams of Mississippi endorsed this racist view and supported emigration, asking Secretary Robert Lansing to implement it. Williams went so far as to promote inclusion of his racist and emigrationist ideas into upcoming treaties with Haiti and Santo Domingo, as a "provision that American negroes should have the privilege of purchase and settlement upon public lands of either republic. Most negroes would infinitely rather stay with white people, but there are a few who would welcome an opportunity to exploit their supposed powers as administrators and governors in building up or helping to build up a peculiarly negro civilization, or what they, at any rate, imagine as such."[17]

Official Washington rejected these requests, concerned more with the occupation of the land than the inhabiting of it. The American treaty was legalized when the U.S. Marines marched into the Haitian legislature. The treaty demanded that Americans control civilian and military services through the appointments of a general receiver, a financial adviser, engineers for public improvement, and an efficient constabulary. In 1918 a new Haitian constitution was drafted in Washington. Incidentally, the author was none other than Franklin Delano Roosevelt, then assistant secretary of the U.S. Navy. To lure American companies to the island, the occupiers eliminated the foreign-ownership provision dating back to Dessalines' rule.

The American press, which viewed the U.S. invasion as a natural course of action, echoed the benevolent yet powerful image of a neighbor trying to improve the Haitians. According to an editorial in *World's Work*, "It has taken the United States a very long time to intervene in Haiti. To find an example in recent history of greater forbearance, greater patience, would be difficult. . . . Having exhausted every possible resource in giving the Haitians time and repeated occasions to put their own house in order, now that we have gone in to do that work for them we are going to do it properly and thoroughly."[18] To many, intervention was a call to duty for the United States, to restore the Haitian republic. *Washington Times* editorial writer George Marvin illustrated this when he writes that Haiti was "dragged dumbly out into the light of what we call twentieth century civilization." He describes this event as "the great experiment of a great government trying to help a small misgovernment help itself; the great experiment of minding your neighbor's business better than he can mind it himself; of holding and directing the dark brother's hand while he writes a few pages of his current history."[19]

Haitian Nationalism

The American occupation unified Haitians against the Americans. First, the masses, experiencing their occupier's brutality firsthand, protested the revival of the *corvée*, an old forced-labor law, by the American colonel Littleton Waller. This long-standing law allowed the marines to build roads for military transportation. Under Charlemagne Péralte, Haitians staged a guerilla war from 1918 to 1919. Péralte's army of peasants—the *cacos*—were armed with machetes, knives, pikes, a few pistols, and two or three hundred rifles, anything they could get their hands on. They were no match for the marine firepower.[20] Péralte was silenced when the marines stormed into his camp and killed him.

The Haitian upper class, disillusioned, fought to reclaim its dignity and freedom. In bringing their own brand of racism to the country, Americans rekindled the long dormant racial nationalism that originally had made Haitian independence possible.

Though the elite and the Catholic Church first welcomed American intervention for political stability, they were soon disillusioned by American racism. For instance, Americans segregated themselves by closing their social clubs to Haitians, and Jim Crow standards were set up in hotels catering to them. Americans directed their resentment primarily toward the elite, viewing them as agitators who were "living off the people." General Eli K. Cole, American brigade commander from November 1916 to December 1917, noted, "The Negroes of mixed type have the general characteristics of such people the world over, vain-loving, excitable, changeable beyond measure, illogical and double faced. Many of them are highly educated and polished . . . Under strain, however, they are almost sure to revert to the black type of characteristics." Cole also described the country people as generally hardworking, "almost invariably our friends and thoroughly content with our presence and administration of affairs."[21]

John Houston Craige, a former U.S. Navy officer stationed in Haiti during the occupation, defended the American sentiment: "This is a mass-belief of Americans at home and a man cannot change the beliefs of a lifetime overnight. Of course, the native aristocrats resent this feeling. Equally, of course, the Americans resent the superior attitude of the native aristocracy."[22]

Blacks and mulattoes, feeling that they were treated as inferiors, objected to the American attitudes. Professor Pierre Hudicourt of the mulatto faction claimed, "It is an open secret that race prejudice has played a great role in the irritation which exists among those people, the Haitians and the Americans. The Haitian people, in their own territory conquered by their own forefathers, and which they have to consider their own for the future, are treated with much contempt by the newcomers. Those difficulties will be prevalent, predominant in Haiti until the Black man has been restored to his privileges."[23]

Jean Price-Mars, the leader of the ethnological movement that emerged because of American racism, defined the attacks on the elite as a deliberate strategy to keep the country under American control. In 1919, he wrote in his book *La vocation de l'élite*, "I know well that the current storm may destroy the bases upon which our intellectual élite is nurtured, from which it draws its directives and from which its thought is developed, but I also know well that the eventual plan they would like to see fulfilled would be to cause the gradual leveling of the Haitian society so that, by taking the intellectual level of the elite down a few pegs and by lifting the masses from the misery of their ignorance, they might establish the framework for the domination of the foreign element."[24]

Haitians used American racism to reexamine the nation's culture. Haitians rejected Captain Charles Young's reforms that ran counter to the cultural nationalism. As American military attaché, Young suggested that Haitians "close high schools and libraries, and engage on a new course, keeping constantly before [their] eyes the example of the American people."[25] Instead, the nationalists promoted the study of Haitian history and culture by creating the Société d'histoire et de géographie in 1923. Cultural nationalism filtered into the educational system by an ardent resistance to the occupation and the military intervention.

As minister of public instruction, Dantès Bellegarde mounted a resistance to the occupation in order to protect national institutions. In 1919, the first University Day was celebrated and the Haitian flag was honored, so that "teachers of our educational system at all levels may feel more strongly the solidarity which unites them in the great task of national education."[26] Haitian students began to learn history not so much from French and European traditions, but rather from an African perspective.

Investigation by the NAACP

The NAACP's decision to fight for Haiti's liberation was a blow to the United States' image of itself as a benevolent occupier. In March 1920, the NAACP board of directors asked James Weldon Johnson to investigate reports of brutality in Haiti. Johnson's selection was appropriate because he was familiar with the region, having served as United States consul at Puerto Caballo, Nicaragua. In addition, his forbears came from Haiti. His maternal great-grandmother, Hester Argo, was a Haitian who left in 1802 during a revolutionary independence period.[27]

Johnson enlisted important Republicans, a strategy that enhanced the black offensive. Before leaving for Haiti, Johnson sought the advice of Theodore Roosevelt. Roosevelt was just as dissatisfied with the Wilson administration's management of the Haitian situation as was Johnson. With Roosevelt's blessing, Johnson sailed for Port-au-Prince, accompanied by Herbert Seligman, NAACP publicity agent. Johnson spent three months in Haiti, meeting with every Haitian political group. On his return, he published his report in *The Nation*, *The Crisis*, and other leading periodicals. He also lectured on the need for Haitian self-determination.

In his reports Johnson made three distinct arguments. First, he said that, contrary to the official version from Washington, the marines did not intervene to restore peace. Twice in 1914, the American government forced Haiti to submit to "peaceable intervention." As in Santo Domingo, the Haitian government was asked to sign a document authorizing U.S. control of Haitian finances. The Haitian government rejected the terms. But the United States had the opportunity to intervene when, on July 27 and 28, 1915, President Vilbrun Guillaume Sam was assassinated and riots broke out. This time, the American government not only controlled Haitian finances but also the military force.

Second, Johnson discredited the American business community's role during the intervention. He pointed out that the military conquest was due to "dollar diplomacy." As proof, Johnson said that Roger L. Farnham, vice president of the National City Bank of New York, was influential in the development of State Department policy regarding Haiti. His bank exercised a monopoly over the Haitian economy by controlling the Banque Nationale of Haiti, the only bank in the country throughout the period of occupation.

Third, Johnson exposed the brutality of the American army. When Haitian patriots, under the command of Charlemagne Péralte, armed themselves and retreated into the hills, the U.S. Marines launched a full-scale attack to reduce those they called bandits and outlaws. Johnson reported that some 3,000 Haitians and 13 U.S. Marines were killed. He also exposed press censorship, the plight of the peasantry, and the use of force to maintain control. Finally, he charged the American government had failed to honor any of its promises to aid in the development of Haiti financially, educationally, or otherwise. As he explained it, "If the United States should leave Haiti today, it would leave more than a thousand widows and orphans of its own making, more banditry than has existed for a century, resentment, hatred and despair in the heart of a whole people, to say nothing of the irreparable injury to its own tradition as the defender of the rights of man.[28]

Johnson was successful in exposing the harshness of the occupation, largely due to a publicity blitz that began with the publication of his papers. As he confided to Oswald Garrison Villard, "I did not go to Haiti to make merely a calm and judicial survey of conditions . . . I went for the purpose of finding out if there were certain wrongs being perpetrated there and to expose those wrongs."[29] Johnson provided a thorough examination of American involvement in Haiti and attracted attention to both Haiti and the United States.

Johnson's ultimate objective was the liberation of the island so that the Haitian people could regain their sovereignty. He urged African Americans to help bring about that outcome, for "Haiti is the one best chance that the Negro has in the world to prove that he is capable of the highest self-government."[30] His reasoning was consistent with that of nineteenth-century African American leaders who played a major role in Haitian civil and political development.

Johnson's investigation rekindled the Haitian nationalistic spirit. From the hills of Pétion-Ville, Price-Mars forwarded his comments, "I am grateful to you as is any Haitian for the splendid work you are doing in the American press in revealing the truth about the Haitian situation to the American people. We are all happy and proud that such a generous action has been done by a prominent member of the Negro race."[31] From Port-au-Prince, former president Légitime agreed, "I rejoice about the success of the campaign you are leading on behalf of Haiti and for the triumph of the Negro cause in the United States. The whole nation is grateful to you."[32] Haitians living in the United States were similarly heartened by Johnson's efforts, finding them a source of pride.

About 500 Haitian émigrés in the United States supported Johnson's action. They had resettled in the New York area, hoping to escape the political chaos in Haiti. These early émigrés came from urban areas and were more literate than the other non-English-speaking black immigrants of this period.[33] One of those, J. Joseph Adam, a member of the NAACP branch in San Francisco, affirmed that Johnson helped the Haitian people to make themselves heard: "You made them feel that although everything looked towards the annexation of the country by withholding its freedom of action they could depend on twelve millions or more kindred people speaking the English language to help them fight their battle against race prejudice and exploitation."[34]

The most prominent Haitian American involved in the liberation campaign was Bishop John Hurst. From the very beginning he was perceived as a prime inspiration for finding a solution. A month following the American intervention, *Nation* editor Oswald Garrison Villard suggested to Secretary of State Robert Lansing the creation of a commission to study the whole Haitian situation. Villard also asked Lansing to appoint influential African Americans to serve in Haiti. Among those recommended were Major Charles Young, James Weldon Johnson, and H. W. Furness. He also said that "Bishop Hurst of the A.M.E. Church, a native Haitian, but a naturalized American citizen" was worthy of consideration.[35] Emmett J. Scott, former secretary and associate of Booker T. Washington, also recommended Hurst to Senator Medill McCormick: "I know of no man among our colored people in the United States who is in better position to give an opinion with respect to the Haitian situation."[36] Hurst said he was pleased with the way Johnson conducted the investigation. He acknowledged that the measure of goodwill Johnson had created for "the Haitian people, and incidentally the Negro in America, through this special work, cannot be estimated."[37] He denounced the occupation as "an unredeemable shame and disgrace" and criticized the Americans for creating an intolerable social atmosphere in Haiti. In his view, "A situation strictly Southern has been developed there. The difference between Texas and Haiti, speaking from a social standpoint, is hardly perceptible."[38]

In black America, too, Johnson was hailed as a hero. From Washington D.C., James Cobb reacted, "*The Washington Post's* leading article this morning is on the Haitian condition and you are on the lips of all the colored people of moment who have sufficient self-respect to be interested in their own problem."[39] J. Moseley, another well-wisher from Decatur, Alabama, reminded Johnson that he was doing "a great work for the race" and that his actions had the desired effect. Moseley even suggested that Johnson be elected to the U.S. Senate.[40]

Johnson also had critics. Prentice Abbot of New York disagreed with placing the blame on the government of the United States. "I maintain that to attack our Government along lines of race prejudice and money-interest in these days of dangerous radicalism is unwise and not the part of a conservative and far-seeing citizen."[41] Others felt that Johnson focused on the injustices committed in Haiti and not any positive accomplishments.

Johnson's activities with Haitian nationalists raised concern, too. Military commander John Russell blamed Johnson for rumors against the occupation and the Dartiguenave government. He claimed that "The only trouble in Haiti today was caused by the agitators and politicians here at the capital, and that I understood now that a society had been formed with Pauléus Sannon as President, to form a provisional government in Haiti and that this society was in communication with a Negro in the United States named James Weldon Johnson."[42]

Nevertheless, Johnson continued with his campaign. For the added publicity Johnson succeeded in securing the Republican nominee for the United States presidency for Ohio senator Warren Gamaliel Harding, when Haitian independence was made a national campaign issue. Johnson wrote to Lewis Einstein, "I made an effort to have the National Republican Campaign Committee get out the mediums of publicity. All along I felt sure that the Haitian exposé would become one of the issues of the campaign and I felt that the facts ought to be in the hands of all of the agencies which have to do with the forming of public opinion."[43] Harding did respond as Johnson hoped.

Harding was eager to win the black vote, which made him a likely ally of Johnson, now a member of the Republican National Advisory Committee. At the request of the NAACP Board of Directors, on August 9, 1920, Johnson met the Republican presidential nominee in Marion, Ohio. He said he would give Harding his endorsement if the Ohio senator would call for antilynching laws, federal aid, and the end of the U.S. occupation of Haiti as part of his platform. Harding showed interest in only the Haitian occupation, since he knew he could exploit this for his election campaign. Johnson felt that Harding "looked upon the Haitian matter as a gift right off the Christmas tree. He could not conceal his delight."[44] Armed with copies of documents that substantiated Johnson's charges regarding Haiti, Harding seized the chance to include the issue in his campaign.

Harding also denounced Franklin D. Roosevelt, Democratic vice presidential running mate for James M. Cox, for his boasts that he wrote the Haitian constitution of 1918. Harding charged that this alone represented an official admission of the rape of Haiti and Santo Domingo by the present administration. He also charged that "Thousands of Haitians have been killed by American Marines and many of our gallant men have been sacrificed." Statements like these shocked official Washington, and forced the Wilson administration to defend itself. Josephus Daniels, secretary of the navy, rejected the senator's charges, claiming that "The Marines have rendered a real service to the people of that country."[45] Secretary of State Bainbridge Colby underscored "the benevolent purpose" for which the United States had sent troops to Haiti in 1915. The

anarchy that reigned there, he claimed, had ended through the "bounte-
ous altruism" of the United States. General John A. Lejeune, U.S. Marines commandant, suggested that his men "had intelligently, zealously,
efficiently and courageously fulfilled their mission. That mission was the
suppression of banditry and the maintenance of peace and tranquility."[46]

Johnson's different view focused on the effectiveness of Harding's
charges: "I see that you have finally gotten under the skin of the Wilson
administration on the Haitian question. You have smoked them out and
got them on the run and I hope that you will keep them running."[47] The
board of the NAACP sent Harding a congratulatory telegram for a job
well done: "The National Association for the Advancement of Colored
People congratulate you on the result of your inquiry into the unconstitutional and brutal invasion of Haiti stop The facts as to which were first
exposed by James Weldon Johnson acting Secretary of this Association
and by Herbert J. Seligmann in the *Nation* stop We urge that you continue to place the facts before the American people to the end that the
illegal misrule in Haiti may be brought to a conclusion."[48]

Johnson maintained the pressure by providing Harding with new facts
about financial dealings of the National City Bank and the State Department. Johnson's report led to the awakening of public opinion. The issue
made front-page news in American papers. The press, which in the five
years before had supported the administration's Haitian policy, was now
posing questions about recent developments. These coincided with postwar efforts to establish the League of Nations, designed to protect the
rights of small nations. The press exposed the discrepancy between the
emphasis on democracy at home and American intervention abroad, in
the Caribbean republics. The *New York Times* demanded an inquiry "in
order to bring out the truth about the conditions in Haiti and to fix responsibility for military inefficiency and official mismanagement of a
policy that was undertaken for the welfare of the Haitians."[49] For the first
time since 1915, the Wilson administration was on the defensive and
forced to reconsider its Haitian policy.

The NAACP also pressed for the truth behind the Haitian occupation.
Eventually, the secretary of the navy ordered an inquiry of "all persons,
officers and enlisted men of the Marines and *Gendarmerie d'Haiti*
against whom existed any evidence of illegal or brutal conduct and a further Court of Inquiry to examine all the high officers of the Marine
Corps connected with the Haitian administration."[50] Hearings took place

in Washington, attended by military officers such as Admiral H. S. Knapp, commandant of the marine forces in Haiti, and General George Barnett. Haitian President Sudre Dartiguenave, in his statement to the board of inquiry, bitterly denounced the arrogance of American officials and their failure to honor the terms of the treaty.

The public viewed this investigation with skepticism. It was believed that Admiral Knapp presented his case through the eyes of the marine corps. Because investigators were also American military officials, the court of inquiry not surprisingly absolved the marines. *The Nation* reacted by asking Congress to send an unbiased commission to Haiti, insisting that "Congress at its coming session must be prompt to investigate, and must tolerate no official white-washing."[51] Senator Medill McCormick of Illinois asked for "a searching investigation of the charges made against the Corps and individual officers." He also insisted that "Prosecution should be instituted if the facts call for it."[52] Despite the failure of the investigation, the NAACP took credit for exposing the horrible realities of the American military occupation and for bringing this important issue to the American political scene.

While Johnson was able to influence public opinion, he also wanted constructive changes. A closer relationship between Haitian and African American leaders around the issue of defending the race was one particular result of his activity. The goodwill generated by his investigation affected both Haitians and African Americans.

Even at this stage, Haitians and African Americans both feared that the concept of blacks running their own government still remained in question. "The theory that colored people cannot govern themselves if found its application in Haiti will hold good for all colored countries," commented J. Joseph Adam.[53] Comparing the two peoples, Adam wrote, "Every Negro with any race pride, feels that the subjugation of the people of Haiti, means that the white race does not intend only to deny the Negro in the United States the rights granted him by the constitution, but intends to go everywhere and destroy the weak Negro governments instead of helping them to hold their places among the smaller Nations of the world."[54]

Walter White, assistant secretary of the NAACP, requested that a network of black editors carry a unifying message: "It is exceedingly necessary that the colored people of America unite with their brothers in Haiti to bring pressure to bear that would restore to Haiti its sovereignty and independence. The Negro in Haiti has the best chance in the world to prove that he is capable of the highest self-development and self-government."[55]

The NAACP national office used this interest as a fund-raiser. White asked the branches to organize large meetings for the Johnson tour, not only to place the facts before the people but also to "realize a substantial sum for the branch treasury as the net proceeds can be divided on the basis of sixty percent to the National Office and forty percent for the branch."[56] Three months later, White informed the branch officers that, thanks to the work of the national office, the Haitian cause commanded the attention of the entire country. He asked, "Are you going to support us to your fullest ability? If you don't, we can't do a greater job, that is all. And there are plenty more jobs to do."[57] The jobs he referred to were not in Haiti but at home, especially concerned with antilynching, Jim Crow cars, and disfranchisement of blacks. The similarity to the Haitian problem was inescapable.

Impact of NAACP Action on Haiti

The American expeditionary forces succeeded in maintaining control over Haiti, with the occasional friction from Charlemagne Péralte's guerrilla soldiers. Even that resistance was short-lived when the guerilla soldiers were crushed by the overwhelming military superiority of the marines. Charlemagne himself was killed in an ambush in November 1919. His death marked an end to any armed resistance against American forces in Haiti.

James Weldon Johnson's visit allowed Haitians to escalate the fight to a diplomatic level. His reports revitalized the nationalists against foreign occupation. Johnson used the opportunity to talk with Haitian civic and intellectual leaders, including former president François Légitime, President Sudre Dartiguenave, Louis Borno, and Jean Price-Mars. Johnson wanted to unite Haitians of different political and ideological persuasions. He agreed with B. Danache, President Dartiguenave's chief of staff, who wrote, "The government and the opposition should back each other since they only faced one enemy: the American."[58] Cooperation was not an easy task since nationalists had opposite views from those who collaborated with the occupation forces.

Johnson convinced opposing factions to adopt methods for "organizing sentiment among the Haitians and for setting up machinery by which they could take united action."[59] He described the central idea and the working methods of the NAACP, demonstrating how a unified front would help free the country from American domination. He convinced them that Haiti should establish a similar organization with the same tenets, headquartered in Port-au-Prince, with branches in other regions.

Price-Mars tried to create an NAACP branch in Haiti but was unsuccessful. "Until now I have not been able to have sufficient persons to take out memberships—at least 50 according to the third point of the pamphlet you sent me."[60] Poet and political leader George Sylvain was more successful in getting Johnson's recommendations started. He revived *L'union patriotique*, an organization he created in 1915. The group, opposed to the occupation, was disbanded under the terms of the Treaty of 1916.

Johnson's involvement in *Union patriotique* brought new life. The first edition of its monthly bulletin, called *La Patrie*, acknowledged Johnson's role in the rebirth of the organization:

On November 17, 1920, in accord with the cherished wish of Mr. James Weldon Johnson, the devoted Secretary-General of the National Association for the Advancement of Colored People, eighteen Haitian citizens, at the call of M. George Sylvain, former Minister plenipotentiary of Haiti to Paris, met at Port-au-Prince in his law office, and decided to form an association having as its prime object the working in accord with the defenders of the Haitian cause in the United States for the abolishment of all restrictions placed upon the full exercise of sovereignty and independence on the part of the Haitian government.[61]

The *Union patriotique* became a powerful force in the struggle for national liberation. Fourteen chapters were established throughout the country. Union leaders sent a delegation to the United States "to make known the plight of the Haitian people, open proper channels of communication necessary for the success of our cause and make preparation for official negotiations between the two countries."[62] This was not an easy task since the money for such a project had to be raised in impoverished Haiti. To help raise money some 200 female volunteers in Port-au-Prince solicited contributions door-to-door and encouraged passersby to donate.

As a result, a commission, composed of historian Pauléus Sannon, statesman Sténio Vincent, and Percéval Thoby, former secretary to the Haitian legation at Washington, was sent to the United States in February 1921. On May 9 a memorandum describing the political, economic, and financial conditions existing in Haiti under American occupation was shown to the Department of State and to the Senate Foreign Relations Committee. Delegates charged that the occupying forces had ignored Haiti's constitutional law: "The American military authorities had taken possession of the custom houses, had invaded the territory of the nation, and, by the establishment of martial courts, had practically suppressed the Haitian administration of justice."[63] They also charged that Haiti had not received any aid "for the development of its agricultural and industrial resources, and no constructive measure had been proposed, for the purpose of placing its finances on a really solid basis."[64] The delegates demanded an end to martial law and the withdrawal of military forces so that Haitians could form a national assembly to draft a constitution reflecting national sentiment. The report was published in *The Nation*.

At Johnson's urging the NAACP organized a branch of the *Union patriotique* in New York in 1923 to send out "appeals to various individuals together with literature on the Haitian situation." Joseph Mirault, for the *Courrier Haitien*, presided over this branch. He informed Johnson of political developments in Haiti such as the cancellation of legislative elections by President Borno and the imprisonment of political prisoners.[65] These included Joseph Jolibois Fils, Elie Guerin, Antoine Pierre-Paul, and George Petit, all of them nationalist leaders jailed by the forces of the American occupation.

In Haiti, the *Union patriotique* maintained a high profile, continuing its pacifist campaign against the occupation. Mass meetings were staged, usually energized by Sylvain's poetic and oratorical verve. In a speech delivered on June 8, 1921, he exhorted his fellow citizens, "Be united, so by fighting for the independence of your fatherland, you might give a vigorous response to your adversaries . . . Remember that there stand behind you all those who, in our country, in South America, in Central America, dread the dangerous consequences of the awful American imperialism."[66] Besides sending the three-member commission to the United States, the *Union patriotique* furnished the NAACP with materials to continue its publicity campaign against the occupation.

Pressure by the NAACP

The election of Warren G. Harding as president of the United States brought new hope for Haiti. President Dartiguenave pleaded with Harding: "The Haitian people stand in great need of justice . . . They stand in great need of benevolence . . . The Haitians have placed their hope in you."[67] Harding seemed committed to American troop withdrawal. In 1922, he ordered the removal of the marines from Camaguey, an important step toward normalization of relations with Cuba. But the military occupation of Haiti was strengthened during the Harding administration.

When Harding took office, he asked his secretary of state, Charles Evans Hughes, to send Sumner Welles, chief of the Latin American division of the Department of State, to Haiti to review conditions there. In July 1921, Welles recommended that an American loan be granted to relieve the country's financial instability, that the Haitian gendarmerie be improved, and that a marine officer be selected as the president's personal representative and empowered to effect various reforms.

In February 1921, California senator Hiram Johnson called for a Senate investigation of America's invasion of Haiti and Santo Domingo. A Senate committee of inquiry was then formed. Chaired by Senator Medill McCormick, the committee included Senators Tasker L. Oddie of Nevada, Atlee Pomerene of Ohio, Philander C. Knox of Pennsylvania, and William H. King of Utah. Hearings were held during August 1921. American officials made a deliberate effort to justify the intervention and emphasized material improvements brought about by the occupation. Throughout the hearings, the NAACP pressured Washington by asking their members to write senators on the committee to urge them to "withdraw the United States Army from Haiti and to treat black republics in the way in which white republics want to be treated."[68] Johnson and Ernest Gruening, attorney for the Haiti–Santo Domingo Independence Society, testified. Johnson reported on Haitian resentment of the occupation force, the harshness of military rule, the blatant violations of treaty agreements, the *corvée*, and the drawing of the color line. He urged "the quickest withdrawal of the United States, and almost as immediate as possible, the withdrawal of the military forces, and as prompt as possible, a withdrawal of even civilian rule or oversight . . . We will never be able to do anything in Haiti unless we have the goodwill of the Haitians . . . and the best way to do it is to assure Haiti we have no ultimate aims against her independence."[69]

Hearings continued in Port-au-Prince. The *Union patriotique* coordinated Haitian efforts. Sylvain, along with law professor Pierre Hudicourt and *Courrier Haitien* journalist Joseph Jolibois, described Haitian feelings toward the American occupation to senators. Incidentally, Jolibois had just been released from prison following slander charges for his anti-American reporting. Throughout the hearings, the *Union patriotique* provided witnesses willing to testify that they saw their fellow countrymen victimized by American military forces. This was not a simple matter because of what Sylvain described as "a situation of intimidation and terrorizing conditions."[70] Many witnesses feared they would be persecuted after the committee's departure from Haiti.

The committee, however, reaffirmed the need for maintaining American control of Haiti. Johnson, trying to console his Haitian friends, wrote to Sylvain, "The Report is far from being what we expected, but the friends of Haiti in the United States are not at all discouraged, and we are not ready to slow down our efforts in the interest of the Haitian people."[71] Sylvain had hoped that some form of compensation would be given to those victimized by the marines. Most observers believed the Harding administration would not deviate from its policy of strengthening the military occupation. According to historian Hans Schmidt, the decisions to reorganize and rationalize the occupation had been made in advance of the inquiry.[72]

The Politics of Race and Color

In spite of the apparent cooperation between Haitian nationalists and African American leaders, sharp differences divided them. These differences emerged as American officials implemented U.S. Senate Committee of Inquiry recommendations. The committee urged the military occupation to undertake a program of industrial and agricultural education for the masses. An imbroglio of the politics of race and color followed within the triangular relations created among Haitians, African Americans, and the U.S. government.

The Harding administration asked Dr. Robert Moton of Tuskegee Institute in Alabama to investigate the feasibility of implementing the

Senate's recommendations. Robert Church of Memphis was to make recommendations on industrial and business matters. Neither man accepted, for Moton was already committed to giving a series of lectures in England and Scotland, and Church thought it unwise to leave the United States because of his business. But their very nomination demonstrated the politics of race and color as Washington sought to pacify black activists in the United States and a Haitian elite bent on maintaining French culture.

Harding hoped to dazzle Haitians with Moton's strong reputation, in the process covering up any wrongdoings of the military occupation. As McCormick wrote, a report "coming from the most prominent Negro in the country would have an excellent effect of allaying hostile criticism of our occupation."[73]

The Haitian elite not only expressed its disdain for the technical and industrial education that typified the Tuskegee tradition, but also its unwillingness to welcome African Americans as official representatives of the United States in Haiti. Léon Déjean of the Haitian legation in Washington said that "As a general rule, the Haitians prefer a white man to a Negro for work in Haiti as the former has more influence and authority, and on account of certain prejudice existing against foreign Negroes."[74]

American officials demonstrated similar racial prejudices during the occupation, particularly in their favoritism for lighter-skinned mulattoes in public affairs. Washington officials reasoned that "The educated Haitians who, for the most part, are mulattoes, rather than full blooded Negroes, sharply draw the line between themselves and full blooded Negroes and resent being classed as such."[75] Not surprisingly, Harding chose Church because of his light skin color: "Church is nearly like a white man that one has to look the second time to know the difference."[76] Despite Haitian opposition, Dr. W. T. Williams, a faculty member of Tuskegee, went to Haiti as Dr. Moton's personal representative with the charge to make a survey of Haitian education.

Haitians had another opportunity to express their dissatisfaction with the idea of receiving African Americans on mission in Haiti. The U.S. government sent a commission to instruct Haitians about improved agricultural methods, but Déjean objected to Moton's presence on the commission: "The upper classes in Haiti . . . have even more race prejudice than the people of the United States, and it would be very embarrassing from a social point of view if an American Negro should be sent there."[77]

The State Department concurred. Secretary of State Hughes called for caution because "The very delicate question of improving the social relations between the American treaty officials and the more prominent leaders in Haiti is one of the most important problems arising in our relations with that Republic, and one to which General Russell has been giving special attention."[78] This appeasement demonstrates concessions made to Haitian mulattoes during the occupation by American officials.

The Final Push for Liberation

The struggle against the American presence in Haiti continued unabated during the 1920s and gradually included a new tactic. The NAACP turned its attention to the freedom of the press under High Commissioner John Russell and the newly elected president, Louis Borno, who had used their power to stifle the press. Haitian journalists, especially Joseph Jolibois of *Courrier Haitien*, countered by asking the NAACP to make the problem known to the American public. In May 1922, Jolibois complained of the arrest and hard-labor sentences for several journalists. He asked "the publication of the present in your interesting paper . . . to make known to the civilized world the situation that is made to the poor Hayti."[79] Johnson forwarded to the press information concerning the treatment of the Haitian journalists.

In 1923, the NAACP protested the investigation and arrest of *La Poste* editor Louis Edouard Pouget for writing "that the place of Haiti's president, M. Borno, was the National Penitentiary." Johnson condemned the suppression of opinion. "We do not believe that the United States Government can continue to allow such a record to be made in Haiti, because it was for the abolishment of just such practices we are there."[80] In 1924, he protested the latest arrest of Jolibois, his eighth arrest in three years, where he was kept in solitary confinement, deprived of books and newspapers, and denied sanitary decencies.

Opposition to the American occupation continued with a collaboration of Haitian and African American leaders through the Pan-African Movement. W. E. B. Du Bois hoped for a unity of black leaders to defend the rights and welfare of people of African descent. In a statement issued by the Second Pan-African Congress, participants argued that "The independence of Abyssinia, Liberia, Haiti, and Santo Domingo is absolutely necessary to any sustained belief of the black folk in the sincerity and honesty of the white. These nations have earned the right to be free; they deserve the recognition of the world."[81] The Pan-African Congress defended the equality of all races as the foundation of world peace and human advancement.

The crusade against the occupation involved students of the American-controlled *Ecole centrale d'agriculture* who went on strike in October 1929. The strike spread to other schools throughout the country. Opponents of the occupation organized a nationwide protest, and bloody riots broke out. In one battle between the marines and Haitians, at least five Haitians were killed and twenty others wounded.

The riots of 1929 thrust the NAACP to the forefront of the Haitian struggle. Walter Francis White was now secretary. White, born on July 1, 1893, of African and white parentage, was a journalist and writer about Haiti. White was an advocate against lynching and had worked toward making it a criminal offense. For the next three decades, White managed to maintain a friendship with Haitian leaders and continued to publicize the plight of the Haitian people. When White learned that "the youth of Haiti are the ones who are leading in the revolt against the iniquitous American occupation," he sent "a story to the press of the country today revealing that the Haitian youth are alive to the situation."[82] The riots revived hope among Haitians for an end to the occupation.

Forced to take action, President Herbert Hoover asked Congress to create a commission to investigate conditions in Haiti. Cameroun Forbes, former governor general of the Philippine Islands, chaired the commission. The NAACP asked Hoover to include an African American on this commission for two reasons. First, a person of high caliber and "wholly unpurchasable" would guarantee the commission would not "whitewash our mistakes and justify any international crime in the name of patriotism and our divine mission to interfere with and rule smaller and weaker American nations,"[83] and second, the NAACP wanted to show that African Americans had an interest in Haiti. The telegram to Hoover emphasized that "Twelve million American citizens of Negro descent are deeply and vitally interested in the matter which touches their legitimate racial pride and the fate of over two million fellow black folk."[84] To add to the pressure, the NAACP sent the following telegram to the branches: "National Office urges your branch to send telegram in its name to both senators from your state and to each member of Congress urging that he support move for impartial thorough investigation Haitian situation and especially appointment on that commission of at least one Negro member who is both qualified and who commands full respect and confidence of Negroes themselves. Haitian situation most alarming. Your part necessary to secure Negro representation on commission which can prevent whitewashing on American occupation."[85]

Hoover did not listen and refused to appoint a "Negro member," but rather asked Moton to form a commission to examine the educational situation. Haitians and African Americans did not like the idea. Raoul Lizaire, chargé d'affaires ad interim in Washington, voiced his disapproval. He restated the past Haitian position: "The Haitians are very disturbed because they fear that Dr. Moton will recommend a program of agricultural and vocational rather than cultural education. The Haitian elite is deeply attached to classical studies and to the French system of education."[86]

African Americans were disturbed by the apparent second-class status of the commission. None other than James Weldon Johnson, veteran crusader against the occupation, voiced his opposition: "I feel that you would be placed in an awkward and embarrassing position to be sent to Haiti as a sort of adjunct to the Commission proper." Johnson interpreted Hoover's action on the ground of the current race relations.[87] He rejected Moton's invitation to join the commission. African American editors complained about the unfair treatment of the Moton Commission, charging that President Hoover "anointed his white men but appointed his colored men."[88] Unlike the Forbes Commission, the navy refused to recognize the Moton Commission by providing them with accommodation for fear of setting a bad precedent.

Meanwhile, the Forbes Commission submitted its report to Hoover. The commission recommended American withdrawal from Haiti and called for the election of a legislature and a president there. Hoover agreed and withdrew occupation forces from Haiti. This American policy also called for the haitianization of the services that were controlled by Americans, including the *Service technique*, the agency that provided for vocational education and agricultural development in Haiti. This did not come about easily.

When elections finally occurred in 1930, Sténio Vincent, a nationalist leader who had resisted the occupation, became president of Haiti. His election symbolized a victory for Haitian nationalists and resulted in congratulatory notices from the NAACP. White extended "warmest felicitations" and wishes for prosperity and peace.[89]

White traveled to Haiti only to return with a mixed review. He reported that Haiti remained "a world race laboratory" and reminded African Americans that "Haiti is the unique and outstanding demonstration in the Western Hemisphere of the Negro's ability to govern himself and administer his own affairs."[90] White stressed the danger that existed despite the fact that the president's commission recommended the evacuation of the marines along with the restoration of all administrative duties to Haitians. White also denounced the almost absolute American control of Haiti's finances through American financial advisers. White declared that "Between now and the presidential campaign of 1932, American public opinion must be mobilized to free Haiti. Franklin Roosevelt and Herbert Hoover must answer to Black America on this subject and answer with great frankness if they expect Negro votes."[91]

President Vincent's appointment of Dantès Bellegarde as Haitian minister to Washington and the Pan-American Union contributed to the end of the occupation. Bellegarde was a prominent diplomat who earlier had served Haiti at the Permanent Court of Arbitration (The Hague Court) and as minister to France. He also served as honorary president of the Second Pan-African Congress and had excellent relations with African American leaders. Du Bois considered Bellegarde's performance in the international arena as representative not just of Haitians but also of African Americans. He wrote, "I am very gratified at your activities at the League of Nations and congratulate you upon them. I want to let the colored people of the United States know how splendidly you have represented them as well as Haiti."[92] Du Bois kept his promise. In a 1926 article in The Crisis, he praised Bellegarde's public career and fight against imperialism, calling him "the international spokesman of black folk."[93]

When Bellegarde arrived in Washington, he vowed to bring about the military and financial liberation of Haiti. He solicited White's support, stressing the common interests binding the two peoples. He wrote, "The struggle we are leading to regain our independence is very difficult. To have victory, we need the assistance of all men of good faith, lovers of justice and respecters of the law. But we are entitled to the right to first of all rely on the cordial assistance of our race brothers who, like us, suffer social injustice. As I said in 1927 at the Pan-African Congress presided by

Dr. Du Bois and as you yourself affirm with strength, the fall of Haiti would be the fall of black Americans. Our interests are bound."[94] This message was repeated to Du Bois on the same day. Bellegarde told him, "I am happy, when arriving in this country, to renew cordial relations with one of the men who has best served, by his talent and faith, the cause of my small nation."[95] The attainment of that objective was yet another challenge to the relationship between Haitians and African Americans. Though they agreed on the agenda, they were divided on the methods of implementing it.

The Forbes Commission recommendation provided the basis for the liberation of Haiti. On August 5, 1931, Americans announced that on October 1 they would return to the Haitians control of the governmental departments operated by the Americans under the treaty. This announcement signaled another shot dividing Haitians and African Americans. White, who was dissatisfied with the announcement, immediately enlisted the help of Vincent, Bellegarde, and other prominent Haitians to decide on the next steps toward Haitian independence. But Bellegarde declared, "The government and the Haitian people are very satisfied of the result obtained by the signing of the Accord of last August."[96] Bypassing the Haitian government, White petitioned Hoover to adopt three provisions: "1) complete restoration of financial and political autonomy to Haiti; 2) withdrawal of the U. S. Marines . . . ; and 3) negotiation of a new treaty constitutionally negotiated with the consent of the legislatures of both nations."[97] Because of these three conditions, it was apparent that White wanted control of the Haitian liberation agenda.

Port-au-Prince and Washington reached an agreement, ironically called a "treaty of friendship," to be ratified by their respective legislatures. White again sharply criticized the treaty because Americans, in his view, continued to control Haitian finances through a fiscal representative. "They will hold the purse-string. They will remain the real rulers of Haiti," he warned. He asked Bellegarde to make a statement "which we might use for publicity purposes but which would not make difficulties for you as the Haitian Minister."[98] Bellegarde refused and sided with his government: "I want to give you the full assurance that this act is advantageous for Haiti, because, if it was otherwise, President Vincent, whose patriotic feelings you personally know, would have never accepted to give it his consent."[99] The minister reminded White of his status as a diplomat that forbade him from meddling in the internal matters of the United States.

Relations between the Vincent administration and the NAACP inevitably soured. Vincent, concerned with keeping his power, mistrusted the Haitian nationalists and the NAACP. He saw Washington and the marines as the most reliable force to maintain his political survival. Haitian officials tried to end the occupation while holding on to Washington backing. The president accepted whatever they could get from Hoover before the arrival of Franklin Delano Roosevelt, whose past wheeling and dealing heightened their fears.

Unlike Vincent, the NAACP chose an uncompromising approach to the Hoover administration, focusing on Haiti's interests instead of Vincent's personal quest for power. Vincent's high-handed tactics widened the gap between his administration and the NAACP. White stole the thunder from Vincent because he had the support of Haitian nationalists. Siding with the secretary, Haitian law professor Pierre Hudicourt translated and publicized his letter to Hoover. Worse for Vincent, the Haitian legislature unanimously rejected the treaty.

A final accord between the Vincent administration and the new Roosevelt administration was signed in 1933. By signing an executive agreement, they bypassed the United States Congress and avoided certain fire from the Haitian legislature. Even then, White refused to accept the agreement, complaining to Vincent, "It appears incredible that any Haitian could be guilty of approving this accord at the very time when fifteen years of struggle seems about to result in full freedom for Haiti."[100] The secretary also asked Bellegarde to "resign as soon as possible in order to create a repercussion throughout Haiti, Central and South America, and the United States, emphasizing that Haiti would be lost unless such an outbreak occurs."[101] Bellegarde chose not to join in the squabble because, in his view, "such action was contrary to diplomatic usage and unfriendly to President Vincent."[102]

Despite his efforts, Bellegarde was blamed for the tensions between the NAACP and Vincent. Vincent fired him for his relationship with the NAACP. The prominent Bellegarde got caught in the crossfire for trying to pacify and please both Vincent and White and lost favor with both. When Haitian negotiators rejected Bellegarde's views, he remained in contact with Vincent. White shared some of these confidences with the president: "I was most astounded to learn that he knew no more about the proposed treaty than I did and M. Blanchet had not informed him of anything concerning the treaty, nor any of the details, and in fact had not even written M. Bellegarde since last June."[103]

Such a statement sealed Bellegarde's fate. For his refusal to resign, he lost White's respect. Even though he had been fired, the minister announced his resignation at the Pan-American Union governing board. Wearing the white enamel cross of the French Legion of Honor, he announced his protest against the agreement. Privately, Bellegarde vowed: "I go back to private life, that is I return to my country with the very definite plan to live away from this Haitian politics made of intrigues, gossips, and maliciousness."[104]

American troops finally withdrew from Haiti on August 24, 1934, allowing the country its political sovereignty. The NAACP was responsible in large part for this freedom from U.S. domination. When the last contingent of marines finally left Haiti, the *Twenty-Fifth Report of the NAACP* judiciously noted, "This event served to recall the part played by the association in stirring public opinion in the United States against the Occupation of Haiti by the Marines. Throughout the occupation, the Association was the leading organization in the United States which had campaigned for the evacuation of Haiti and for the end of the financial control by the Americans and American banking houses."[105]

The Haitians acknowledged that African American leaders had greatly contributed to the liberation of their country. Vincent expressed his gratitude and that of the people of Haiti "to all those American friends, colored or white, who, so willingly and so courageously have taken part, on our side, in the long and hard struggle of which the day of last August 21st marked the crowning victory."[106] Yet the tension between Vincent and the NAACP continued to boil.

The Twenty-sixth Annual Conference of the NAACP in St. Louis, Missouri, adopted the following resolution: "We regret and condemn the suppression of free speech by the Vincent administration in the republic of Haiti, and the imprisonment of critics of the Vincent government, among them such distinguished Haitians as Jacques Roumain, poet and patriot. We urge upon Vincent and the present Haitian government that they reverse their course before it is too late."[107]

Notwithstanding these conflicts, Haitians and African Americans had pulled together to restore the sovereignty of the only black republic in the western hemisphere.

The Rise of Black Consciousness, 1920–1940

I know, in any case, that the most crucial time in my own development
came when I was forced to recognize that I was a kind of bastard of the
West; when I followed the line of my past I did not find myself in Europe
but in Africa. (1949)

James Baldwin, *Notes of a Native Son*

The ongoing Haitian and African American struggle to overcome racism
and oppression gave rise to a bolder movement for cultural nationalism.
Historians John Bracey Jr., August Meier, and Elliott Rudwick explain the
orientation of this new movement: "The cultural nationalism of the
twenties expressed pride in the race's past, celebrated the black man's
unique cultural achievements and contributions, called for specifically
black literature, art, and theater that would reflect the life, interests, and
needs of the Negro people of America, and explored with equal verve and
sensitivity the experience of both the Negro elite and the black masses."[1]
Cultural nationalism led to a new consciousness among people of color to
value their African heritage. Because of this new awareness, African
American writers and artists freed themselves from Western techniques
to discover their own cultural heritage.

Haiti, traditionally considered by African Americans as the torchbearer of freedom, took on the distinction of becoming a new mecca for
black culture. Hannibal Price described the new Haitian consciousness: "I
am from Haiti, the Mecca, the Judea of the black race, the land where one
finds the sacred fields of Vertires, where every man with African blood in
his veins should go in pilgrimage at least once in a lifetime, because it's
there the Negro had made himself a name."[2] Many African American
intellectuals listened and went to the Caribbean nation to explore the
folklife and better understand their own heritage.

Exploring the History and Culture of Haiti

At the beginning of the twentieth century, W. E. B. Du Bois distinguished himself as the main proponent of an ideology that sought the cultural and economic elevation of black people. In 1897, he published a paper, "The Conservations of Races," in which he affirmed that "We believe that the Negro people, as a race, have a contribution to make to civilization and humanity, which no other race can make."[3] African American writers agreed and produced works that put greater value on African culture. They marshaled their energies to revive their own cultures, traditions, and institutions.

A study by Alain Leroy Locke, *The New Negro*, captured the new African American assertiveness. Locke, a critic, educator, and philosopher, published his collection of essays, poems, short fiction, and artwork on contemporary African American life in 1925. He wrote, "The Negro has been more of a formula than a human being—a something to be argued about, condemned or defended, to be 'kept down' or 'in his place'; or helped up." Locke believed the "New Negro" should cast off the burden of stereotypes. His mind "seems suddenly to have slipped from under the tyranny of social intimidation and to be shaking off the psychology of imitation and implied inferiority." What was taking place, Locke suggested, was a form of spiritual emancipation.[4] Locke said the "New Negro" was "interested in the race and its past; he was becoming more conscious of his relationship with other colored peoples and with Africa."[5] Blacks showed a greater interest in discovering African culture of both the United States and the Caribbean islands.

Haiti became a focal point for exploration of the historical past, culture, and folklore of Haitians and African Americans. Black nationalist leader Marcus Aurelius Garvey, who had fought passionately for the elevation of the race, emphasized both the relevance of Haiti's historical past and the paramount importance of Africa itself. He viewed Haiti as a source of pride to people of African descent.

Garvey was born in Jamaica, where he began a crusade for the advancement of the Negro race. As a political activist in Kingston, he participated in the Printers' Union strike. He later set up a newspaper called *The Watchman*. In 1914, Garvey created the Universal Negro Improvement Association (UNIA) as a channel for blacks to create their own institutions and businesses. In 1916, he moved to New York where he established a chapter of the UNIA. Capitalizing on the strain and stress of the black masses living in hostile communities, Garvey was very successful. By 1919, thirty UNIA branches had sprung up across the United States. A man of action, Garvey also launched some ambitious business ventures, notably the Black Star Line (a black-owned steamship company) and took steps to bring to pass his "Back to Africa" campaign for the resettlement of blacks in Africa. Garvey appealed to black pride and promoted African heritage, urging blacks to take on "the toga of race pride and throw off the brand of ignominy which has kept you back so many centuries."[6] He stressed that African Americans should identify with the pharaohs of Egypt, with Toussaint Louverture and Dessalines. Though the white man suppressed the great black leaders in America and elsewhere, Garvey saw Haiti as an exception. Haiti was the land where "one Negro repelled them [whites] and established an independent republic."[7] Inspired by Toussaint Louverture, Garvey envisioned the restoration of Africa and sought to lead blacks back to the motherland. Through Garvey, the nationalist ideology supported a separatist and emigrationist orientation.

Garveyism, as it came to be called, spread from the United States to the West Indies and Haiti. Activist Napoléon Francis established a UNIA branch in Port-au-Prince and circulated a French version of the *Negro World*, the official movement publication. When Francis attended the 1920 UNIA convention, he expressed support for his Haitian comrades: "I represent the division from the land of Toussaint L'Ouverture. We have heard your voice in America and have sent a delegate to bring you greetings and to say to you that when the time shall arrive to blow your bugle and cross the ocean to Africa we shall send you every available officer of the Haitian army."[8]

Haitians held top UNIA administrative positions in the United States. Professor Jean Joseph Adam joined the UNIA in San Francisco and after a year became president of the local division. In 1922, Adam, fluent in French, English, and Spanish, served as secretary and official UNIA interpreter at the League of Nations in Geneva.

Businessman and activist Elie Garcia played a major role in the UNIA as general secretary of the Philadelphia division. He led a 1920 commission visit to Liberia to acquire land for business, agricultural, and industrial programs. He also looked into transferring UNIA headquarters to Liberia in keeping with the back-to-Africa philosophy.

Garveyism was not popular in Haiti, probably due to deeply rooted social and cultural traditions. Haitian intellectuals saw Garvey as a "workman who does not possess . . . that beautiful Latin culture, that civilization of which we are so proud and which distinguishes us from all the other Negroes in the world."[9] These same intellectuals followed such men as James Weldon Johnson and W. E. B. Du Bois. When Garvey tried to declare October 26, 1924, as a day to celebrate the restoration of Haitian independence, the response was lukewarm. Only 200 people attended the celebration.

Garveyism failed to make headway because of the Haitian attitude toward race and color, a feeling of superiority over foreign blacks. High Commissioner John Russell said that "The intellectual and wealthier classes, who are generally mulattoes, do not identify themselves with the Negroes of pure African strain and feel themselves culturally and racially allied much more closely to the Caucasian race, particularly to the French, from whom their culture has been derived."[10] Finally, the social and intellectual elite had openly repudiated their African heritage. Though American occupation forced them into a nationalist mold and even into the deeper depth of indigenousness, they managed to keep aloof from Garveyism.

Even American black intellectuals kept Garvey at arm's length. W. E. B. Du Bois viewed Garvey as a "hard-working idealist" but called his methods "bombastic, wasteful, illogical and ineffective and almost illegal."[11] He regarded Garvey's intolerant attacks on the NAACP and black opponents as repugnant. Garveyism eventually faded when Garvey was jailed in Atlanta on a mail fraud charge.

Garvey used Haiti's history as a motivational force. The writers of the *Harlem Renaissance* went one step further, embracing Haiti's history and its folklore, integrating the two into literary works. Jamaican-born Claude McKay, who later lived in the United States, was a vanguard writer for the *Harlem Renaissance*. His collection of poetry, *Harlem Shadows*, set the tone for the exploration of Haitian culture and began the Harlem Renaissance movement.[12] A West Indian by birth, McKay injected his works with tales of Haiti's heroic past. *Home to Harlem* describes a railroad trip to Pittsburgh, where Ray, a Haitian working and studying in America, takes the opportunity to teach the main character, Jake, about the heroes of Haiti: "For the first time he heard the name

Toussaint L'Ouverture, the black slave and leader of the Haytian slaves. Heard how he fought and conquered the slave-owners and then protected them; decreed laws for Hayti that held more of human wisdom and nobility than the Code Napoleon."[13]

As African Americans pursued their interest in Haitian history, the life of Toussaint Louverture occupied center stage. The January issue of the *Negro History Bulletin* carried various articles featuring "The First of the Blacks." One was a reprint of Wendell Phillips's "Eulogy of Toussaint," portraying him as a man ranked above Napoleon, Cromwell, and Washington.[14]

Arthur Schomburg kept Haitian history alive by writing several articles. He coordinated a display of literary works by African Americans and Haitians at the New York Public Library, including eight original proclamations by Toussaint Louverture. The editor of the *New York Herald Tribune* called the Louverture pieces perhaps the most unusual items of the exhibition because one of these proclamations was as yet unpublished.

In the arts, Jacob Lawrence explored Haitian history. Lawrence, born in Atlantic City, studied under Harlem Renaissance artists and authors Langston Hughes, Alain Locke, and Augusta Savage. Lawrence painted forty-one gouaches documenting the life of Toussaint Louverture. These paintings were exhibited in 1940.[15]

Langston Hughes was the central figure of the Harlem Renaissance. His writings explored Haitian history and its folk culture. Hughes used the arts and literature to combat cultural and social oppression in the United States. His first poem published in *The Crisis,* "The Negro Speaks of River," addressed the fundamental issues of the cultural awakening: a keen interest in the glory of Africa's past and the need to celebrate the best of the black man's unique cultural achievements.

Closer to home, Hughes's great-uncle John Mercer Langston served in Haiti as American minister for a number of years. As a result of his reading of Haitian history—"I had read of Toussaint L'Ouverture, Dessalines, King Christophe, proud black names"[16]—Hughes wanted to make a pilgrimage to Haiti and did so in 1931. He described his journey from Cuba to Port-au-Prince, and to Cap-Haitien "where the slaves, years ago, planned the revolt that shook the foundations of human bondage in the Western world."[17] Hughes searched for "folk life" as he mingled with the common people, going out with fishermen in the morning and enjoying the company of simple country people who knew how to play drums and dance the conga at night.

Hughes visited the Citadel, the massive building erected during Christophe's rule. The Citadel, built to stop the French from threatening Haitian independence, remains one of the wonders of the world. This fortress made a lasting impression on Hughes, and he described it as a splendid monument to the genius of a black king. "The immensity of the citadel, towering on a mountain peak whose slopes would create a problem for modern builders, is beyond belief. A hundred years ago, when motors and machinery were lacking ... the rearing of its walls, was one of the great feats in the history of human energy and determination. The fact that beauty as well as strength went into its making is cause for further wonderment, for the Citadel is majestic, graceful in every proportion, with wide inner staircases and noble doorways of stone, curving battlements, spacious chambers and a maze of intricate cellars, dungeons, terraces and parade grounds."[18]

Haiti proved to be a major resource of black culture for Hughes, who drew from the island material for plays and stories. Cap-Haitien was his inspiration for a drama originally titled *Drums of Haiti*, then revised and renamed *Emperor of Haiti* and finally reworked into the libretto for the opera *Troubled Island*. The play focused on the rise and fall of Dessalines, the "Emperor, First Liberator of the blacks and Chief Ruler of Haiti." It highlighted Haiti's socioeconomic plight and the class and the color struggle. Underlining the mistrust between black and mulatto, the character Congo says that the "mulattoes think they're white for us." Hughes described Dessalines as a mighty soldier with the dream of building a civilization as "good as any the whites have in their lands." Dessalines could not accomplish this because, as Hughes's play claims, Dessalines "is not a statesman."[19] Hughes explored Dessalines' life in terms of Haitian culture, emphasizing the practice of Vodou and the emperor's opposition to the cult.

While in Haiti Hughes also wrote the story *Popo and Fifina*, in collaboration with Arna Bontemps. This work follows the lives of a Haitian girl and boy whose parents left their village because of the harsh economic conditions. The family moved to Cap-Haitien in search of a better life. *Popo and Fifina* was used in American schools and was translated into many foreign languages because it appealed to children, readers, and students of that literature.

Popo and Fifina contrasts the beauty of the Haitian landscape, its lush flowering trees, and delicious fruit with the plight of Popo and the bare-footed peasant farmers who lived in huts. These people were in "no hurry or excitement," in contrast to the grinding hustle and bustle of New York City. Hughes contrasted these poor, hardworking, and productive peasants with the rich people of the cities who lived on government sinecures. Poor Haitian artisans were woodcarvers, but their spirit radiated through their beautiful handmade serving trays, tables, and ornaments. The folk culture shone through their recreational activities. In Hughes' story, Popo tells of going inside under a thatched roof "where many people were dancing, and at one corner three black men were playing on tall drums of different sizes, swaying back and forth, their hands moving at a rapid rate, beating out the vibrant music."[20]

Through *Popo and Fifina*, Hughes and Bontemps documented Haiti's historical significance. The theme of one of the stories was Popo's diligence in learning the "heroic things" of the old days. Popo learned the stories about the slaves of Saint-Domingue, the life of Christophe, and the gigantic and sumptuous buildings built by Christophe.

Zora Neale Hurston, novelist, anthropologist, and folklorist, is a second major Harlem Renaissance writer who wrote about Haiti as a mecca of black culture. Hurston's book *Mules and Men* used as its major theme black folklore in America. She developed a fascination with Vodou when she learned about it in Louisiana. Later, spending two years in Jamaica and Haiti afforded her the opportunity for an in-depth study of Vodou.

Hurston wanted to rescue Vodou from those who thought the religion was sensationalist or primitive. She defined it as "a religion of creation and life. It is the worship of the sun, the water and other natural forces, but the symbolism is no better understood than that of other religions and consequently is taken too literally."[21] She deviated even from Haitian social scientists: "Some of the other men of education in Haiti who have given time to the study of Voodoo esoterics do not see such deep meanings in Voodoo practices. They see only a pagan religion with an African pantheon."[22] She interpreted Vodou as an African religion and discovered ties with African American folk beliefs.

Hurston traveled throughout Haiti to unravel the mysteries of the cult. In the process, she became an active participant in some ceremonies she attended. She identified with the devotees. That is the impression she offered after attending a ceremony at a new *hounfort* (Vodou temple) in Arcahaie. "We were given some delicious hot tea called chanelle before breakfast and it was a most refreshing and surprising thing." Then, she added, "Mambo Etienne tied my red and yellow handkerchief on my head in the proper loose knot at the back of my head. We removed our shoes and went into the hounfort.[23]

Throughout her work, Hurston reveals Haiti's African heritage. She describes a village where a Vodou priest fulfills his role of leader, "the African compound where the male head of the family rules over all of the ramifications of the family and looks after them."[24] Haiti's African background came not out of isolation but by a link of African Americans and people of African descent, she believes.

As interest in Haitian folklore spread in the United States, Haitian writer J. B. Cinéas, in collaboration with American anthropologist George E. Simpson, contributed "Folk Tales of Haitian Heroes." Cinéas was a novelist who depicted country folk's daily struggles with nature, superstitions, and illiteracy. One of these features a story about Henri Christophe. Staging a military review for Franco de Medina, a spy of Louis XVIII, Christophe "demonstrated the discipline and devotion of his soldiers by ordering them to jump from the top of the citadel into the abyss. The first battalion had already docilely executed this maneuver when Franco de Medina, filled with pity, begged Christophe to show mercy and declared he was convinced of the invincible fervor of the Haitian people and its fidelity to the Dessalinian oath of being as free and independent men or of dying."[25]

Haitian poet Jean Brierre wrote a one-act sketch, "Famous Women in Haitian History," for African American readers. Women included are Sanite Belair, wife of the revolutionary Charles Belair, and Marie-Jeanne, a soldier in her own right during the war of Haitian independence. The poet highlighted the contributions each woman made towards the emancipation of Haiti. Sanite shared the ideal with her husband, Charles. She was also a leader of the insurgents. Suzanne Louverture fought at her husband's side against such potentially destructive adversaries as "Anxiety, Discouragement, Cares, and Fatigue." Marie-Jeanne fought for liberty in the ranks of the revolutionaries. These women symbolized an untold number of Haitian women who embraced the cause of freedom.[26]

These examples established Haiti as the preeminent source of black culture in the western hemisphere. Major African American writers and artists helped reveal the richness of Haitian folklore and the greatness of her revolutionary past. As cultural nationalism bloomed, Haiti became a vital force for preserving the African past. African Americans showed more interest in their African heritage as the climate became more conducive to the appreciation of Africa. Ethnic and artistic discoveries in Europe resulted in a reevaluation of African civilization. The German anthropologist Leo Frobenius established in his three-volume *Und Afrika Sprach* the existence of an African civilization. In the United States, the African American artistic revival also became popular through the proliferation of Negro spirituals and jazz.

The Awakening of Black Consciousness in Haiti

While African Americans explored Haitian culture and folklore, Haitian writers were discovering a greater appreciation of their own heritage. This new attitude coincided with a cultural awakening in Haiti that began in the 1920s. While race consciousness constituted the fundamental element of Haitian independence, the artistic focus of black people and racist practices of the occupation forces motivated Haitians to renew "racial pride," "linguistic and cultural authenticity," and the "popular ideology."[27]

Haitian statesman and diplomat Dr. Jean Price-Mars is credited with launching the black-consciousness movement in Haiti. He studied medicine at the University of Haiti and the University of Paris before launching a career in politics, diplomacy, education, and literature. He argued for the relevance of Haitian scholars and journalists such as J. C. Dorsainvil and Arthur Holly, son of emigrationist Bishop J. T. Holly. He also asked Haitians to return to their ancestral heritage to celebrate their own cultural achievements.

Price-Mars suggested this theory in *Ainsi parla l'oncle* (Thus Spoke the Elder), a 1928 book that made an impact on the black-consciousness movement at both national and international levels. Price-Mars thought the book would "uplift in the eyes of the Haitian people the value of its folklore." He criticized Haitians for their inferiority complex about their color and African roots. He compared this feeling with what the French writer M. de Gaulthier called "*bovarysme collectif*,"[28] the tendency for a "society to perceive itself other than it really is." Price-Mars wrote that this misperception had led Haitians to believe that they were "colored French" and bound them to servile imitation of French ideas, literature, and customs. He challenged his countrymen to accept themselves for what they are. That included embracing their culture and African past.[29] He studied Haitian folklore, including its stories, legends, maxims, and religious beliefs. Three chapters were devoted to Africa, its people and civilization, its relations with the outside world, and its religions.

In his search for a new Haitian literature that embraced African and national cultural values, Price-Mars found relevant African American models. He called on contemporary writers to create literature that reflected Haitian life even though written in French. As he asked, "Who has ever prevented the English language from expressing the state of mind of American Negroes as in the works of James Weldon Johnson, Du Bois, Booker T. Washington, Chestnut?"[30] He compared this literature to the Harlem Renaissance writers. In literary-review articles published in *La Relève*, he asserted that Langston Hughes's poem "Our Land" contained a rhythm and possessed "a savor that is difficult to find in our Haitian production handicapped by the taste of French imitation."[31] Price-Mars advised that Haitians express their individuality and draw themes from their environment for truly original work.

Works circulated by African American writers belonging to the Harlem Renaissance helped this pursuit of originality in Haitian literature. One Haitian scholar, René Piquion, translated African American writings into French and introduced Haitian intellectuals to Hughes's works in *Langston Hughes: Un chant nouveau*. He pictured Hughes as a giant in the liberation struggle for African descendants throughout the world. In Piquion's estimation, Hughes was the quintessential black writer who intoned, as Piquion wrote, the "hymn of liberation." He stressed how Hughes managed "with the highest consciousness, talent, and courage, to express the yet inarticulate interests, aspirations, and feelings of a great mistreated race."[32] Hughes's works were a catalyst for Haiti's literary revival. Historian and critic Roger Gaillard praised Hughes as a poet with a racial, social, and revolutionary tone aimed at protecting the identity and authenticity that characterizes Afro-American literature. The new generation of Haitian writers refused to imitate European cultural patterns. Jacques Roumain, the leading poet and novelist of Haitian writers of that period, celebrated Africa and its civiliza-tion.[33]

This return to Africa and its civilization had an effect on literary and artistic works of the black francophone world. It took the name "negri-tude," coined by Aimé Césaire of Martinique and Léopold Sédar Senghor of Senegal while both were studying in France in 1945. Although it is difficult to specifically define negritude, René Piquion describes its fun-damental features as "racial awareness, evocation of passed black valor, rejection of assimilation, development of African personality, hatred of colonialism, resistance to neo-colonialism, the blossoming of the new African, aspiration to the lost greatness."[34] Understood in those terms, the movement found its very roots in Haiti with the work of Price-Mars, whose *Ainsi parla l'oncle* influenced not just Haitians but writers and artists throughout the world.[35]

Social Consciousness

As African American writers explored Haiti's folklife firsthand, they also discovered Haiti's socioeconomic problems. In the nineteenth century, Booker T. Washington, T. Thomas Fortune, and Arthur Schomburg com-plained of Haiti's lack of economic and technical progress. The Great De-pression of the 1930s in the United States even worsened the Haitian economy. Bellegarde, Haitian minister in Washington during that period, underscored that the Vincent administration faced the most terrible fi-nancial and economic crisis Haiti had ever known because "the prices of the exportation products have considerably plummeted, which led to an extremely strong decrease of the treasury receipts." Compounding the problem, Cuba dismissed some Haitians who were working in its sugar industry. They returned to their homeland and joined Haiti's unem-ployed.[36]

Haiti's depressed economy did not go unnoticed by the African Amer-ican intellectuals who were on a pilgrimage. Their reaction was in keeping with the level of social consciousness exhibited by black intellectuals of the 1930s. Their new awareness coincided with the emergence of Com-munism in Russia in 1917. The Bolsheviks' success at ending czarist rule began with a revolution that affected the world. Communism's em-phasis on an even distribution of wealth to all the world's people had an impact on black writers and artists fighting their own oppression. Those who traveled to Haiti paid particular attention to the tenets of Communism and its implications that could improve Haiti's socioeconomic predicament.

That concern was described in Hurston's *Tell My Horse*, though her work was primarily anthropological. Probing the causes of Haiti's underdevelopment, she illustrated Haiti's social problems of the traditional divides of class and color: "Haiti has always been two places. First it was the Haiti of the masters and slaves. Now it is Haiti of the wealthy and educated mulattoes and the Haiti of the blacks. Haiti of the Champ de Mars and Haiti of the Bolosse. Turgeau against the Salines."[37] This stark contrast between class and color characterizes practically every period in Port-au-Prince.

Hurston portrayed the selfish maneuvering of irresponsible politicians who believed that "a national election is a mandate from the people to build themselves a big new house in Pétion-Ville and Kenscoff and a trip to Paris."[38] In her view, these politicians became mired in a "fog of self-deception" while they spoke about Haiti's past glory. Hurston wrote that African American orators were eager to "mount any platform at short notice and rattle the bones of Crispus Attucks; tell what great folks the thirteenth and fourteenth amendments to the constitution had made out of us."[39] African Americans, however, grew impatient with political rhetoric. Instead, they called for jobs and houses and food for their people. Unfortunately, the Haitian poor could not do the same since they never knew about a life of prosperity.

Langston Hughes portrayed the social issues of the period. He was concerned with the struggle of the disenfranchised in the United States. The African American economic situation got worse during the Great Depression. Black workers were probably the first to fall on hard times, as businesses, banks, and mines shut down.[40] Most African American workers lost their jobs and sought relief through a nonexistent public-assistance policy. This situation made a lasting impression on Hughes. As he wrote, it was "impossible for me to travel from hungry Harlem to the lovely homes on Park Avenue without feeling in my soul the great gulf between the very poor and the very rich in our society."[41] He became a radical socialist and, because of his political beliefs, was denounced by the House of Representatives Special Committee on Un-American Activities and labeled a dangerous radical.

Hughes's social interests extended beyond the borders of the United States. On a 1931 trip to Haiti, Hughes expressed his distaste for Haiti's rigid class distinction, which was the basis for the alienation of the masses from the upper class. He shunned the Haitian elite. "It was in Haiti that I first realized how class lines may cut across color lines within a race, and how dark people of the same nationality may scorn those below them. Certainly the upper class Haitians I observed at a distance seemed a delightful and cultured group. No doubt, many of the French slave owners were delightful and cultured, too—but the slaves could not enjoy their culture,"[42] he wrote. He viewed the upper class as composed of irresponsible citizens who contributed nothing and drained any progress out of the country. He said their time was spent "living for years on under-paid peasant labor and lazy government jobs . . . writing flowery poetry in the manner of the French academicians . . . , creating bloody civil wars and wasteful political party revolutions, and making lovely speeches on holidays . . . Borrowing government money abroad to spend on themselves." Hughes identified himself with the lower class. He called them "people without shoes,"[43] noting that all of the work that "keeps Haiti alive, pays for the American occupation, and enriches foreign traders . . . is done there by Negroes without shoes." For Hughes, there was a parallel between the reality of class and color distinction in both Haiti and the United States. "I was reminded strongly of my years in Washington where Negro society, too, was stratified—the government workers, college professors and schoolteachers considering themselves much better than the usually darker (although not always poorer) people who work with their hands."[44]

Race and class were factors in the social distance that existed between the Haitian elite and African Americans. Du Bois writes, "There was a time when the Haitian Minister to the United States avoided Negroes like a pest. He had no social connection with them in Washington and the Haitian government several times expressed its desire to have a white man in Haiti as United States Minister."[45] Du Bois also acknowledged that Bellegarde changed that situation when, as Haitian minister, he opened the doors of the legation to American Negroes.

While in Haiti, Hughes met Jacques Roumain, a Haitian writer and a member of the Haitian elite despised by Hughes. Despite their political differences, the two formed a lasting friendship. Their works shared "essential themes, images, and language techniques whose comparable patterns infer a neo-African literature that crosses national and linguistic frontiers."[46] The two used literature as a tool for economic, political, and social change, a practice used throughout the Afro-American world. Writers clarified and tried to solve social, political, and economic problems through their art. The critic Lilyan Kesteloot described the central themes of the works of Hughes and Roumain: "analysis of ancient and multiform sufferings that the race endures as an implacable destiny, the titanic revolt that it prepares against its executioners, the vision of a future and ideal world from which would be banned racism and the exploitation of man by man."[47]

Roumain also dedicated his life and work to social issues and the defense of Haitian sovereignty. When Roumain returned to Haiti from Europe in the 1920s, he campaigned against the American occupation primarily to mobilize Haitians. To try to improve the social and economic conditions, Roumain, grandson of former President Tancrède Auguste, denounced his bourgeois roots and declared himself a Communist.

In 1934, Roumain founded the Communist Party of Haiti, promoting his commitment to a unified society. Since affiliation with the Communist movement was illegal in Haiti, Roumain was brought up on sedition charges and sentenced to a three-year jail term. Hughes tried to secure Roumain's release with his famous "Appeal for Jacques Roumain," sent to editors in the United States and beyond. In those appeals, he discussed Roumain's commitment to social and economic reforms in Haiti. Hughes argued, "He is one of the very few upper-class Haitians who understands and sympathizes with the plight of the oppressed peasants of his island home and who has attempted to write about and to remedy the pitiful conditions of 90 percent of the Haitian people exploited by the big coffee monopolies and by the manipulations of foreign finance in the hands of the National City Bank of New York."[48]

Roumain's ideology of proletarian consciousness was described in his novels. In *Masters of the Dew*, Roumain focused on the daily life of oppressed country folk. With the skills of an ethnologist, he depicted the poverty, superstitions, and struggle for survival. Manuel, the leading character of the novel, "watched the peasants as he drank, seeing in the wrinkles of their faces the deep marks of poverty. There they were around him barefoot, and through the holes of their patched garments, he saw their dry earthy skin. All of them carried machetes at their left sides, from habit no doubt, for what work was left now for them?"[49]

Literary critic Martha Cobb said Roumain conveyed the importance of liberation through the eyes of Manuel. He takes measures to "free his people from superstition, from outworn customs, from exploitation and from dependency on the vagaries of nature and the deities."[50] In his books Roumain wrote about his dream of the liberation of the entire human race from the evils of racism and exploitation. He spoke for all the outcasts of the world. In the poem "Dirty Niggers," he prophesied a day of liberation for "all the damned of the earth."

As Haitian writers focused on national cultural life, they developed a greater affinity for their African American brothers. In 1945, Mercer Cook wrote about the similarities in the works and interests of Haitian writers including Jean Price-Mars, Jacques Roumain, Jean F. Brierre, and René Piquion. These observations convinced him that "The American Negro is now being described as a brother."[51] Cook attributed this fraternal feeling toward African Americans to the sense of kinship Haitians shared with other oppressed and exploited peoples. Haitian poet Jean Brierre, while attending Columbia University, explored this sense of solidarity in a poem to Paul Robeson called "Here in Harlem."

Black brother, here I am no less poor than you,
No less sad or more great, I am part of the crowd
The anonymous passer-by who fattens the convoy,
The fraternal black drop within your sea swell.

See, your hands are no less black than our hands,
And your footsteps across centuries of misery
Strike the same death knell on the same path:
Our shadows are entwined on Calvaries' steps.

For we have already fought side by side.
When I stumbled, you took my arms,
And with your whole great body labor sculpted,
you blocked my fall and smiled through tears.[52]

In the 1930s, involvement in social issues was not limited to literature. African Americans were outraged over the 1937 massacre of Haitians in the Dominican Republic. In that massacre the armies of Rafael Leonidas Trujillo y Molina slaughtered an estimated 15,000 Haitians who were agricultural-production workers in the Dominican Republic. The National Negro Congress held a fact-finding conference and asked President

Roosevelt to send an official delegation "from America to Haiti and to the Dominican Republic. This delegation would be charged with the responsibility of obtaining the complete facts relative to the reported troubles, and of making suggestions for removing the fundamental causes of such troubles."[53] Similarly, the NAACP asked the government to send a distinguished American, such as diplomat James Weldon Johnson, to Haiti and Santo Domingo to report on the situation. The State Department refused to send a special American delegate. Since an international conciliation commission was to deal with the crisis, Under-Secretary of State Sumner Welles argued that "The United States Government has no connection with this commission and is without authority or intention at this time to constitute any other American delegation with respect to the Haitian-Dominican controversy."[54]

Intercultural Exchanges

Burning social and economic issues in the United States led to political changes in Haiti. After an eleven-year rule, Sténio Vincent was ousted as president and replaced by Elie Lescot, former ambassador to Washington. Lescot ruled during the years of World War II (1941–45). He aligned himself with the United States and declared war on Germany. With unusual rhetoric, Lescot argued his "unequivocal decision to bear the ordeal of bombs and to see if necessary our country burn like a torch rather than yield under the hell of Nazism and Fascism." [55]

Under Lescot, intercultural exchanges began to take place between African Americans and Haitians. Dr. L. D. Reddick, who visited Haiti from the start of Lescot's regime, maintained that the president had a "cordial feeling for American Negroes and welcomes closer ties between Haitians and colored Americans."[56] Lescot favored inviting African American businessmen to cultivate enterprises in Haiti.

In addition to businessmen, prominent African American intellectuals promoted better cooperation and understanding while on cultural missions in Haiti. As chairman of the Atlanta University Department of Modern Languages, Mercer Cook spread the English language to Haiti, in a project sponsored by both the Haitian and American governments. Cook wrote an English handbook for Haitian teachers. As literary critic, Cook published several articles about Haitian literature that emphasized the cultural links between Haitian and African American writers. He also translated into English Jacques Roumain's masterpiece *Masters of the Dew*.

W. E. B. Du Bois traveled to Haiti again, providing the endorsement of the U.S. NAACP. Though he did not stay as long as either Hurston or Hughes, he focused on their themes of culture and social consciousness. In 1942, Du Bois had said he wanted to hold the Fifth Pan-African Congress in Haiti, after World War II, but his plan never materialized. In 1944, Du Bois was a guest of the Haitian government for the Philosophical Congress in Port-au-Prince. The trip was his opportunity to increase "the cultural unity of the Caribbean area and the Negroes of the U.S., as well as white friends."[57]

Du Bois liked the Haitian landscape, describing it as "that amazing island, whose beauty surpasses anything I have ever seen." Haiti represented a place of great historical significance, "the most dramatic and colorful center of human history in the Western hemisphere."[58]

During Du Bois's stay, he met with Bellegarde, Price-Mars, President Elie Lescot, and Lescot's cabinet. He presented his paper "La conception de l'éducation" at the Philosophical Congress. He was deeply moved that young Haitian intellectuals supported his views on the question of colonization and on postwar conditions. Du Bois addressed the issue of colonization in his lecture at the conference. Against the view that the black nations of Haiti, Liberia, and Ethiopia were not an integral part of the community of nations and could therefore be left out of the ongoing process of social, economic, and political development, Du Bois sharply reacted, "As for us . . . we are persuaded of our equality with humanity and our ability to be a part of the modern culture."[59]

Du Bois was greatly concerned for the Haitian poor: "The principal matters which Haitians [have] got to face and act upon are education, land, and the peasantry, work and wage, industry and housing."[60] Although Du Bois recognized that the peasants maintained "a folklore and culture pattern, which leads directly back to Africa and has survived with beauty," he felt they had more pressing needs. He maintained that it was "extremely necessary through industrialization, reforestation and scientific agriculture to enable this peasantry to earn a decent living."[61]

During that same period, Alain Leroy Locke, a Howard University philosophy professor, visited Haiti as an exchange professor with the American Committee for Inter-American Artistic and Intellectual Relations sponsored by the Haitian Ministry of Education. Locke was an articulate interpreter and defender of black culture, including Haitian culture. Locke delivered six lectures that were published in French as *Le rôle du nègre dans la culture des Amériques* (The Role of Blacks in American Culture). In the opening lecture, he greeted the Haitian people "with the most fervent and sincere wishes of happiness and prosperity from an admirer, a fellow Black, and friend." He defined his mission as one of cultural rapprochement between the two peoples.

During these lectures, he cited numerous examples that demonstrated how Haitians, African Americans, and other African Caribbean nationalities enriched the cultural heritage of the western hemisphere. These contributions gained recognition because they were rooted in the culture of their own people or stemmed from national inspiration. Such artistic products transcended national boundaries. Haitian writers Philippe and Pierre Thoby-Marcelin, who won the Pan-American Prize for their *Canapé-vert*, focused on the struggle of the Haitian peasants. A condensed version was published in the June 1944 issue of *Negro Digest*. Locke explained that, in their works,

> We have a concrete illustration of what I am discussing here, that risen to the level of an universal expression and art, what appeared as local and national, can acquire an international significance, and a positive influence, and can substantially become representative of a race. We thus notice instantly the impact of this prize, and its significance from a human and international standpoint because of the subject selected by these young writers who, instead of escaping to an ivory tower of pale cosmopolitanism, have deeply dug the fertile ground of their native soil.[62]

Locke described the particular achievements and contributions that African Americans have given to American society in the arts and humanities, science, education, and politics. He maintained that their "intellectual contributions were able to affect poetry, art, and music, [and] their political contributions, perhaps more important, have quite widely influenced the mood of the country, its way of life and sensibility, its songs, dances, and popular stories."[63]

To attain a true cultural democracy, Locke called for equality and fraternity beyond geographical boundaries and beyond the barriers of race and nationality. At the close of the lectures, President Lescot honored

Locke with inclusion in the National Order of Honor and Merit, with the rank of commander.

Haitian intellectuals were involved in black institutions, cultural activities, and communities in the United States. Bellegarde served as an exchange professor at Atlanta University during the summers of 1937 and 1940. His students described him as the professor "who revived for them Toussaint Louverture, Dessalines, Pétion, Christophe; who depicted with vivid colors the exotic grace of Haiti."[64]

Once again, the shared interest in Africa, its history, and cultural heritage coalesced with Haitian and African American artists during the 1920s and 1930s in producing some creative works reflecting their cultural nationalism and in promoting some unprecedented cooperation between the leaders of the two peoples.

Promoting Human Rights
and Economic Development, 1940–1956

> We want to see more people know and love Haiti as we do. We want en-
> lightened and unselfish investment capital to flow to Haiti. We want to
> see the economic, educational, health and the cultural status of the most
> impoverished Haitian raised to a more affluent and permanent level.
> (June 9, 1950)
>
> Walter White, *Papers of the NAACP*

Following the American withdrawal in 1934, Haitians found the energies
they had spent battling imperialist occupation were now available for
human-rights and economic-development concerns. During this time,
African Americans continued to explore Haitian culture, reaffirming that
Haiti held a special place in the western hemisphere. They maintained
that events in Haiti would somehow redound to black America's benefit.
NAACP head Walter White symbolized continuity of attitude among
African Americans. He described the perception in this way: "Haiti is a
symbol of what Negroes can do in self-government. Thus what happens
in Haiti has repercussions which far transcend Haiti itself."[1] Blacks everywhere considered this statement poignant, especially those in Africa
who still struggled against colonialism and in the United States, where
African Americans faced segregation and the denial of their civil and political rights.

White was determined to promote the development of Haiti. "We
want enlightened and unselfish investment capital to flow to Haiti. We
want to see the economic, educational, health and the cultural status of
the most impoverished Haitian raised to a more affluent and permanent
level."[2] This appeal became the outline for close collaboration between
the NAACP and two Haitian administrations during the forties and fif-
ties.

The NAACP and the Estimé Administration

In August 1946, Dumarsais Estimé became leader of Haiti when the General Constituent Assembly replaced the three-man military junta that had ruled since the overthrow of President Lescot in 1946. The assembly elected Estimé who, backed by the military, obtained a majority of the ballots among the eight candidates.

Estimé was born in Verettes in the peasantry. He studied in Port-au-Prince at the Lycée Pétion before becoming president of the Haitian legislature and then minister of education in the Vincent administration. He was considered a black moderate and came to power in the aftermath of what is known as the Revolution of 1946.

The Revolution of 1946 was but another episode in Haiti's long-standing class and color struggle. Lescot perpetuated the racist policy of the American occupation by solidifying the dominance of the mulatto bourgeoisie. During his presidency, he "not only pursued the U.S. practice of systematically placing light-skinned individuals in the top echelons of the public service, but he also extended color favoritism to all levels of the administration without the slightest bow to the rule of perceived competence."[3] In that way, mulattoes added political clout to their perennial economic control.

The middle class, aspiring for some political power as well, opposed Lescot's policies and launched a revolution by reversing the status quo. The president also lost the support of the United States and strongman R. L. Trujillo of the Dominican Republic. Students rioted, causing a general strike that paralyzed communications, transportation, and industry for a week. The strike accomplished the resignation of Lescot, who left the country for Montreal to practice law.

African Americans were also aware of this new round of uprisings in Haiti. Rayford Logan, a scholar on Haiti for the *Pittsburgh Courier*, saw three fundamental causes for this new uprising: "the inherent interest of some of the elite to have a democratic government, the revolt of the masses against a tight economic situation and the insistence of students that civil liberties shall exist in reality." But he also emphasized that African Americans "should not look upon it as a manifestation of the inability of a Negro people to govern themselves."[4] Logan concluded that such revolutions were commonplace in Latin American republics.

Raymond Pace Alexander traveled to Haiti and wrote a five-part special report on the revolution for the *Pittsburgh Courier*. He explored the events connected with the dictatorial practices and corruption of the Lescot regime. He placed special emphasis on the class and color issue. In his view, the revolution stemmed from the racist policies of the American occupation, which not only created a "color caste" in Haiti but also drained Haitians of the desire to "know and understand American Negroes." They have come to believe that the "American Negro is perhaps the world's most uncommon man. They have this new regard and recently acquired belief in the American Negro as a result of what they have been able to learn about him in the last ten years. They want to know more about him and he should attempt to learn more about them. American Negro progress, the progress of this great black republic, the progress of the Negroes throughout the world and respect for the Negro in world affairs go hand in hand. The American Negro must not fail to grasp the significance for this new political and social movement in this island."[5]

Alexander was correct that the American occupation had an effect on the color issue in Haiti. He also realized that the majority of African Americans of his time had hardly heard of Haiti. He wrote that many of his friends "among the educated class actually confess ignorance as to the location of the island of Haiti."[6] His report aimed to eliminate this ignorance.

The revolution triggered drastic social and political changes by bringing darker-skinned black politicians to power. Estimé committed himself to defending the cause of the masses when he became president: "We shall work for the financial liberation of the country—the education of the masses—the rational organization of agriculture, the progressive and systematic organization of cooperatives to work for the benefit of the producer and not the middleman. We shall increase the salary of the artisan and the worker."[7]

Estimé's ascension to power provided an opportunity for new cooperation between Haitian and African American leaders, with the NAACP resurrecting its role as Haiti's publicity agent. With the end of the occupation, the association promoted goodwill to help Haiti's progress. Walter White, the association secretary, cooperated fully with Estimé to this end.

White wanted to create a positive image of the sole black nation of the western hemisphere. He deplored the common depiction of Haiti in the United States "as a poverty-stricken, illiterate, hopelessly backward country whose people are little removed from the jungle and practically all of whom practice voodoo."[8] He felt the wide circulation of William Seabrook's *Magic Island* and Kenneth Robert's *Lydia Bailey* contributed to this opinion. To correct this, White suggested that the Estimé administration begin a vigorous public relations campaign beginning with the naming of a public relations officer in the United States. The office would be modeled after those of Russia, Great Britain, France, and other European nations.

White suggested the Haitian government ask distinguished American writers, educators, financiers, and agricultural scientists to visit Haiti at their own expense. He believed "an educational conference to analyze, improve and unify educational systems for the Americas in the democratic processes could be so sensational and successful that it would attract educators from all of the Americas to talk about building civilization instead of making war and erecting tariff and other barriers between nations."[9] Such great names as Mordecai Johnson, John Dewey, and Ralph Bunche and foundations like the Rockefeller Foundation, the National Educational Association, and the American Teachers Association would be persuaded to attend such a conference, he reasoned.

White suggested a 1954 celebration in grand fashion of the 150th anniversary of Dessalines' proclamation of Haiti as a free and independent nation. That celebration might have started as early as 1953 with the commemoration of the victory of the indigenous troops over Rochambeau. White suggested, "It would be possible for us to induce whoever is president of the United States at that time to go to Haiti for that celebration. Undoubtedly the heads of other governments over the entire world, or at least of the Western Hemisphere, would be present or would send diplomatic representatives."[10] Estimé endorsed the plan. Ambassador Joseph D. Charles acknowledged that "The Government approves the idea of organizing as you proposed, a Public Relations service in the United States and that I am authorized to discuss plans immediately."[11] The Haitian Bureau was created and operated out of New York.

White strongly supported Haiti's efforts to secure a $30 million loan from the Export-Import Bank to pay off the balance of outstanding private loans and to fund necessary projects to develop Haiti's natural resources. Estimé sent a diplomatic mission to the United States to conduct the appropriate negotiations. When the State Department failed to approve the request, the characteristically aggressive White went on the offensive. He reminded President Truman that "The United States has made loans running into billions of dollars to other countries. . . . Some of these loans have been to countries which clearly indicated that they had neither the ability nor the intention to repay such loans."[12] After invoking Haiti's good credit record in repaying past loans, he attributed the rejection to racism: "What was done is still held up as an example of 'Yanqui imperialism' and racial bigotry."[13] He asked Truman to approve the loan because U.S. assistance, if given to Haiti, would help Haiti solve its economic problems and pay rich dividends to the United States in goodwill throughout Latin America.

Haitians loudly applauded White's firm stance. Ambassador Charles wrote, "It is for us a strong comfort to feel the closeness of our American friends in supporting our efforts among whom you stood in the first rank."[14] The Haitian senate agreed, thanking White: "On the occasion of your brilliant and courageous intervention in favor of the Haitian nation, a victim in spite of international pacts and agreements of the most odious politics of racial discrimination and imperialism of the most ferocious kind, the Senate of the Republic of Haiti extends to you its warmest felicitations and liveliest thanks."[15] Estimé awarded White the Haitian Order of Honor and Merit.

The seeking of this loan illustrated another instance of cooperation between Haitian and African American leaders. As a result of playing the race card, the Export-Import Bank granted Haiti a $4 million loan to finance construction of flood control, irrigation, and drainage works in the Artibonite Valley and agricultural development of the area to be irrigated. White could certainly take credit for the success of these negotiations.

White committed himself to promoting humanitarian work in Haiti. Prior to White, other African Americans had shown similar humanitarian interest. During the American occupation, West Virginia banker Charles E. Mitchell sponsored an effort to ship goods to Haiti. Harriet Gibbs Marshall, the wife of Captain Marshall, a member of the New York colored regiments, coordinated charitable activities. She was involved with some progressive young Haitian women to furnish clothing for poor children and to educate these children.[16]

White enrolled Mary McLeod Bethune and her National Council of Negro Women to support Mrs. Lucienne Estimé, the president's wife, in her works with the orphans of Haiti. He viewed Mrs. Estimé, head of Abri des Orphelins, as a woman of simplicity and modesty. White was instrumental in persuading Dr. William L. Mellon of Pittsburgh, Pennsylvania, to establish the Albert Schweitzer Hospital in the Artibonite Valley in 1953.

Under Estimé, White participated in the bicentennial celebration of the founding of Port-au-Prince. The government began some grandiose projects, constructing new hotels, guest cottages, and elaborate buildings on the seafront at Port-au-Prince, and building new roads and highways. The Haitian Information Bureau helped bring a large number of tourists to Haiti. White visited Haiti in 1949 when he talked with President Estimé about plans for the bicentennial exposition. White pledged to generate a large amount of publicity for the exposition. He tried to get President Truman and Eleanor Roosevelt to attend the opening ceremonies. Though they did not attend, the U.S. Senate and House of Representatives did establish a commission known as the "United States International Exposition for the Bicentennial of the Founding of Port-au-Prince." This Commission would represent the United States in the world's fair and the celebrations connected with the bicentennial.

At the bicentennial celebration, Marian Anderson performed a concert in Port-au-Prince as guest of President Estimé. Historian René Piquion and poet Jean Brierre wrote a thirteen-page booklet introducing Marian Anderson to the Haitian people. Brierre compared Miss Anderson to the Haitian *oiseau musicien* (musician bird) that sings day and night in the landscape of Forêt des Pins. Whatever the season, the bird bravely endures the elements, storms, and human threats to keep singing. The poet showered the famous singer with praise:

O Black Virgin, on the altar of our love
We enthroned you this evening and for ever
To You, our Pain, our Art and our Grace
To You our Soul, our Glory and our Race.

The authors hailed Marian Anderson's triumph as a victory for all Haitian people. Anderson was featured as "a form of beauty more than human, the symbol of the black race in its aspiration to impose itself through its talent or competence."[17]

Under Walter White's leadership, the NAACP promoted greater collaboration between Haitian and African American leaders, resulting in further economic development of Haiti. The cooperation between these leaders advanced freedom and the betterment of the socioeconomic status of blacks in the world.

The Struggle for Human Rights

In the second half of the twentieth century, the crusade for human rights gained new fervor. The United Nations initiated the effort in 1948 by proclaiming the International Covenant on Civil and Political Rights. The states that were party to the covenant recognized the inherent dignity of each human and their right to enjoy civil and political freedom. They agreed in Article 1 that "All peoples have the right of self-determination. By virtue of that right they freely determine their political status and freely pursue their economic, social and cultural development."[18]

African American leaders and civil-rights organizations demonstrated particular interest in the human-rights issue in Haiti. Haiti was a democratic nation with the motto of "Liberty, equality, and fraternity," but the sense of these words had been lost in the maze of dictatorship and the human- and political-rights violations traditionally practiced by Haiti's system of government. Despite Haiti's lofty creed, it was soon business as usual with the overthrow of President Estimé in another coup d'état. The leader of this new coup was Paul Eugène Magloire, a powerful figure in Haiti's political arena.

Magloire was born to a military family in northern Haiti. His father, Eugène, was a general. After studying at the Lycée national Philippe Guerrier in Cap-Haitien, Magloire studied at the military academy, an end product of the American occupation. In 1946, Magloire became a member of a three-man junta, along with General Franck Laveaux and Colonel Antoine Levelt. Though Magloire and his fellow military officers played a major role in propelling Estimé to the presidency, they were also instrumental in undermining his power in 1950.

Like most Haitian chiefs of state, Estimé sought reelection at the end of his four-year term. In April 1950, he spearheaded a campaign to revise the constitution so that he could stay in office. After approval in the lower house of Parliament, the measure stalled in the Senate. To show their displeasure, a mob supporting the president invaded the senate building and manhandled fleeing senators. The army intervened and played the trump card on behalf of Magloire. The same military junta of three officers who had presided over Estimé's victory in 1946 now took over, with Magloire as the strongman.

Undoubtedly, Magloire was the rising star in Haitian politics. He gained support from the elite, the army, the Church, and the United States, and ultimately became the president later in the year through an army-controlled election. Magloire's administration included those who were described in the African American press as the "Rulers of the world's proudest Negroes."[19] Playing the class and color card Haitian style, Magloire's administration included both blacks and mulattoes.

African Americans watched these developments. Walter White, still executive secretary of the NAACP, explained in a letter to Magloire, "Because of my long term interest in Haiti and the numerous articles I have written in the United States . . . regarding what I call my second country, I have been deluged by newspapers and individuals for information regarding recent developments in Haiti. The same has been true of the National Association For The Advancement of Colored People, because it has . . . been interested in Haiti as far back as the early 20's when it led the fight against military occupation and financial control of Haiti by the United States."[20]

In response to White's request for an explanation of events in Haiti, Magloire cunningly drafted what he called "Comments on the circumstances surrounding the fall of the Government of President Estimé." He had two major goals in mind: First, he wanted to keep the NAACP in his corner as an effective publicity agent. It was one that had been reaching and influencing the American public on behalf of Haiti since 1920. That was Magloire's implication in his statement to the NAACP secretary that "You will always do everything in your power to help to make Haiti known under her real name." Second, Magloire wanted to justify Estimé's overthrow. As Magloire explained, the army had no choice but to intervene because Estimé had lost control. In Estimé's reelection attempt, opposition from the very senate he vowed to dissolve hindered him. In the heat of this struggle, Magloire wrote, "The President conceded that he was no longer master of the situation and that he was placing the country in the safety of the Army. Faced with the gravity of the situation the Army resolutely accepted its responsibilities."[21] In White's view, Magloire's document was actually ambiguous and lent itself to various interpretations.

Magloire's ascent to power was a continuing threat to democracy and human rights in Haiti for the next six years. Within months after he became president, Magloire tried to squelch all his detractors. He dissolved the Peasant Workers Movement (MOP) and Popular Socialist Party (PSP) on December 30, 1950, by a communiqué from the Council of Secretaries of State. In the order, he tried to prevent any meeting of their members with the idea of propagating ideas that would create a disturbance in Haitian life and tend to destroy American unity.[22] This decree severely restricted the freedom of Daniel Fignolé, who was very popular with the masses. Fignolé's popularity stemmed from his charisma as a demagogue who used his witty, exciting Creole speeches to incite the working class of Port-au-Prince. As the head of the MOP, his political party, and as a union leader, he was able to establish himself as a defender of the masses. Emile St. Lôt, the minister of justice, prohibited Fignolé from printing and circulating MOP's newspaper.

Other human-rights organizations with less threatening agendas were allowed to survive. Working under the umbrella of the Ligue Féminine d'Action Sociale, Haitian women rallied for the right to vote. Women's rights leader Madeleine S. Bouchereau wrote, "Our campaign has been progressing very well in the last month. We have now in Port-au-Prince more than 10 committees in all the districts with women of all classes working together to obtain equal rights under the constitution."[23]

The Ligue Haitienne des Droits de l'Homme (Haitian League for Human Rights) was not as fortunate. Roger Baldwin, the U.S. chairman, complained that the organization "has been unable to operate because of government oppression. Even its offices are closed."[24] Baldwin asked for an investigation into this and other problems including the shutting down of the newspapers La Nation and Le Réveil, the dissolution of political parties opposed to the administration, and the restricted nature of amnesty for political prisoners. It was evident to Baldwin that Magloire was engaged in stifling the fundamental democratic quest for human and political rights.

Evidently, Haitian officials tried to justify Magloire's actions. From Port-au-Prince, the president's secretary, Luc Fouché, in a description of the League for the Rights of Man leaders, charged that these "troublemakers, whose subversive activities have been suppressed, have skillfully decked themselves out in sheep's clothing to make an appearance before the League for the Rights of Man to voice their complaints. In this way they transform a domestic problem into an international issue."[25]

The task of defending Magloire's actions proved to be much more difficult in New York for Ernest Chauvet, the Haitian representative to the United Nations. Chauvet had been a friend of White for twenty-five years. White described him as "a charming and delightful person. But I am a little puzzled by his patent attempt to cover up Magloire."[26] White condemned the oppressive practices of the Magloire regime. Confronted with this criticism, Chauvet answered that "only a few political opponents who have lost the Government jobs they had during Estimé's regime"[27] were attacking the administration.

White did have two effective weapons at his disposal. Haitians relied on the NAACP to promote a positive image of Haiti. White knew this when he threatened to launch some form of propaganda campaign exposing Magloire's repression. He reasoned that "It would be tragic right now for a number of reasons for Haiti and Liberia to be guilty of the kind of fascist repression of liberty which we denounce when they are perpetrated by Malan and Talmadge. The one thing that may deter them is threat of exposure."[28] Chauvet, who was also a journalist, could sense the disaster that could result. He promptly asked White, "Please . . . don't start any press campaign or public action. It would be more desirable to approach privately and confidentially those who can come in contact with the Haitian authorities after the investigation and inquiries made by the judge are over."[29]

The second weapon, just as powerful as the first, used White's influence as a power broker for Haiti in private and governmental circles. White played this card by warning Chauvet, "I have refrained . . . from intervention in the form of advice or recommendations to certain individuals with respect to considerable financial and other aid to Haiti."[30] Dodging the threat, Chauvet asked for patience: "Dear Walter, I know how deeply you love, and to what extent you have helped my country. I do not see how local incidents and rumors could make you change your attitude, as far as not advising or recommending certain individuals, with respect to considerable financial and other aids to Haiti."[31] White never carried out his threats since his relationship with Magloire gradually improved.

While Haitians were struggling for their human rights, African

Americans were in the midst of their own crusade for civil rights. Even though the Civil War brought about freedom for African Americans, segregationist policies had kept them from enjoying full equality since they were still treated as second-class citizens under "separate but equal" practices.

During the first half of the twentieth century, the NAACP established a Legal Defense and Education Fund to fight segregation in education. Thurgood Marshall, before he became the first African American to sit on the United States Supreme Court, won many cases against segregation in higher education. In 1954, through the case *Brown v. Board of Education*, Marshall succeeded in having segregation outlawed in public schools.

The first breakthrough in eliminating segregation on buses came about on December 5, 1955, when Mrs. Rosa Parks was arrested for refusing to surrender her bus seat to a white man. Since Dr. Martin Luther King Jr. led the cause for Rosa Parks, the case propelled him to national prominence. After a year-long bus boycott organized by King's Montgomery Improvement Association, the United States finally affirmed "a decision of a special three judge U.S. District Court in declaring Alabama's state and local laws requiring segregation on buses unconstitutional" in December 1956.[32]

King and his lieutenants forged ahead in the struggle to eradicate the evil of segregation. This crusade took him to Atlanta, where he founded the Southern Christian Leadership Conference, dedicated to bringing about social change through nonviolent resistance. Dr. King believed in integration through nonviolence. He described it best himself: "Through nonviolent resistance the Negro will be able to rise to the noble height of opposing the unjust system while loving the perpetrators of the system. The Negro must work passionately and unrelentingly for full stature as a citizen, but he must not use inferior methods to gain it."[33]

The movement spread throughout the country and took on various forms. In Greensboro, North Carolina, black students used sit-ins to request service at "Whites only" lunch counters. In Birmingham, Alabama, African Americans marched for fair employment opportunities and for school desegregation. In Selma, they demanded the right to vote. Their tactics worked: In 1964 Congress enacted the Civil Rights Act that guaranteed all races protection against segregation practices.

Toward Social and Economic Development

In Haiti White's attitude toward Magloire warmed up considerably in the early 1950s. In August 1951, White and his wife visited Haiti as the guests of President and Madame Magloire. From Haiti's beautiful Hotel El Rancho, White described his conversion from a skeptic to a believer in Magloire's policies: "That skepticism has been almost entirely obliterated. President Magloire has surrounded himself with an able cabinet. He appears to be winning increasing support from the people. Instead of talking about housing, roads, new opportunities for agriculture and business and other governmental improvements, he and his government are proceeding to accomplish these desirable and desperately needed benefits without waiting for outside help but instead using the quite slim resources which the government here possesses."[34] As a result of the trip, Poppy Cannon, White's wife, was appointed public relations consultant for Haiti. Poppy was to "act as adviser to the Haiti Tourist Information Bureau in New York and will cooperate with the bureau director, Gérard de Catalogne on all phases of tourist and economic promotion in the furtherance of plans for the development of Haiti."[35] This was a shrewd move for Magloire. By enticing Poppy into his camp, the president gained her husband's ear as well.

By all accounts, White's collaboration with Magloire was successful. White suggested five notable improvements in the areas of (1) government and politics, (2) economic development, (3) tourism, (4) public relations, and (5) advertising.[36] His suggestions were included in Magloire's five-year economic-development plan at a projected cost of $40 million. The plan included the creation of hundreds of new roads into the rural centers, more supervision of agriculture, new schools for the locals, and new hotels and beaches for tourist industry development. Some African Americans began believing that Magloire could pull Haiti by "its bootstraps from poverty and dissension"[37] to a position as a secure and productive nation.

Walter White convinced the Ford Foundation to conduct projects in Haiti on the same scale as its activities in India and Pakistan. He recommended Magloire in glowing terms: "Under President Magloire a phenomenal job has been done in raising the economy of the island with very little outside aid. The most extraordinary of these is the development of the 120,000 acre Artibonite Valley."[38] Socioeconomic conditions had improved under Magloire through the five-year basic development and industrialization plan.

With Poppy Cannon as adviser in the New York public relations office, tourists flocked to Haiti. In an interview with White over WCIB radio in New York and affiliated stations, Magloire announced "the more than doubling of the number of tourists to Haiti from the United States during the past four years and the anticipated increase of at least 30% in 1952."[39]

Meanwhile, White was proving to be one of Magloire's new apologists. In 1953, Baldwin wrote Magloire to denounce the roadblocks Magloire's administration raised before the Ligue Haitienne des Droits de l'Homme. "We understand that the organization is unable to function because of interference and intimidation by agencies of the government. Reports indicate that meetings have been put under police surveillance, that publications of any sort are impossible because of fear of prosecution, and that rightly or wrongly for the officers feel it dangerous to carry on any activity."[40]

White, once considered a great crusader for human rights, soft-pedaled the issue. He was skeptical and counseled Baldwin for patience: "The only basis I can think of for the report you have received is that Haiti has been alert to any possible infiltration or activity by Communist or other trouble-makers which includes agents of the Dominican Republic, Argentina, and other countries which for one reason or another may try to stir up trouble in the Caribbean. But as far as I know, this has been done legally without infringement on the rights of assembly or a free press."[41] This argument bore striking resemblance to those offered by dictators to justify oppression. White, who was traveling to Haiti with Poppy to research an article for Collier's Magazine on the progress that had been made under the Magloire administration, promised to report the facts.

This report served to set up White as a defender of Magloire. Haiti was once again believed to have obstructed the appointment of a black as American ambassador. The candidates were Mrs. Jessie Vann from the Pittsburgh Courier and eight other prominent African Americans. At the Forty-fourth Annual Conference of the NAACP in St. Louis, Missouri, there were impassioned pleas to draft a resolution criticizing Haiti. White halted the proceedings pending a discussion with Magloire. "I took the liberty of assuring those who were eager to introduce such a resolution that Haiti was concerned only with the caliber and influence of the ambassador to be named and not with the race of the ambassador."[42] The Haitian government later offered the most vigorous denial of what it called "a fantastic assertion." However, even before Haiti had the opportunity to react, White had already quenched the fire on behalf of Magloire. One can easily understand Magloire's appreciation for White's labor on his behalf. As he wrote White, "I . . . appreciate your efforts to establish the prestige and moral credit of my government in the United States."[43]

One of the most fruitful benefits of the White collaboration was the visit Magloire made to the White House in 1955. From the beginning White was orchestrating his scheme to get Magloire to visit an American president. In 1951, he suggested to Secretary Acheson that Magloire deserved an invitation because of his achievements for the socioeconomic development of Haiti and for "the consideration of the relationship of a Negro Republic in the Western Hemisphere upon the opinion of the United States among colored peoples throughout the world."[44] In 1953, White repeated the request to Edward R. Murrow, a renowned broadcaster for the Columbia Broadcasting System (CBS): "Most Southern American and Caribbean countries, knowing our racial attitude, send the lightest skinned spokesmen to the United States. I believe that inviting a quite dark-skinned head of state like President Magloire would have beneficial repercussions both in the Caribbean and in Asia and Africa."[45]

The request was rejected because of Truman's busy schedule and competition from other nations. World leaders who wanted an audience with Truman included Magloire's neighboring strongman generalissimo R. L. Trujillo of the Dominican Republic. White confided to Luc Fouché, Magloire's secretary, that Trujillo "vehemently demanded to know why he has never been invited to Washington since, as he phrased it, 'I have done everything the American Government has asked me to do for the past 20 years.'"[46] Though Trujillo believed his faithful service deserved recognition, politicos in Washington did not want either of the two leaders to visit.

Despite objections, White continued to try to secure Magloire's invitation—always with the overtones of race. In 1953, he wrote to Secretary of State John Foster Dulles: "I believe strongly that an official visit to the

United States of the President of the only Negro republic in the Western Hemisphere will have beneficial repercussions throughout the world and particularly in Latin America, Africa and Asia."[47]

In 1955, Magloire finally came to the United States as the official guest of President Dwight Eisenhower. Magloire spent a night in the White House and stayed at Blair House for the rest of his visit. White sent him this welcoming telegram: "We of the National Association for the Advancement of Colored People which has long been deeply interested in your great country extend to you a warm welcome to the United States. We are confident that in the excellent program which has been arranged for your visit there will come an even closer bond between our two countries."[48]

Magloire enjoyed all of the trappings of an official state visit. He addressed both houses of Congress. Magloire was honored in a ticker tape parade in New York City sponsored by Mayor Robert Ferdinand Wagner Jr. Congressman Adam Clayton Powell (D-NY) organized a reception for the Magloire party at the Abyssinian Church. Columbia University and Fordham University awarded him honorary doctoral degrees. Back in Haiti, Magloire underscored the importance of his visit to the United States in improving Haitian and African American relations. In a letter to White, Magloire acknowledged, "I take great pleasure in thanking you personally and give you my conviction that the excellent relations which now exist between the Negroes in the United States and Haiti have been strengthened."[49]

The Sesquicentennial Anniversary of Freedom

On January 1, 1954, Haiti celebrated the 150th anniversary of its independence, bringing together Haitian and African American leaders. White acknowledged to Magloire's chief of staff Mauclair Zéphirin, "Mrs. White and I are also talking with *Life Magazine* about plans for extensive coverage of the sesquicentennial celebration of Haitian freedom."[50] It was an opportunity to showcase the achievements of the black republic and the black race.

The festivities began in Gonaives, at the site of the battle of Vertières, which was reenacted by Haitian cadets. It continued in Port-au-Prince with the dedication of monuments to the heroes of independence. The Grand Ball in the National Palace was touted as a regal event for blacks.

"Nowhere on earth among Negroes is there a match for the classic finery, in dress, in drama, in art, as was exhibited the day of the festival."[51] During the ceremonies, depictions of memorable events of Haitian history were presented. Haiti seemed to shine as the star of freedom she was perceived to be through the years, as distinguished blacks from the United States, South America, Africa, and the West Indies descended on Port-au-Prince. Contralto Marian Anderson, who returned to Haiti to perform, ended her program with the Haitian national anthem.

The celebration boosted black consciousness and pride. It gave both Haitians and African Americans an opportunity to appreciate the accomplishments of the race in this hard, long-fought battle for liberation. Against a thousand odds, the flame of freedom had been maintained in the New World for 150 years. To demonstrate appreciation for the importance of this momentous event, Walter White suggested to unionist Patrick E. Gorman of the Amalgamated Meat Cutters and Butchers of Chicago "on January 1, you fly the flag of the Republic of Haiti because on that date Haiti will celebrate the sesquicentennial of its emancipation."[52] For this brief period, the parties that were frequently at odds with each other were unified.

The task of honoring the heroes of Haitian independence was given to "the ablest Negro talent in the world." They were Blanco Ramos, Cuban professor at the National Institute of Art of Havana, and Richmond Barthe, renowned African American artist and sculptor. Barthe sculpted four giant monuments honoring Haiti's historical leaders, Toussaint Louverture, Jean-Jacques Dessalines, Alexandre Pétion (displayed in Port-au-Prince), and Henri Christophe (placed on the northern shores of Haiti). In the black media, these statues were described as "the Greatest Negro Monuments on earth."[53]

African American pride in Haiti was strong during this period. Featured articles describing the sesquicentennial events heightened public awareness and were evident in both the white and black media. The NAACP sent the following congratulatory message:

The National Association For the Advancement of Colored People expresses its warmest congratulations to Republic of Haiti on its 150 birthday. Yours has been a gallant battle against odds, which would have crushed a weaker people. Your fortitude is bringing fruit and the world is beginning to recognize the part Haiti has played in the struggle for freedom from economic and political tyranny. The U. S. especially is recognizing that its own prosperity and size is in part due to Haiti's successful fight for this freedom, since that victory forced Napoleon to sell the enormous Louisiana territory to the U. S. We felicitate your great nation and people and pledge our continued help in your struggle to provide a more abundant life for Haiti's people and to strengthen democracy in the western hemisphere. We have asked Dr. Ralph J. Bunche, a member of the Board of Directors, to represent us at the sesquicentennial celebration.[54]

Underlying all the celebration of pride was some ugliness. President Magloire used the celebration to ignore the good wishes of the telegram and flex his muscles at his presumed enemies. Ironically, he used the very army that was trained by the Americans to exercise political control and to brutally repress the Haitian people. His military police, headed by the ruthless Marcaisse Prosper, arrested and imprisoned political opponents, silenced the press, and dissolved the legislative chambers.[55]

Magloire's term in office ended in December 1956. Like most of his predecessors, Magloire tried to extend his mandate beyond the Constitution. He failed, and the president was overthrown by popular pressure. Following his departure, Haiti declined into a state of political and economic turmoil from which it is still recovering.

Managing the Haitian Political Quagmire, 1957–2000

The black American relationship has already proven to be extremely important to us. Now what we will increasingly see is the 300,000 Haitians born in the United States who are black Americans as well as Haitian-Americans serving as a vital bridge. This is our hope for modernizing, politically, culturally and economically. (1994)

Leslie Delatour, *Haiti-Observateur*

Haiti remained in the African American consciousness throughout the twentieth century. New social and political events altered the links between the two peoples and their perceptions of each other. Haiti's distinction as a symbol of freedom to blacks throughout the world became tarnished as the country slid further into the depths of repression and human-rights violations.

Congressman Walter E. Fauntroy, during the Haitian March on Washington in 1981, sharply criticized the Haitian leaders for allowing their nation to decline into such repression. He described the feelings African Americans felt towards Haiti, declaring to Jean-Claude Duvalier's corrupt regime, "You will not get over by just talking that talk of negritude and Black pride and brotherhood but you will have to walk that walk by reordering your priorities and structures so that the voices of freedom can be allowed to speak and the Haitian people can benefit from the fruit of their labor . . . Haiti, which once symbolized Black liberation struggle as the world's first Black republic, under your present and corrupt repressive policies can no longer lay claim to this proud heritage."[1] In the eyes of many African Americans, Haiti now has become a troubled land: a land of authoritarian government and of human-rights abuse, a land of Vodou, boat people, and AIDS. Although the links remain between Haitians and African Americans, it is undeniable that a reversal of attitude and even of role has taken place.

In the Grips of Tyranny

There are a number of factors that contributed to Haiti's decline into a quagmire of oppression. Heading the list is the overwhelmingly authoritarian government. Add to this dictatorship the role of political corruption and mismanagement. In its two centuries of independence, the nation has never known democracy.

Haiti lacks an adequate system of public education, a prerequisite for any democratic society. Georges Anglade quantified this problem: "Out of 400 children, 120 will attend school, 20 will reach the level of primary studies certificate, and five will continue until the exams of secondary studies and only one of them will pass those exams."[2] Nearly 60 percent of the population of Haiti has no formal schooling, according to the *Encyclopedia Britannica: 1996 Yearbook*. Rural Haiti, constituting the overwhelming majority (69.3 percent in 1996) of the populace, has no political voice.

François Duvalier epitomized the Haitian tradition of dictatorship. Duvalier was the product of Haiti's resistance to the racist policies of the American occupation, which catered to the upper-class mulatto interests over the dark-skinned masses. After gaining valuable political and administrative experience during the rule of his mentor Dumarsais Estimé, Duvalier emerged as the torchbearer of noirist ideology. All the while, he shrewdly packaged himself as a defender of the masses' legitimate interests. In September 1957, Duvalier was elected president of Haiti.

As Duvalier began his presidency, African American leaders continued their interest in Haitian affairs. Eural Grant Jackson of the New York Public Schools described the civil crises in light of the socioeconomic conditions prevailing in Haiti. For Jackson, the disturbances were associated with the country's abysmal poverty, economic difficulties, widespread illiteracy, soil erosion, shocking malnutrition, and acute hunger. Jackson challenged the United States to reach out and help the Haitians: "More economic assistance and technical aid are the present needs of this Negro republic. These proud indigent people may not be very anxious to accept a quixotic doling out of charity with 'strings attached.' We must show cogent insight by helping the Haitians help themselves."[3]

Duvalier also knew of Haiti's socioeconomic problems. Having witnessed the overthrow of Estimé, though, he was determined to prevent a repeat of Estimé's humiliating experience. His desire to perpetuate his rule was an overwhelming obsession for him. The intense effort of his enemies increasingly drove him to autocratic rule.

Duvalier had staunch opposition; some key political figures went into exile. Most of them settled in New York City, including former president Paul Magloire, ex-senator Louis Déjoie, and Daniel Fignolé, who had served as provisional head of state for nineteen days. These men created political groups aimed at overthrowing the Duvalier government. As leader of the Democratic League of Haiti, Déjoie sent a note to Duvalier in 1959 demanding that he resign his presidency. He charged the president with ruining Haiti. Déjoie and members of the league picketed the Manhattan residence of Haiti's ambassador.[4] The secretary of the league, Dr. Camille Lhérisson, an ex-minister in Magloire's cabinet, tried to stop aid to Duvalier through his Friends of Haiti, a nonpolitical group that sought to improve the welfare of the Haitian people. Lhérisson charged that the help offered to the republic's citizens would not be beneficial "until an atmosphere of democracy and human liberty was restored to the Republic."[5]

Duvalier exploited his enemies' attacks to fortify his autocratic rule. He went on the offensive, first targeting the very army that won him the presidency. He emasculated its authority by dismissing all officers with questionable allegiance. He counterbalanced its strength by creating a private militia called Volontaire de la Sécurité Nationale, better known as Tontons Macoutes, who murdered thousands of innocent citizens.

The dictator weakened Haiti's traditional institutions that resisted his ambition for absolute power. To quell all opposition, he shut down opposing newspapers like the *Haiti Miroir, Indépendence, Le Patriote,* and *La Phalange*.[6] Journalists who opposed his regime were imprisoned or driven underground. The parliament and the judiciary system became mere puppets. Members of the hierarchy of the Catholic Church were expelled: Monsignor François Poirier, the French archbishop of Port-au-Prince; Monsignor Rémy Augustin, his assistant and the first appointed Haitian bishop; Bishop Jean-Marie Robert of Gonaives; and Jesuit priests who, according to Duvalier, were a threat to national security.

Having neutralized the Catholic Church, Duvalier revived Vodou as the political force it had been during the revolutionary period of the eighteenth century. During the 1957 electoral campaign, Duvalier rallied Vodou priests to his side. These same priests later occupied key government positions and became "informants spying on members of their congregation, and Tontons Macoutes within the boundaries of their communities and neighbourhoods. Through the network of voodoo priests, it was possible to reach the masses and also to control them. Their temples are used for the diffusion of the Duvalierist ideology."[7] Like the old colonial-era political leaders, Duvalier projected an image of infallibility because of the protective power of the Vodou gods.

Duvalier's dictatorship occupied center stage in the American media. The image of a country that stood as a symbol of freedom was replaced with one of tyranny. In the chorus of critics, Serafino Romualdi, the AFL-CIO inter-American representative, wrote, "Duvalier came to power on September 22, 1957, by fraudulent elections, and undertook to govern by terroristic methods."[8] Graham Greene, one of Duvalier's harshest critics, described Haiti under Duvalier as "a nightmare Republic . . . surely never has terror had so bare and ignoble an object as here—the protection of a few tough men's pockets."[9] Greene's *The Comedians* described how the regime severely tarnished Haiti's image.

The black media also spotlighted Duvalier's ongoing repression. At the beginning of Duvalier's regime, some African American journalists were first to raise the red flag over Haiti's chronic political instability. The *Afro-American Baltimore* sharply criticized the violence marring Duvalier's electoral campaign and his preinstallation days. Its reporter in Haiti, Louis Lomax, described the country as being "on verge of national suicide," as military men reminiscent of Nazi Germany "rampaged the streets of Port-au-Prince declaring merchants enemies of the army and forcing open doors."[10] A year later, the *Afro-American Baltimore* editorialized against the reign of terror in Haiti, during which hooded men raided the printing plants and destroyed their presses. The editor compared these events to the activities of the white-based "Ku Klux Klan, the most despicable of American institutions."[11] David Smithers, writing in the *New York Amsterdam*, depicted Haiti as "a leper among nations." He substantiated these claims by describing the bogeymen who are "Duvalier's own special contribution to the comic opera of Latin-American dictatorships."[12] In his description, the Tontons Macoutes used violence and extortion to steal money for Duvalier. These thugs specialized in rape, even in public.

The Haitian government took the counteroffensive against both the anti-Duvalier factions and African American critics in the United States. In 1959, the consulate of Haiti in New York sharply criticized Lhérisson, secretary of the Democratic League, for his "shameful letter" to the Friends of Haiti. Lhérisson was branded "a turncoat under the cloak of a magistrate."[13] In 1960, Haitian ambassador to Washington Ernest Bonhomme criticized African American journalist Lynn Grossberg for a "one sided slanderous attack on the administration of President Duvalier."[14] Miss Grossberg retorted, "If Mr. Bonhomme is attacking me for calling Dr. Duvalier a dictator, why doesn't he attack the *New York Times* and all the other press and personalities . . . that do likewise?"[15] The debate over the state of despotism in Haiti heated up.

In spite of harsh criticism and conflict over his reign of terror, Duvalier had some support in the African American community. The *New York Age,* for instance, covered Duvalier's rule to the advantage of his administration. In 1959, Lancelot Evans spent two weeks in Haiti as a guest of the Haitian government. He met with Duvalier and wrote a series of articles for the *Age* in which he depicted the president as a man "with a soft voice and a grim determination to lead his country to a new era of progress."[16] These articles included publication of "Haiti's 2-Year Plan" of economic and developmental programs. To Evans, Duvalier's opponents were more "interested in toppling his government, than helping him fight disease and poverty. Two scourges which unfortunately, is the lot of the republic's largest segment."[17] The *Age's* series concluded with an editorial referring to the "esteemed François Duvalier" as a man with a will to make Haiti one of the most solvent and progressive countries in this hemisphere.[18] Duvalier's African American supporters identified Haiti as a nation with whom they shared a common African origin.

On the sociological level, African American journalists differed in their interpretations of events. David Smithers, for instance, believed the Haitian political crisis was the result of a class and color struggle: "Between black and brown is a gulf almost as wide as between black and white in the United States."[19] He saw the black Duvalier as being the major opponent of the brown, for "Duvalier hates the brown with such consuming zeal that despite impartial brutality of his regime he holds the respect of millions of blacks."[20]

Lancelot Evans analyzed these events in the same way, pointing out that while the "creoles" still controlled the economic life of the country, dark-skinned Haitians who are in a majority stood solidly behind Duvalier.[21] Other African American leaders attributed the chaos in Haiti to the dichotomy between French and Anglo-Saxon political systems. They saw Haiti's government structure "patterned after the French whose unsteady performance gives it a sorry model to follow."[22] In spite of the worsening conditions, African Americans continued to envision positive change in Haiti within the rule of democracy.

While Haiti slid toward dictatorship, African Americans were climbing upward in their quest for freedom. The segregation walls came tumbling down. Martin Luther King Jr., a young Baptist minister, propelled the civil rights movement to the national agenda. As president of the Montgomery Improvement Association, he led the crusade that resulted in the Supreme Court's decision declaring "Alabama's state and local laws requiring segregation on buses unconstitutional."[23] Then, at the head of the Southern Christian Leadership Conference, King and his lieutenants continued the struggle through nonviolent resistance. The civil rights movement brought about revolutionary change in American society, culminating with passage of the civil rights bill in 1964, a century after emancipation from slavery. It was the most far-reaching step in the struggle for equality for African Americans.

When Martin Luther King was gunned down in Memphis, he was also mourned in Haiti as a hero and defender of the race. To honor his memory, Duvalier wrote a book entitled *Hommage au martyr de la non-violence, le réverend Dr. Martin Luther King, Jr.* In the book Duvalier presented a biographical sketch of King, highlighting the philosophy of the slain civil-rights leader. The president also described how his government honored King. These included a telegram to his widow Coretta in the name of the Haitian people. A communiqué from the Department of Foreign Affairs announced on April 6, 1968, that four days of mourning would be observed. During that time the national flag was flown half-mast on all public buildings. Public theaters closed and radio stations broadcast somber music to remember King's life and works. Furthermore the city council of Port-au-Prince changed the name of Ruelle Nazon, one of the main arteries in the capital, to Avenue Martin Luther King Jr.

Duvalier's response to the King assassination loudly echoed his commitment to Haiti's traditional role as leader of the black-liberation struggle. Duvalier's minister of interior, Dr. Aurèle Joseph, spoke of

Haiti's historic mission at the United Nations General Assembly: "American by her geographic position, active member of the Organization of American States, and African by race and culture and rightful member of the future Organization of African States, Haiti will not fail in her historic mission as a bridge between two worlds which are inspired by the same ideals of freedom, brotherhood and human solidarity."[24]

As for the Haitian masses, their plight worsened. In the grip of terror, Haitians fell victim to human-rights violations. The International Commission on Human Rights tried to investigate conditions in Haiti, but Duvalier refused to cooperate. Through his secretary of foreign affairs René Charlmers, he claimed a visit by the commission "might be interpreted as a form of interference in the internal affairs of the Republic of Haiti that affects its sovereignty."[25] Making a mockery of the commission, Duvalier provided only irrelevant and incomplete information.

Throughout the sixties, "Papa Doc" successfully thwarted all attempts to overthrow his regime. Political exiles launched ill-fated invasions that the dictator used to tighten his grip on the people. In 1971, before Duvalier died a natural death in the national palace, he made provisions to be succeeded by his nineteen-year-old son, Jean-Claude, known as "Baby Doc."

Early on, Jean-Claude Duvalier functioned as a detached president, leaving the business of government to his late father's cronies and to his mother, who still held on to the title of first lady. Based on their own greed, they managed Haiti by relying on the repressive machinery still in place. By 1977, the twentieth anniversary of the dynasty, Jean-Claude promised to begin an economic revolution on the assumption his father had already completed the political revolution. He boldly referred to this new era as "Jean-Claudism." The president explained the new ideology by stressing that the Duvalierist revolution was achieving its explosive phase and entering into its economic phase to finish its work because it was evident that a revolution could not be successful unless it completely ensured the rehabilitation of the masses.[26] Probably out of desperation, this new policy heightened the hope of many Haitians.

African Americans saw no real change in the Duvalier dynasty from father to son. Congresswoman Shirley Chisholm of New York charged, "Human rights violations were so widespread and serious under the regime of François Duvalier that they were virtually institutionalized during his rule from 1957 to 1971. Despite a much publicized, but ill-defined liberalization that was proclaimed by his son, 'President-for-life' Jean Claude Duvalier, the Duvalier system of authoritarian government and political persecution based on the military and the Tonton Macoutes has not been significantly altered."[27]

As president for life, Jean-Claude found himself in the same predicament as his father, and it was understandable that he adopted the same repressive measures. The handpicked Haitian legislature backed him by investing in him, as if by a ritual, *pleins pouvoirs*, or full powers.

African Americans tried to reverse Haiti's repressive trends. In August 1977, Andrew Young, then U.S. ambassador to the United Nations, carried the Carter administration's human-rights crusade to Haiti. In his discussions with Jean-Claude, Young tied U.S. economic aid to human rights. He made it clear that "Improvement in the human rights situation will directly affect the aid cooperation Haiti receives from Washington."[28] Following those talks, Young denounced the lack of voices of dissent and the refusal of the Haitian government to offer due process to its citizens. Jean-Claude backed down and even pledged to allow an investigation by the Organization of American States.

Far from improving human rights in Haiti, however, Jean-Claude worked instead to enhance his own standing with the Carter administration. He hired the law firm of Peabody, Rivlin, Lambert, and Meyers to influence policy makers in the State Department and Congress. Additionally, the firm of Edelman International was retained to polish the Haitian government's political image.

Cosmetic changes labeled "liberalization" vaporized as soon as Ronald Reagan became U.S. president in 1980. Jean-Claude and the *macoutes* cheered when Carter lost his bid for reelection. They celebrated by crushing dissent against the regime, rounding up and detaining without charges journalists and human-rights activists. Lame-duck officials at the U.S. State Department criticized this offensive, but it was a calculated move. Duvalier felt the inauguration of the conservative Reagan signaled the death of any human-rights policy practiced by the Carter administration.

Once again, African Americans criticized the new waves of human-rights violations. In "Repression in Haiti," the editor of the *New York Amsterdam* wrote, "In what appears to have been a spasm of fear, the government of President Jean-Claude Duvalier has spun off into a wave of repression that is repugnant to civilization."[29] The editor called for a halt to all aid to "Baby Doc" until he returned "some semblance of freedom" to Haitians.

The decision to deny foreign aid to Haiti was another effort African Americans were willing to support in the hopes of destroying Duvalier's oppression. They blamed Haiti's abysmal poverty on Duvalier's mismanagement and greed. U.S. Congressman Walter Fauntroy of the District of Columbia said, "While I am concerned about economic development in Haiti, I am particularly anxious that our economic development assistance help the least of these—the poor—and not merely support the lifestyle of the rich."[30] He later protested political conditions in Haiti and warned that if they were left uncorrected, the U.S. government would sharply reduce aid to the nation.

As had been the case with his father, other African Americans came to the defense of Jean-Claude Duvalier. Former commerce secretary Ron Brown, as a member of the Washington law firm Patton, Boggs, and Blow, worked for him from October 1982 until 1986 at an annual salary of $150,000. In a 1983 memo to Duvalier, Brown reported on his duties: "We continue to pay a great deal of attention to the Black Caucus and to other 'liberal' members of Congress. The leader of the Black Caucus, Representative Julian Dixon, has been extremely positive and has helped us a great deal; also, a large number of 'liberal' members of the House of Representatives and of the Senate are now, thanks to our efforts, ready to help. Although some of them continue to make negative comments about Haiti, all, without exception, have proved to be cooperative on the issue of aid."[31]

Brown defended his involvement with Jean-Claude Duvalier on the ground that he was helping Haiti. He noted that, in the eyes of the Black Caucus, "it was a positive thing" that Haiti had turned to an African American for lobbying help,[32] even though it allowed Duvalier's repressive policies to continue.

Besides Brown, U.S. Senator Edward Brooks of Massachusetts reflected racial identification and unity when he drew attention to Haiti in the Senate. In 1976, Brooks underscored the severe drought causing much suffering in the country. Insufficient rainfall led to crop failures in northwest Haiti and in La Gônave. Brooks asked Congress to "stand ready to provide the assistance the Haitians need to meet this latest disaster and improve their capacity to become more self-sustaining in the future."[33]

Despite widespread criticism of his regime, Duvalier did not change his policies but rather used the traditional theme of a Communist threat to reinforce them. He enacted an anti-Communism law providing that "persons who make any declarations of belief in Communism, verbal or written, public or private, or propagated communist or anarchist doctrines by inferences, speeches, conversations, by leaflets, posters, and newspapers will be charged with crimes against the state, tried by a military court and if convicted may be punished by death penalty."[34] That law led the Lawyers' Committee for International Human Rights to charge that Jean-Claude Duvalier's regime was continuing to tolerate and perpetuate past abuses.

Two decades of tyranny under the Duvalier dynasty could not overshadow Haiti's contribution to liberty. On the 200th anniversary of the Declaration of Independence of the United States, Representative Dante Fascell of Florida stood in the halls of the U.S. Congress to extol Haiti's significance in the western hemisphere: "Haiti's participation in the American Revolution aided our country in becoming the foremost symbol of freedom and independence throughout the world. We must not forget the courageous efforts of Haitians who sacrificed their lives for American independence."[35]

The Boat People Crisis

Immigration has been an important factor in the relations between Haitians and African Americans. The 1791 Haitian Revolution triggered a mass exodus of French colonists, mulattoes, and their slaves to the United States. During the nineteenth century, African American freedmen migrated to Haiti in two emigration waves, one in 1824 and another in 1859. They were drawn to the island by the promise of freedom and the hope of economic betterment. The second half of the twentieth century brought about a reversal in the migratory patterns. It was now the Haitians who were forced from their country by poverty and political oppression. They left their land to escape cruelties by their own government and seek refuge in the United States.

This migration took place in two distinct phases. First, professionals, including doctors, lawyers, teachers, engineers, and public administrators chose to go primarily to Africa, where they brought much needed skills to the newly liberated nations. According to Robert I. Rotberg, by 1963, 1,000 Haitians were employed in the Congo (Kinshasa), and from 1960 to 1962, 310 Haitian professionals were working in Guinea for either President Sekou Touré or the United Nations. By 1968, more than 75,000 professional Haitians had settled in the United States, another 10,000 in Canada, 300,000 in the Dominican Republic, and 50,000 in Cuba.[36] With the "brain drain" going on in Haiti, members of the underclass found themselves wanting for medical help, good teachers, and other services once provided by Haiti's exiled professionals. That led to a second phase of migration, where the masses tried to escape Duvalier's tyranny. Rather than go through official channels, they escaped by sea and became known as the "boat people." They sailed for Miami in overcrowded and unsafe small boats. Some died during the journey from starvation, exposure, and dehydration. This form of escape began in 1972, gaining in numbers from 1978 to 1981. In August 1978, Congressman Joshua Eilberg of Pennsylvania brought the Haitian refugees' situation to the attention of his colleagues by informing them that "Currently there are approximately 8,000 Haitian nationals in the Southern Florida area awaiting either deportation or exclusion proceedings."[37]

These trips often ended in disaster. The *New York Times* of July 23, 1978, revealed that "A small boat carrying 28 Haitian refugees heading for Florida was hit by a storm and capsized; Bahamanian officials reported that 10 refugees drowned, 3 were missing and 15 survived."[38] On August 14, 1979, a similar accident occurred when 5 children and 1 adult drowned after being pushed overboard by men allegedly paid to help them enter Florida illegally from Haiti; 10 others survived and 2 are missing. In November 1981, the Haitian refugees' plight got the attention of the American public when bodies of refugees drifted onto the shores of posh Hillsboro Beach, in Fort Lauderdale. Some thirty people were killed in that accident.[39]

On reaching the American shores, Haitian refugees preferred the larger cities where other Haitian refugees now lived. They especially moved to neighborhoods where "skin color enables the Haitians to merge easily with the American black population."[40] But cultural and language differences set them apart. Miami became the city of choice because of its proximity to Haiti. In 1982, the U.S. General Accounting

Office (GAO) reported that the Immigration and Naturalization Service (INS) "had apprehended 47,666 Haitians entering or attempting to enter Florida without authorization since the early 1970's."[41]

In Miami, the boat people settled in a burgeoning Haitian American community known as "Little Haiti," situated in the Edison-Little River section just north of Miami's central business district. Throughout the 1970s, following the example of black-owned businesses in the area, Haitians set up a network of bakeries, dry cleaning shops, cafés, photographers, and auto and television repair stores. In Little Haiti, the refugees found community support from storefront churches and agencies organized to help Haitians, including the Haitian-American Community Association of Dade County, the Christian Community Service Agency, and the Haitian Community Mental Health Center.[42]

The boat people's legal status became hotly debated. Since the United States supported any government that was anti-Communist, President Jimmy Carter refused to grant asylum to the refugees. And as economic rather than political refugees, the American government said that these Haitians should be sent back home. The INS took the necessary steps to that end. In statements made before the Subcommittee on Immigration of the House Judiciary Committee, John A. Bushnell, deputy assistant secretary for Inter-American Affairs, declared that "The stark contrast between living conditions and economic prospects in Haiti and the United States is the principal factor motivating emigration to this country."[43] U.S. policy had allowed people from Communist countries or the Middle East to enter as political refugees and to be given favorable consideration for admission. Haitians fleeing the hellish Duvalier dictatorship were declared to be economic refugees and had to be sent back.

The Haitian government, eager to receive American financial aid, agreed with the INS. It offered strong assurances that those who returned would suffer no reprisals or recriminations. In a letter to the American ambassador, the Haitian secretary of foreign affairs, Edner Brutus, assured the ambassador that "the Government of the Republic has no objection to the return to this country of Haitians classified in the United States as economic refugees or illegal immigrants, and that punitive measures of any kind against those unfortunates who left in search of remunerative work has never been considered. Hundreds of our compatriots have returned and are living at home in peace."[44]

These reassurances reinforced the administration policy to send refugees back. Stephen Palmer Jr., deputy assistant secretary of human rights and humanitarian affairs, declared that most "applications contain no allegation that the applicants or their families suffered persecution before they left or that other factors in their background would make them suspect politically in Haiti. We do not believe that such applications support a finding of a well-founded fear of persecution, and in such cases we recommend denial of the application."[45] This policy was consistently implemented, for Mr. Palmer could claim that the State Department had only favorably recommended 250 Haitian boat people for asylum out of the thousands of cases seeking admission.

Human-rights organizations, including the Haitian Refugee Project, the Haitian Fathers of Brooklyn, the American Committee for the Protection of Foreign Born, and the National Alliance of Postal and Federal Employees, rejected the American government assertion that the Haitians were economic refugees. In 1979, religious organizations under the umbrella of the National Council of Churches urged Carter to grant political asylum to the 8,000 Haitian boat people who had entered the country since 1972. They also appealed to the judicial system. In *Haitian Refugee Center v. Civiletti*, 4,000 Haitians brought a class action suit against the INS, opposing the INS policy of mass deportation. The case was heard by federal judge James Lawrence King.

In a strongly worded 180-page opinion, Judge King rejected the administration's argument and said the INS had followed a "systematic program designed to deport them [the Haitians] irrespective of their asylum claims." The judge denounced the Haitian political situation as "stark, brutal and bloody" and rejected the State Department's findings. He forbade the INS from expelling refugees and ruled that the Haitians faced political repression. Judge King also considered discrimination by comparing the official federal policy between dark-skinned Haitians and light-skinned Cubans. He found that 117,000 Cubans were routinely granted asylum, while "none of the 4,000 Haitians were granted asylum. No greater disparity can be imagined."[46]

The matter of the Haitian boat people reinforces the linkages between Haitians and African Americans. Both peoples were involved in issues rife with racial overtones, issues they could not ignore. African American leaders and civil-rights activists alike vehemently embraced the Haitian cause. Lois Colbert, a former worker in the Haitian-American Community Association of Dade County Inc., asserted that "Blacks . . . are very concerned about Haitian asylum and those helping Haitians are using this factor in influencing President Carter."[47] Congressman Fauntroy set the tone of black support by emphasizing the solidarity binding Haitians to African Americans. He said, "We, as black people, want to make it clear that we understand the connection between the treatment of the Haitian refugees and the regard which this administration may have for black people at home. . . . We, the Congressional Black Caucus, plan to stand with our Haitian brothers and sisters in their quest for simple justice and will be taking this issue to every forum and community available to us."[48]

Haitians themselves brought up the race issue in their plea: "We are asking why you treat us this way. Is it because we're Negroes? Why are you letting us suffer this way, America?"[49] The GAO agreed, pointing out that State Department officials "recommended disapproval of 97 percent of all Haitian asylum claims on which the Department issued advisory opinions in 1980 and 1981." It further acknowledged, "Haitians were maintained under Spartan conditions, with unsuitable housing and services.[50] For instance, a detention center in Florida called Krome was built as a short-term facility to house 524 prisoners; yet up to 1,500 Haitians lived there in 1981.

Prompted by racial identification, African American leaders wanted to secure the same due process for Haitian refugees that was granted to all others. They pressured the American government to respect the rights of Haitians. At the forefront was the Congressional Black Caucus, which formed a special task force to deal with Haitian refugees in the United States. In the beginning, Congresswoman Shirley Chisholm of New York, caucus chairperson, led the congressional offensive. On October 24, 1979, she called for action:

> The Congressional Black Caucus strongly urges the Department of Justice, through its Immigration and Naturalization Service, to adhere to this nation's fundamental tradition of equal protection for all persons under law by granting work authorization and due process to Haitians seeking political asylum in our country. The Caucus must stand firm in its insistence that the United States human rights and refugee policy be administered on an evenhanded basis so that no government activity or decision may be viewed as tainted with race, class or ideological prejudice.[51]

Chisholm rejected the economic-refugee claim, as well as the State Department's report that Haitians would not be mistreated or punished by Duvalier's military thugs when they returned. She denounced the unfairness of the Miami INS district office for its handling of Haitian refugees under "special procedures," different from the manner in which other refugees were treated. While the normal rate of deportation hearings is ten a day, as many as 150 deportation hearings a day were held concerning the Haitian refugees.

Congressman Mickey Leland of Texas complained that the American government's handling of the Haitian refugees was a betrayal of its open door policy for the oppressed. He quoted the inscription on the Statue of Liberty:

Give me your tired, your poor
Your huddled masses yearning to breathe free
The wretched refuse of your teeming shore
Send these, the homeless, tempest-tossed to me . . .[52]

He said Washington officials did not follow the wishes of these inspiring words as Haitians were turned away from the American shores. Because Cubans were welcomed with open arms, Leland said the closed-door policy was clearly discriminatory against the Haitians.

During the hearing, Chisholm said the caucus's Task Force on Haitian Refugees worked toward getting political asylum for Haitian refugees. As she explained, "Hundreds of our Haitian brothers and sisters have fled a repressive society only to encounter a sense of injustice and a double standard under the administration of law in the United States."[53] In that quest, the caucus wrote President Carter expressing their concern for the safety and well-being of these refugees.

In June 1980, Chisholm's caucus was successful in getting Congressman Walter E. Fauntroy to raise the issue in the House of Representatives. He suggested that the caucus was shocked, angered, and outraged at the treatment of Haitian refugees, calling them "the black boat people" who were subjected to imprisonment, starvation, and deportation. He complained that the Carter administration's policy on Haitian refugees was carried out in violation of the United Nations protocol regarding the status of refugees. That protocol mandates that "A person should not be returned to a country if they have a well founded fear of persecution because of race, religion, nationality, political opinion or membership in a particular social group."[54]

When Ronald Reagan became president, he took even tougher action to control the influx of Haitian refugees. On the recommendation of a task force headed by Attorney General William French Smith, a policy was adopted to "prohibit bringing undocumented aliens in the U.S., and to strengthen existing authority for the interdiction, seizure and forfeiture of vessels used in violation of our laws."[55] The policy went into effect, and by October 1981, the *Washington Post* reported that the Coast Guard cutter Chase had intercepted a boatload of Haitian refugees and promptly turned them back to Port-au-Prince.[56]

Chisholm's caucus lambasted the Reagan administration for its policy of intercepting Haitian vessels on the high seas. Denouncing this practice, Chisholm said, "Interdiction certainly violates the principle of nonrefoulement in the U.N. protocol relating to refugees. The return of refugees to their country, given the gross and consistent pattern of human rights violations, makes a mockery of International Human Rights Day and the U.S. commitments to uphold our international treaty obligations."[57]

The NAACP supported the Haitian refugees and opposed discrimination against them. Benjamin Hooks, executive secretary of the association, protested the double standard of treatment of Cuban and Haitian refugees. In a letter to President Reagan, Hooks wrote that "The action is clearly discriminatory, because it amplifies a pattern which, for the past five years has singled out Haitian refugees for special and harsh treatment unlike any other refugees and in spite of the fact that we have welcomed and supported more than a half million refugees from elsewhere in the past two years."[58]

The NAACP board reinforced this position in a strongly worded resolution asking Reagan to demonstrate fairness toward Haitians. The resolution asked "that the NAACP call upon the President to demonstrate his commitment to human rights and grant political asylum to the Haitian boat people under his parole authority for those refugees already in the country." The resolution also called on the Washington bureau of the association to "work for the passage of HR 2816, the Refugee Act of 1979, and any companion legislation in the Senate of comprehensive refugee assistance."[59] The NAACP demonstrated its support by having its assistant general counsel, George Hairston, serve as head of a team of investigators probing the drowning of refugees off the coast of Miami. This legal team set a strategy into motion that would seek release of the refugees from detention centers and prisons. The team would then activate "the large network of NAACP branches nearest the centers to monitor all activities and provide as much comfort to the refugees as possible."[60]

The Haitian American community in the United States supported the cause. In May 1980, 200 Haitian Americans marched in Washington to protest the Carter administration's handling of the situation. Haitian community leaders such as Father Antoine Adrien of Brooklyn and Gérard Jean-Juste of Miami denounced the injustices and discriminations against Haitian refugees. In 1981, various Haitian American organizations joined the NAACP in a giant march in front of the White House. Their leaders included Jean Dupuy, head of the Haitian Neighborhood Center in Manhattan; Guy Sansaricq, coordinator of Haitian ministry for the Diocese of Brooklyn; Father Adrien, an Aristide supporter; and Yvon Rosemond, coordinator for the Defense of Haitian Refugees.

Fauntroy used his position as chairman of the Congressional Black Caucus to blast the Reagan administration for its harsh treatment of Haitian refugees. He also criticized Haiti's repressive leaders and denounced Jean-Claude Duvalier's dictatorial government by affirming that "The Government of Haiti should know that the Congressional Black Caucus would be interested in a dialogue but only in a dialogue that is fixed on bringing good news to the oppressed poor of Haiti and not one merely based upon color. Being a brother is a matter of acting like a brother, it is a matter of the content of your character, not the pigmentation of your skin."[61]

Other African American leaders joined with Fauntroy and asked for a fair and just resolution to the Haitian refugee crisis. The Rev. Jesse Jackson criticized the INS for its discriminatory policy toward Haitian refugees. In 1980, at a Haitian rally in Miami, he spoke out: "There is room in the United States for Cubans trying to escape oppression. There is for Haitians trying to escape oppression."[62] Jackson even asked the pope to use his moral influence to come to the aid of Haitian refugees. Since 98 percent of the refugees were Catholic, Jackson argued that Haitians deserved the same kind of attention the pope had granted during the Polish crisis.

Yet not all African Americans welcomed Haitian boat people into their neighborhoods. In 1984, the U.S. Justice Department instituted a loan program to pay for the move of 250 Haitian men from South Florida to Georgia. The organization Economic Opportunities Atlanta (EOA) coordinated the effort. However, only a few Atlanta residents welcomed the plan. Despite the intervention of the Southern Christian Leadership Conference (SCLC), a northwest Atlanta neighborhood opposed converting an abandoned elementary school into a Haitian resettlement center. Community members did not want the Haitians because they were "fearful that jobs will go to Haitians, not to residents."[63]

In the midst of the tyranny and exodus of Haitians, the image of Haiti suffered another severe blow with the acquired immunodeficiency syndrome (AIDS) virus. In the 1980s, the disease spread out of control in the United States, and some theories linked the origins of the human immunodeficiency virus (HIV) to Haiti, using Vodou practices as a scapegoat. The Centers for Disease Control designated Haitians as potential carriers of the disease and classified them as a high-risk group. The U.S. Food and Drug Administration (FDA) followed suit by excluding Haitians and sub-Saharan Africans from donating blood. Although the theory was not founded on research, it made waves in the United States, where the mass media leaped on it and blew it out of proportion.[64]

The Haitian government protested this unsubstantiated accusation. From Port-au-Prince, the administration's minister of public health, Dr. Ary Bordes, declared, "A whole population should never have been given this stigma."[65] The Haitian ambassador in Washington, Fritz Cinéas, echoed the message: "The Republic of Haiti has suffered a severe injustice over the past year in the American press. Countless broadcast and print journalists have related stories attributing the origins of . . . AIDS to Haitians, without sufficient factual data to support this theory."[66]

Since these diplomatic rebukes from the Haitian government went unheeded, Haitians and Haitian Americans alike protested the FDA policy. Putting aside their traditional differences, some 50,000 Haitian demonstrators marched to the Brooklyn Bridge in April 1990 to blast the federal policy. They also complained of the abuse and ridicule they were subjected to in both the media and the workplace.[67] This massive demonstration forced the FDA to back off. It lifted the ban a few weeks later.

The Land of Impossible Democracy

After three decades of political and economic turmoil, Jean-Claude Duvalier fled the country in 1986, ending his repressive rule. But after the dictator's forced exile, human-rights conditions actually worsened. A dossier from the Institute for European–Latin American Relations posed the question "Haiti: An impossible democracy?"[68]

For almost a decade (1986–95) after Jean-Claude Duvalier's departure, Haiti floundered in the same political chaos that characterized the country while the Duvaliers were in power. The government changed hands seven times in six years. Behind the upheaval, a fierce tug-of-war was being fought, pitting progressive against regressive forces for control of the nation. In that struggle, the military had the strong arm. Fortunately, with its abuses the military dug its own grave.

December 1990 signaled the first democratic elections ever held in Haiti. As a result, Jean-Bertrand Aristide was elected to the presidency. Aristide was born in the south of Haiti to peasants. In 1982, he became a priest in the Order of the Society of Saint Francis de Sales where he embraced liberation theology. During the 1980s, the charismatic preacher Aristide used his pulpit to galvanize opposition against Jean-Claude Duvalier's rule of terror and later against the repressive practices of the interim military governments. Two months before the 1990 election, Aristide threw his hat into the race as a candidate for the Front National pour le Changement et la Démocratie. The people elected him by a 67 percent majority.

But the elected government was short-lived. On September 30, 1991, just seven months after the election, General Raoul Cédras, commander of the army, overthrew Aristide. Cedras' action worsened the socioeconomic crisis, perhaps the worst in Haiti's history. African Americans now confronted a new version of refugee influx and contributed to the crusade to restore Aristide.

The Haitian military was ruthless, recalling the successes of Aristide in smashing Roger Lafontant's failed coup a few months earlier. Lafontant was the feared interior and defense minister under President Jean-Claude Duvalier. His presidential ambition was thwarted when the electoral council barred him from running in the 1990 election primarily because of his past connections with Duvalier. In 1991, Lafontant staged a coup. With help from the army, he seized control of the national palace and declared himself provisional president. With lightning speed, Aristide supporters killed the coup by shutting down Port-au-Prince, the capital city. Lafontant was arrested and jailed.

This time, Cédras staged a preemptive strike against the masses. Thousands died violently. Amnesty International reported, "The days immediately following the coup were marked by violent repression particularly in the poor communities, where support for President Aristide had been strongest. Soldiers deliberately and indiscriminately opened fire into crowds, killing hundreds of people, including children."[69] Backed by the reactionary elite, the military and paramilitary forces terrorized the population from 1991 to 1994, stamping out any support for Aristide.

The crisis triggered another exodus of Haitian refugees, with an even greater number flowing into Florida than during Duvalier's reign. In October 1991, an increasing number of Haitians began to sail in rickety boats. By February 1992, the U.S. Coast Guard intercepted some 15,000.[70] The U.S. Naval Base in Guantanamo Bay, Cuba, housed as many as 10,000 refugees.

Once again, African Americans were at odds with their government. In December 1991, the Rev. Jesse Jackson and Congressman Charles Rangel, a New York Democrat, visited the refugees. They asked the president to keep the refugee crisis on the political agenda in America. They were skeptical, however, "for it's hard for poor people to get on the agenda in Washington. And if you're poor, foreign and black, you don't even get on the radar screen of George Bush," Rangel said.[71] On May 24, 1992, their suspicions were confirmed when the president issued an executive order requiring the return of intercepted refugees to Haiti, denying them the opportunity to ask the United States for asylum.

African Americans still identified with the Haitian turmoil and the boat people. In the columns of The Crisis, Garland L. Thompson offered some insight on the fraternity of these two peoples: "It is impossible for Blacks to ignore Haiti. That island nation is not only close by—a mere 800 miles away—it is a Black land which has sent hundreds of thousands of emigrés here, many deeply involved in the business, political and social affairs of Black America."[72] The links of race and historical heritage remained alive despite the tragedy.

African Americans felt the Bush policy for handling the Haitian refugee crisis was tainted with racism. From lobbying the U.S. Congress to demonstrating in the streets, African Americans took action to fight the policy. The Congressional Black Caucus, which had grown from twenty-six to forty members after the 1992 election, was a vital force in shaping Haitian policy. It created a special task force headed by Representative Major Owens of New York to coordinate activities related to the Haitian crisis.

As in the past, the caucus targeted discriminatory practices based on race. Representative Alan Wheat of Missouri denounced such discrimination when he read a new version of a poem written by F. Russell Millin of Kansas that paraphrased the inscription of the Statue of Liberty:

Give me your tired, your poor, your
Huddled masses yearning to breathe free . . .
But not the Haitians nor the dark-skinned refugees.[73]

The caucus reinforced this view in its "Statement of Conscience in Support of Haitian Refugees" that stated, "In light of the grave human rights conditions in Haiti, we can only believe that the real reason these people are being repatriated without due process is because they are black. Soviet and Vietnamese refugees have been welcomed with open arms."[74] They called on President Bush to personally intervene and order a halt to the repatriation program.

The NAACP remained active. Benjamin Hooks, the executive secretary, complained that the racist patterns practiced by the United States were evident not only in Haiti but in South Africa as well, with the Bush administration's support of President F. W. de Klerk on apartheid: "In recent months, African Americans have perceived a racist tinge to American policy toward Haitian refugees. With the acquiescence of the Supreme Court, the United States is repatriating thousands of refugees."[75] In October 1992, the NAACP demonstrated in front of the White House to publicize its grievances with the Bush policy on Haitian repatriation.

The famous dancer and choreographer Katherine Dunham, who lived in Haiti for over half a century, joined the chorus of those who denounced the racist policy of the Bush administration. She was eighty-two years old when she went on a hunger strike in protest in East St. Louis, Illinois, going without food for forty-seven days, stopping only at the request of exiled President Aristide. Explaining her action, Dunham stated, "For 31 days I saw Haitians walking off those boats. And they were sent back. And I got the feeling they [the Coast Guard] were saying, 'Well, they're not people,' and I was outraged."[76] Besides Dunham, Randall Robinson, a

Harvard law school graduate, also used a hunger strike as a tactic to force the Clinton administration to reverse its policy on the black boat people. In 1977, he founded TransAfrica, a think tank on African and Caribbean issues. In 1984, Robinson occupied the South African Embassy in Washington to protest apartheid. With the dismantling of apartheid by the elevation of Nelson Mandela as South Africa's president, Robinson turned to the Haitian crisis as another human-rights issue of great significance.

On April 12, 1994, Robinson launched his well-publicized hunger strike targeting Clinton's stand on Haitian refugees. Clinton entered the world of Haitian boat people with a high sense of idealism. As a presidential candidate, he had opposed President Bush on repatriation. Back in Haiti, as the masses reeled under military oppression, boats were built and the people prayed for Clinton's election. But by the time Clinton took office, he had reversed his thinking. As the boat people continued to take to the rough seas, Clinton embraced George Bush's policy on Haitian refugees.

Robinson's hunger strike forced the president to change his course of action. By May 8, 1994, when Robinson ended his strike, Clinton ordered that Haitian refugees be interviewed on board ships to determine if they were political refugees, rather than automatically sending them back to Haiti. Moreover, under pressure from the Congressional Black Caucus, Clinton adopted a much tougher stand toward the military leaders in Haiti.[77]

From the beginning, negotiation was a key word in reaching a solution. Joao Baena Soares, general secretary of the Organization of American States (OAS), went to Haiti as the head of a delegation of six foreign ministers. The secretary lobbied to reinstate Aristide with a return to constitutional rule. General Cédras and his military party stalled these and subsequent negotiations. Consequently, the OAS began an economic and diplomatic embargo.[78] An accord reached in February 1992 between Aristide and the Haitian Parliamentary Negotiating Committee to find a permanent solution was never implemented.

Despite the OAS failure to negotiate a solution, a new avenue was explored between the de facto government and Aristide on Governors Island, New York. Under the auspices of the United Nations and the OAS, both Cédras and Aristide attended. The agreement provided for the return of constitutional rule via the retirement of the commander in chief of the army and a return to Haiti of President Aristide on October 30, 1993. The United Nations agreed to suspend all sanctions against Haiti. This agreement also went nowhere.[79] Cédras and his cronies persisted defiantly, ignoring all pleas for a diplomatic solution.

In this context, the Congressional Black Caucus pressed the Clinton administration to throw out of power what its members called the "thugs in military uniform." In 1993, the caucus lobbied to have the assets of the Haitian military leaders frozen, to have their visas and those of their supporters revoked, and to have enforced an embargo on strategic materials, including oil. In the strongest language, the caucus demanded that "the military terrorists and the drug smugglers who impose a savage and inhumane oppression on the people of Haiti bring an end to these gross violations of human rights."[80] They endorsed a return of President Aristide and the exile of the military terrorists, even if by force.

Traditional African American attitudes toward Haiti were reversed. African Americans were so outraged by conditions in Haiti that they supported a military occupation. Past leaders like James W. Johnson, W. E. B. Du Bois, and Walter White, who defended Haitian independence with such fervor, would have had trouble with this policy. Times had changed. Haiti had freed itself from slavery and become a haven for African Americans during the nineteenth century. But African Americans now took upon themselves the task of freeing the nation from its own military tyrants.

Because of pressure from the Congressional Black Caucus (CBC) and from Randall Robinson, President Clinton yielded. He not only reversed his position on Haitian refugees, he also fired his adviser, Lawrence Pezullo, the principal architect of the policy of negotiation. William Gray, a former congressman from Pennsylvania and former member of the CBC, assumed the leadership of those promoting this tough new stand against the "military thugs." The president said that Gray's role was to restore freedom and democracy in Haiti, and Clinton endorsed a policy calling for the unconditional surrender of the Haitian military dictatorship.[81]

Gray condemned the leaders of the military coup and eliminated negotiations for solving the crisis. He told a journalist, "We're only open to one negotiation, and the negotiation is: when are you leaving? What time are you departing? There is no negotiation about recognizing the illegal de facto government. No negotiation about any coalition government.

They've had their chance."[82] Gray implemented the CBC's plan to ensure that Haitian refugees got a fair hearing with legal representation and to restore democracy in Haiti, even if by American military intervention.

A final attempt at negotiation came about when a high-level team consisting of former president Jimmy Carter, former chairman of the Joint Chiefs of Staff Colin Powell, and Senator Sam Nunn of Georgia went to Haiti. In the eleventh hour, Haitian military leaders elected to leave, but only when they realized the American military was on its way to occupy Haiti. Relief was in sight for everyone. Walter Fauntroy suggested that the effort helped rescue "the Haitian people and the American people from what would have been a disastrous situation for all, had we been forced to shoot our way into that tortured nation."[83] On September 19, 1994, Americans conducted a friendly takeover of Haiti. Cédras and the military clique capitulated. On October 15, 1994, Aristide returned to Haiti and was officially reinstated as president.

The events reinforced the links between Haitians and African Americans and the perceptions African Americans had of Haiti. African Americans, through race identification, supported aid to the Haitian boat people. They took action with hunger strikes, marches, and protests via the mass media. It is not surprising that they took credit for solving the crisis: This "winning presidential strategy in Haiti started because of Black American activism over Haitian conditions."[84] Besides the actions taken by various African American leaders, one can point to General Colin Powell's involvement. In the eleventh hour of the negotiations, he was the key figure in avoiding hostile military intervention. Even at the end, Fauntroy declared that the plan Clinton executed included the "first two of an eight point plan that I have earnestly tried to get staffers for both you and President Bush to adopt since first this crisis developed three years ago."[85] Haitians, too, recognized the ties between the two peoples. "The horror of the Haiti situation is also an African American catastrophe. We need your prayers. We need your acknowledgment that we are one,"[86] wrote Haitian American novelist Edwidge Danticat. Into the twenty-first century race remains the strong linkage binding Haitians and African Americans.

Epilogue

The Ongoing Struggle

It has also been my experience that the Haitian people are eager to build strong working relations with Africans in America as a vehicle to enhance their struggle. There is a general understanding their struggle is our struggle and our struggle is their struggle. (1999)

Ron Daniels, *New Pittsburgh Courier*

The story of Haitians and African Americans over the last 500 years has been one of a long, hard-fought struggle. Uprooted from their African homeland against their will by slave traders and sold as chattel to New World plantation owners, these two peoples have resisted oppression. Throughout five centuries, they have succeeded in winning many times. Displaying great ingenuity, both Haitians and African Americans have employed comparable strategies to gain the rights and privileges of citizenship.

As the war against oppression continues, economic empowerment is the primary objective driving Haitians and African Americans. It is important to remember that Haiti's political independence has always been in trouble due to her long-standing desperate economic conditions. Today Haiti ranks as the most underdeveloped country in the western hemisphere and among the least developed countries in the world.[1] On the other hand, even though 33.5 million African Americans constitute one of the largest black communities in the world outside Africa and are an integral part of the most powerful economy in the world, a large segment still experiences the social ills of unemployment and poverty.[2] The dreams of nineteenth-century leaders in both societies for rehabilitation and elevation of the race have yet to be wholly fulfilled. This explains why the struggle for freedom and equality still boils at various levels.

On the Racial Front

Racism is the main obstacle standing in the way of the empowerment of African descendants today. In both Saint-Domingue and the American colonies, race was the divider and a cause for slavery. In the cultures of Europe and the western hemisphere, the slave codes reflected deep-seated racist ideologies and attitudes towards both Haitians and African Americans. Seeing these peoples as chattel, those who sold others into slavery usurped a basic right that should be given to all mankind: freedom. Colonists and their supporters used race as a moral and psychological weapon to dehumanize their slave property, propagating a myth of "natural inferiority." On their liberation from slavery, the former slaves discovered that segregation and discrimination became instruments for continuation of racist attitudes.

Today, because of the universal and perpetual mixing of people, even the question of race is up for debate. Modern scholars focus instead on the "gene pool" that generates a "cluster of traits" characterizing people. As explained by anthropologist Audrey Smedley, race as a mode of classifying human beings appeared in the language of the Spanish, Portuguese, Italians, French, Germans, Dutch, and English as these groups established colonial empires in the New World and Asia and set about dealing with the heterogeneous populations of these empires.[3]

The race factor has proven to be the most powerful link between Haitians and African Americans. Leaders from both societies joined hands during the latter part of the nineteenth century in a fight against racism. Prominent Haitian and black American social scientists argued against the racial-inferiority theory.

During the early decades of the twentieth century, the National Association for the Advancement of Colored People played a major role against the occupation of Haiti by the United States. The NAACP saw a correlation between Haitian independence and the dignity of the black race. In an unprecedented move, James Weldon Johnson urged the withdrawal of American troops from the island as he launched the NAACP into international affairs. More recently, African American leaders became deeply involved in the crisis of the Haitian boat people. This intervention was justified solely on the basis of race. The Black Caucus in the United States Congress, along with the NAACP and other human-rights organizations, identified themselves with the refugees' cause, arguing that the treatment of refugees by the United States government was racially motivated.

With the recent arrival of Haitian immigrants, race continues to unite Haitians and African Americans. In New York, as Haitians live in the same neighborhoods as African Americans, these first-generation immigrants maintain their identity by remaining a distinct ethnic group. They remember their Haitian background by establishing a business network that includes grocery stores, restaurants, barbershops, music stores, and travel agencies. The Haitian media now includes the newspapers *Haiti Observateur, Haiti Progrès* in New York, and *Haiti en Marche* in Miami, as well as a number of radio and television programs, thus solidifying Haitian culture and marking out their differences from the African American communities.[4]

Yet Haitian ethnicity takes a back seat when, as with African Americans, Haitian Americans experience racism in the United States. In her study on the relations between the two groups, Flore Zéphir concluded that "The similarities of their experiences as victims of racial discrimination and relegation to the bottom rung of the social ladder . . . draws Haitian immigrants toward native Black Americans."[5] So at times, both groups have put aside their differences to join forces combating their common enemy, racism.

Racism is seen in the unemployment numbers where African Americans and Haitians have fewer jobs than their white counterparts. Opportunities are still limited for people of color. Whites have found justification for their racism in culturally biased intelligence tests; they hire blacks but foster a glass ceiling in corporations where blacks are stopped from promotion to higher-level jobs; they fail or refuse to provide programs that help blacks improve themselves.

Color and Class

While the historical linkage between Africans and Europeans in the Americas is a story of relationships between blacks and whites, this is a gross oversimplification. As Africans, native Indians, and Europeans commingled in the New World, a blending of black and white skin colors resulted.

Mulattoes emerged as a distinct group in both Saint-Domingue and the United States though they experienced somewhat different fortunes in their respective societies. In Haiti, mulattoes joined forces with the black masses in ousting the French. But once that goal was achieved, they quickly seized both political and economic power. Their own class interests superseded any national interests they may have had. To build a separate and ruling class, the mulattoes made themselves superior to the black masses just as the Europeans had done to them. Katherine Dunham, an African American dancer and anthropologist who spent many years in Haiti, observed during the 1930s that "The first social regulation in Haiti was to stay closely knit to your own color or degree of black-white blood-mixture grouping—which was actually a caste, being exclusive, endogamous, inherent, nontransferable, immutable."[6] More than a half century later, the separation of the Haitian peasant and elite classes has yet to be bridged. The class and color issue is one of the most important internal causes of Haiti's underdevelopment.

The fortunes of mulattoes took an altogether different turn in the United States. While the status of free Haitian people of color was elevated after their revolution, the standing of freedmen, both blacks and mulattoes, declined in the United States. The census of 1850 listed 406,000 mulattoes representing 11.2 percent of the Negro population and 1.8 percent of the national total.[7] Mulattoes maintained group cohesiveness, social status, and economic power in the upper and lower South until 1850. During Reconstruction, however, the motivation to maintain white power threatened their growth and freedom. Mulattoes ultimately merged with blacks in the 1920s to become a single ethnic group.

Both Haitians and African Americans have had to grapple with the traditional issue of elitism. In black America, W. E. B. Du Bois championed the idea of a "talented tenth" of the overall black population with the goal of building a black leadership that was necessary for any group's advancement. The civil rights movement of the 1960s allowed that segment of African Americans to climb the political and economic ladder. Unfortunately, there was a growing division between this black middle class and the underclass of blacks who were confined in the inner cities. Historically those in the underclass have "weak connections with the world of productivity, little education, social and geographic isolation, family instability, high rates of crime, drug addiction and dependency."[8]

As Haiti prepares to celebrate the bicentennial of her independence, the elite have failed to develop a nation commensurate with the aspirations of all her citizens. Elitism has transformed the dream of a haven for blacks into an oligarchy of "a few thousand families who continue to embrace a sort of feudal life that is hard to believe exists at the end of the twentieth century. The less than one percent of the population represented by these 'ruling families' controls over 44 percent of the wealth in Haiti."[9] The urban masses and the peasantry, which represent the backbone of the economy, must languish in poverty. Color and class in Haiti impedes the national unity necessary to conquer racism and promote urgently needed social and economic development.

Culture

Since Haitians and African Americans have inherited divergent cultural influences, it is reasonable they would also have disparate cultural views. They are like brothers and sisters, born of the same mother—Africa, who grew up in different homes and developed different values and lifestyles. Though never abandoning their cultural heritage, they each embraced aspects of their former slave owners' customs and institutions.

Cultural differences played a major role in the failed emigration of African Americans to Haiti during the nineteenth century. That same diversity also inspired Booker T. Washington to recommend the Anglo-Saxon educational system as key to Haiti's development whereas the Haitian elite was rooted in a French-style classical education.

Despite these marked differences some very strong ties bind Haitians and African Americans. They share a high level of consciousness of their African cultural heritage. African Americans always thought of Haiti not only as the guardian of freedom but also as a black cultural mecca.

Anthropologist Zora Neale Hurston looked at Haiti for a new direction to her Vodou research. Katherine Dunham found in Haiti endless resources for her dance and anthropology interests. African American writers discovered Haitian history to be inspirational in fulfilling the dream of rehabilitating the race, a dream prevalent during the Harlem Renaissance. They created characters inspired by Haitian heroes. In *Emperor of Haiti*, Langston Hughes portrayed Dessalines as the dreamer of a great civilization. Leslie Pinckeney Hill's play *Toussaint L'Ouverture* refutes the lies that the black race "has no traditions, no characters of world importance, no record of substantial contributions to civilization."[10]

Strong alliances were forged between Haitian and African American writers. Langston Hughes and Jacques Roumain shared a common social and political consciousness. Both produced works that extolled black culture and encouraged other black writers and artists to draw on their own heritage rather than imitate Western art.

Black artists are now making significant contributions to the arts and discovering a new pride in their black identity. Mercer Cook has shown how René Piquion, James Weldon Johnson, Arna Bontemps, Dantès Bellegarde, and others have "tried to bridge the cultural and geographical gap which separates three million Haitians from their Negro brothers in the United States."[11]

In this atmosphere of cooperation, Walter White forged an alliance with Haitian leaders Dumarsais Estimé and Paul Eugène Magloire that has proved productive in improving Haitian–African American relations. With White at the helm, the NAACP became a public relations agency for Haiti. White polished Haiti's image abroad and promoted its economic development.

Religion

Religion is the soul-force that "turns sorrow into joy, crying into laughter, and defeat into victory."[12] It has played a major role in the survival of Haitians and African Americans during five centuries in the New World. It has also liberated them from oppression.

The two groups have experienced religion in the Americas through different routes. In the Caribbean, the officially Catholic Haiti maintained her strong tradition of African religion through the practices of Vodou. African Americans, widely influenced by Anglo-Saxon Protestantism, saw Vodou as an impediment to Haiti's development. African American missionaries crusaded for the extinction of Vodou to promote their Protestant Christianity. Other African Americans embraced Vodou, becoming active practitioners themselves.

Vodou remains deeply rooted in Haitian culture. Today with the Haitian refugees' migration to major American cities, Vodou practice is slowly moving into American culture. For instance, Vodou is beginning to be practiced in New York, Miami, and New Orleans. In 1997, Vodou art was exhibited in such major museums as UCLA's Fowler Museum of Cultural History and New York's Museum of Natural History.

Contrast in Political Traditions

Haitians and African Americans inherited contrasting political traditions. Bishop James Theodore Holly viewed Anglo-Saxon political institutions as wholly suitable for transforming Haiti's system of despotism, yet Haitians held to their French political traditions as they decried America's horrible system of racist supremacy.

The Haitian political system has clearly failed to promote the development of the country since Haiti still ranks as the poorest in the western hemisphere. Haiti has always claimed to be a democracy, yet she has never lived up to this ideal. While African Americans historically considered Haiti the land of freedom, they never overlooked her tradition of dictatorship and violations of human rights. During the nineteenth century, African Americans were dismayed by the chronic political chaos plaguing Haiti, fearing it would hurt their own chances for citizenship in America's democracy.

During the second half of the twentieth century, black America's perception of Haiti as the torchbearer of freedom was overshadowed by the darker image of a country foundering in a political and economic morass. Under the Duvaliers (1957–86), oppression and human-rights violations were common. Even in post-Duvalier Haiti, harsh militarism prevailed.

Since 1994, however, dramatic changes have taken place. President Aristide replaced Haiti's army with a police force and guaranteed the security of all Haitians. A second democratic election resulted in the election of René Preval to the presidency. Haitian democracy still searches for a sure footing.

What does the future hold for relations between Haitians and African Americans? Today countries are moving more and more to the beat of a common drum proclaiming the right to freedom for all of the peoples of the earth. In spite of what the Russians are doing to the Chechnyans, the Serbs tried to do to the rest of Yugoslavia, and the Iraqis have done with certain opposing tribes, freedom and respect for human rights may be growing between old enemies in places like Northern Ireland and Israel and its surrounding area. In the eloquent words of Martin Luther King Jr., "All men are interdependent and thereby involved in a single process. We are inevitably our brother's keeper because of the interrelated structure of reality."[13] Haitians and African Americans will continue to reach out to one another and, building on their cultural and historical ties, develop stronger friendships, understanding, and compassion.

Notes

Introduction

1. Brown, *History and Present Condition of St. Domingo,* 33.
2. Franklin, *From Slavery to Freedom,* 72–73.
3. Franklin, *From Slavery to Freedom,* 208.
4. Price, *Maroon Societies,* 1–30.
5. Ott, *The Haitian Revolution,* 47–51; James, *Black Jacobins, 85–90.*
6. Debien, "Saint-Domingue Refugees in Cuba," 34.
7. Washington, *Writings of Thomas Jefferson,* vol. 4, 20 and 49.
8. Ott, *The Haitian Revolution,* 58–60. James, *Negro Revolt,* 11–13.
9. Tyson, *Toussaint Louverture,* 96.
10. Pickering to Stevens, 20 April 1799, Dept. of State consular dispatches, Cap Haitien series, vol. 4.
11. Dunbar-Nelson, "People of Color in Louisiana," 376.
12. Aptheker, *American Negro Slave Revolts,* 96.
13. Ibid., 96–97.
14. Egerton, *Gabriel Rebellion,* 46.
15. Dupuy, *Haiti in the World Economy,* 73; Trouillot, *La guerre de l'indepen-dence d'Haiti,* 300.
16. Williams, *From Columbus to Castro,* 254.
17. Redpath, *Guide to Hayti,* 66.

Chapter 1. Haiti: The Sun of Hope, 1800–1865

1. Dewey, "Independence of Hayti," 175.
2. Williams, "Discourse in St. Phillip's Church," in *Black Abolitionist Papers,* reel 1.
3. Vashon to Douglass and Delany, *North Star,* 21 August 1848, in *Black Abolitionist Papers,* reel 5.
4. Fishel and Quarles, *The Negro American,* 63.
5. Steward, *The Haitian Revolution,* iv–v. See also Patrick Bellegarde Smith, *Haiti: The Breached Citadel,* 45.
6. Bracey, Meier, and Rudwick, *Free Blacks in America,* 1.
7. Winch, *Philadelphia's Black Elite,* 1.
8. Bracey, Meier, and Rudwick, *Free Blacks in America,* 3.
9. Franklin, *From Slavery to Freedom,* 155.
10. Bracey, Meier, and Rudwick, *Black Nationalism in America,* 20.

11. Ibid., 11.

12. *Freedom's Journal*, 16 March 1827.

13. Payne, *History of the African Methodist Episcopal Church*, 477.

14. Childs, *French Refugee Life in the United States*, 33–35, 51–54, 142–146.

15. Nash, *Forging Freedom*, 141

16. Woodson, *Education of the Negro prior to 1861*, 8.

17. Nash, *Forging Freedom*, 142.

18. Sherwood, *Oblates' Hundred and One Years*, 7.

19. Ibid., 35.

20. Ibid., 37.

21. Hunt, *Haiti's Influence on Antebellum America*, 46–47; Lachance, "1809 Immigration," 110–11.

22. Desdunes, *Our People and Our History*, 7–8, 92–95.

23. Herrin, *Creole Aristocracy*, 95–96; *Collier's Encyclopedia*, vol. 3 (1995), 217–19.

24. McConnell, *Negro Troops of Antebellum Louisiana*, 70.

25. Lachance, "1809 Immigration," 128.

26. Sherwood, *Oblates' Hundred and One Years*, 15–16; Johnson, *Black Savannah*, 61–62.

27. Garnet, "Past, Present Condition, and Destiny of the Colored Race," in *Black Abolitionist Papers*, reel 4.

28. Watkins, "Address," 170.

29. *Genius of Universal Emancipation* 2 (22 December 1822): 93.

30. Dewey, *Genius of Universal Emancipation* 4 (August 1825): 175.

31. Aurora, "Haitien Independence," 20.

32. Douglass to Cornish, 1 January 1838, in *Colored American*, 3 March 1838.

33. Harold to Delany and Douglass, *North Star*, 21 April 1848, in *Black Abolitionists Papers*, reel 4.

34. *Colored American*, 11 March 1836, in *Black Abolitionist Papers*, reel 1.

35. Woodson, *The Negro in Our History*, 134.

36. Rock to Douglass, 19 August 1858, in *Black Abolitionist Papers*, reel 11. See also Rock, speech at annual meeting of Massachusetts Anti-Slavery Society in Boston, 27 January 1860, in *Black Abolitionist Papers*, reel 12.

37. Redpath, *Guide to Hayti*, 66.

38. Bird, *The Black Man or Haytian Independence*, 52.

39. Cole, *Henri Christophe*, 242.

40. Mackenzie, *Notes on Haiti*, vol. 1, 25.

41. Wilson, *History of Pittsburgh*, 704.

42. Rollin, *Life and Public Services of Martin R. Delany*, 29.

43. Aptheker, *Documentary History of the Negro People*, 87.

44. Brown, *The Rising Son*, 172.

45. Crummell, "Hope for Africa," *Black Abolitionist Papers*, reel 8.

46. Phillips, "Eulogy of Toussaint Louverture," 74.

47. Cited in Logan, *Diplomatic Relations*, 172.

48. *Colored American*, 18 March 1836, in *Black Abolitionist Papers*, reel 1; *Niles' Register* 22 (23 March 1822): 49.

49. Proceedings of the Colored National Convention Held in Rochester on 6, 7, 8 July 1853, in *Black Abolitionist Papers*, reel 8.

50. Boyer to Dodge, 16 August 1821, in *Genius of Universal Emancipation*, 23 August 1823, 45.

51. Montague, *Haiti and the United States*, 53.

52. "The Federal Government vs. the Free People of Color," in *Black Abolitionist Papers*, reel 9.

53. *Genius of Universal Emancipation* 4 (August 1825): 168.

54. Ibid., 169.

55. Foner, "John Browne Russwurn," 396.

56. Ibid.

57. Aptheker, *Documentary History of the Negro People*, 84–85.

58. *Freedom's Journal*, 16 March 1827.

59. Asante, *Afrocentricity*, 2.

60. Plummer, "Afro-American Response," 127.

61. Douglass to Cornish, 1 January 1838, in *Black Abolitionist Papers*, reel 2.

62. Hunt, *Remarks on Hayti*, 19.

63. *North Star*, 27 October 1848, in *Black Abolitionist Papers*, reel 5.

64. Vashon to Gerrit Smith, 16 November 1850, in Quarles, "Letters from Negro Leaders," in *Journal of Negro History* 27 (October 1942): 444.

65. Smith, *Lecture on the Haytien Revolution*, 24–25, 28.

66. Ibid., 27.

67. Holly, "Vindication of the Capacity," 22.

68. Ibid., 49.

69. Ibid., 64

70. Holly, "Thoughts on Hayti," 186.

71. *African Repository* 4 (April 1828): 53. See also Fishel and Quarles, *The Negro American*, 82.

72. Bracey, Meier, and Rudwick, *Black Nationalism*, 52.

73. Ripley, *Black Abolitionist Papers*, vol. 2, Canada 1830–65, 274.

74. Aptheker, *Documentary History of the Negro People*, 434.

75. Foner and Walker, *Proceedings of the Black National and State Conventions*, 335.

76. Matthewson, "Abraham Bishop," 151.

77. *Genius of Universal Emancipation* 3 (November 1823): 77.

78. Lundy, "Address to the Public," 1.

79. Garrison to Benson, 18 August 1836, in Merrill, *Letters of William Garrison*, 159.

80. Douglass, *Narrative of the Life of Frederick Douglass*, 49.

81. *North Star*, January 1848, in Frederick Douglass Papers, Library of Congress.

82. Bracey, Meier, and Rudwick, *Black Nationalism*, 75.

83. Garnet, "Past, Present Condition, and Destiny," in *Black Abolitionist Papers,* reel 4.

84. Aptheker, *Documentary History of the Negro People,* 403.

85. Williams, ed., *African American Encyclopedia,* vol. 6, 1640–41.

86. Walker, "Appeal to the Colored Citizens of the World," 146.

87. Berlin, "After Nat Turner," 146.

88. Ibid., 146.

89. *Genius of Universal Emancipation,* August 1822, 44.

90. Carroll, *Slave Insurrections,* 95.

91. Aptheker, *American Negro Slave Revolts,* 275.

92. Brown, "St. Domingo: Its Revolution and Its Patriots," in *Black Abolitionist Papers,* reel 8.

93. Bowers, "How Can It Be Abolished," *Black Abolitionist Papers,* reel 13.

94. Langston, *The World's Anti-Slavery Movement,* 52.

95. Benjamin, letter to editor, *Northern Star and Freemen's Advocate,* 31 March 1842.

96. H. Ford Douglass, in speech 23 September 1860, *Black Abolitionist Papers,* vol. 5, 88.

97. Langston, *The World's Anti-Slavery Movement,* 12.

98. Langston, *The World's Anti-Slavery Movement,* 22.

99. Pennington, *Black Abolitionist Papers,* vol. 1, 106.

100. Rock to Douglass, 19 August 1858, in *Black Abolitionist Papers,* reel 11.

Chapter 2. The Quest for an Asylum, 1824–65

1. *Anglo-African Magazine* 1, October 1859, n.p.

2. Cited in Porter, *Early Negro Writings,* 279.

3. Pemberton to Cuffee, 27 September 1808, in *Black Abolitionist Papers,* reel 16/ 0815. See also Cuffee to Pemberton, 14 September 1808, reel 16/0814.

4. Miller, *Search for a Black Nationality,* viii.

5. Meinig, *The Shaping of America,* vol. 2, 191; Garrison, *Thoughts on African Colonization,* 111.

6. *Niles' Register,* 3 July 1824, 284.

7. Jefferson to Monroe, 24 November 1801, in Washington, *The Writings of Jefferson,* 419–23.

8. Finley to Mumford, 14 February 1815, in the *African Repository* 1 (March 1825): 2.

9. Staudenvaus, *The African Colonization Movement,* 19–20.

10. *Black Abolitionist Papers,* reel 17/0242; Garrison, *Thoughts on African Colonization,* part 2, 9.

11. Cornish to Cox, 4 December 1834, in *Black Abolitionist Papers,* reel 8.

12. *Rights of All,* 16 October 1829, in *Black Abolitionist Papers,* reel 17/0630.

13. Garrison, *Thoughts on African Colonization,* part 2, 4.

14. *Liberator,* 12 March 1831, in *Black Abolitionist Papers,* reel 8.

15. Harvey, *Sketches of Haiti,* 237.

16. Griggs and Prator, *Henri Christophe and Thomas Clarkson*, 124.

17. White, "Prince Saunders," 526–35.

18. Prince Saunders, "A Memoir," in Porter, *Early Negro Writings*, 272.

19. Ibid., 274–75.

20. Staudenvaus, *The African Colonization Movement*, 64–65.

21. Griggs and Prator, *Henry Christophe and Thomas Clarkson*, 229.

22. Dupuy, *Haiti in the World Economy*, 95; Plummer, *Haiti and United States*, 25–26.

23. Coradin, *Histoire diplomatique d'Haiti*, 138–40.

24. *Niles' Register* 18 (1 July 1820): 326.

25. Leon, *Propos d'histoire d'Haiti*, 196–97; *Genius of Universal Emancipation*, 17 September 1825, 28.

26. Dewey, *Correspondence*, 3–11.

27. Ibid., 7.

28. Ibid., 15.

29. "Emigration to Haiti," *Niles' Register*, 14 August 1824, 400.

30. Cited in Jackson, "Origins of Pan-African Nationalism," 233.

31. Plummer, *Haiti and the United States*, 31. See also Winch, *Philadelphia's Black Elite*, 56.

32. *Genius of Universal Emancipation* 3 (September 12, 1825): 19.

33. *New York Commercial Advertizer*, 21 June 1824, in Granville, *Biographie*, 122.

34. Staudenvaus, *The African Colonization Movement*, 84.

35. *Genius of Universal Emancipation* 4 (September 1825): 86.

36. Granville, *Biographie*, 146.

37. *Niles' Register*, 13 November 1824.

38. *Genius of Universal Emancipation* 4 (November 1824): 27.

39. *New York Daily Advertiser*, 26 June 1824, in Granville, *Biographie*, 160.

40. Granville to Boyer, 9 July 1824, in Granville, *Biographie*, 216 (my translation).

41. *Niles' Register*, 23 October 1824, 114.

42. Lundy, "Emigration to Hayti," *Genius of Universal Emancipation* 4 (November 1824): 18.

43. Dewey to Granville *fils*, 23 May 1865, in Granville, *Biographie*, 244.

44. Garrison, *Thoughts on African Colonization*, part 2, 5.

45. Hunt, *Remarks on Hayti*, 11.

46. Armstrong to Adams, 4 January 1825, Dept. of State consular dispatches, Port-au-Prince series.

47. Leon, *Propos d'histoire d'Haiti*, 205 (my translation).

48. National Gazette, 19 June 1824, in Granville, *Biographie*, 116.

49. *Commercial Advertizer*, in Granville, *Biographie*, 144.

50. Hunt, *Remarks on Hayti and the Mulatto*, 14; Winch, *Philadelphia's Black Elite*, 55.

51. Jackson, "Origins of Pan-African Nationalism," 116.

52. Ibid., 262.

53. Bird, *The Black Man or Haitian Independence,* 152.

54. Léon, *Propos d'histoire d'Haiti,* 204.

55. Cited in Bell, *Black Separatism and the Caribbean,* 2.

56. Delany, *Condition, Elevation, Emigration,* 14.

57. Bracey, Meier, and Rudwick, *Black Nationalism in America,* 67. See also McAdoo, *Pre–Civil War Black Nationalism,* 67.

58. Delany, *Condition, Elevation, Emigration,* 45–46

59. Bell, ed., *Minutes of the Proceedings of the National Negro Conventions,* 9.

60. Miller, *Search for a Black Nationality,* 101; Sterling, *Making of an Afro-American,* 39.

61. George Lawrence Jr., "Aid to Hayti," *Weekly Anglo-African,* 21 April 1861.

62. H. Douglass Ford, "The Haytian Movement," *Weekly Anglo-African,* 20 April 1861.

63. William Wells Brown, "Lecture on Haiti," *Pine and Palm,* 31 August 1861.

64. William Watkins in speech at meeting of Colored Education Institute, *Liberator,* 30 August 1861.

65. Cited in Bell, *Black Separatism,* 65.

66. A. P. Smith, letter to editor, *Weekly Anglo-African,* 23 February 1861.

67. Desdunes, *Our People and Our History,* 109–10.

68. Ibid., 112–13.

69. Holly to Blair, 30 January 1858, *Journal of Negro History* 10, no. 4 (October 1925): 496.

70. Whitfield to Blair, 1 February 1858, *Journal of Negro History* 10, no. 4 (October 1925): 765.

71. Vashon to Redpath, 3 June 1861, in *Pine and Palm,* 3 August 1861, in *Black Abolitionist Papers,* reel 13.

72. "Emigration to Haiti," *Douglass Monthly* 3 (January 1861): 386.

73. Redpath, *A Guide to Hayti,* 97.

74. "Emigration to Haiti," *Douglass Monthly* 3 (January 1861): 387.

75. Ibid., 386.

76. *Weekly Anglo-American,* 18 February 1806, in *Black Abolitionist Papers,* reel 12.

77. *Black Abolitionist Papers,* reel 12.

78. Newman's letter from Haiti, in *Black Abolitionist Papers,* reel 12.

79. "Emigration to Haiti," *Douglass Monthly* 3 (January 1861): 387.

80. Redpath, *A Guide to Hayti,* 9.

81. "Haytian Advertisements," *Douglass Monthly* 3 (August 1861): 3–4.

82. Hunt, *Remarks on Hayti,* 3–4.

83. Delany to Holly, 15 January 1861, in *Chatham Planet,* 21 January 1861; Sterling, *Making of an Afro-American,* 221.

84. Smith to Garnet, 5 January 1861, in *Black Abolitionist Papers,* vol. 5, 101.

85. William to *Chatham Planet,* 21 June 1860, in *Black Abolitionist Papers,* reel 12/0583.

86. J. B. Smith, letter to editor, *Weekly Anglo-African*, 15 December 1860, in *Black Abolitionist Papers*, reel 13.

87. Cary to Redpath, 26 August 1861, in *Black Abolitionist Papers*, vol.2, 449–451.

88. Miller, *Search for a Black Nationality*, 242.

89. Bell, *Black Separatism*, 7–8

90. Sanchez to Hamilton, *Weekly Anglo-African*, 1 March 1862.

91. Isaiah Jones, letter to editor, *Weekly Anglo-African*, 15 April 1862.

92. Harding to Steward, 4 September 1867, Dept. of State consular dispatches, Port-au-Prince series, 1835–1906.

93. *Weekly Anglo-African*, 15 March 1862.

94. Mary Ann Shadd to Robert Hamilton, *Weekly Anglo- African*, 28 September 1861.

95. "Haitian Emigration in New Haven," *Weekly Anglo-African*, 25 January 1862.

96. Buckeye, "Haytian Movement Dead in the West," *Weekly Anglo-African*, 12 April 1862.

97. See *African Repository*, October 1862, in *Black Abolitionist Papers*, reel 14.

98. "Letters from St. Mark Emigrants," *Douglass Monthly* 5 (July 1862): 677.

99. Certificate of naturalization of A. B. Williamson of Maryland in Archives of Schomburg Center, New York.

100. Montague, *Haiti and the United States*, 76; Seraille, "Afro-American Emigration to Haiti During the Civil War," 192–93.

101. Seward to Whidden, 6 January 1863, Dept. of State Consular dispatches, Port-au-Prince series, 1835–1906.

Chapter 3. Religion as a Weapon, 1824–1900

1. Payne, *History of the African Methodist Episcopal Church*, 476–77.

2. Holly, "Disabilities," 220.

3. Simpson, *Religious Cults of the Caribbean*, 305. See also Genovese, *From Rebellion to Revolution*, 28.

4. Mbiti, *Introduction to African Religion*, 9.

5. Mbiti, *African Religions and Philosophy*, 188.

6. Barrett, *Soul-Force*, 95.

7. Métraux, *Haiti: Black Peasants and Their Religion*, 59.

8. *International Encyclopedia of the Social Sciences*.

9. Laguerre, *Voodoo and Politics in Haiti*, 35.

10. Bellegarde, *La nation haitienne*, 65 (my translation).

11. Korngold, *Citizen Toussaint*, 41.

12. E. L. Blackshear to Secretary of State, 13 May 1912, Records of the Dept. of State, file 838.404.

13. Bodin, *Voodoo Past and Present*, 9–13.

14. Tallant, *Voodoo in New Orleans*, 56.

15. Du Bois, *The Negro Church*, 5.

16. Starobin, *Denmark Vesey*, 5.

17. Sobel, *Trabelin' On*, 58.

18. Simpson, *Black Religion in the New World*, 216.

19. Smith, *Climbing Jacob's Ladder*, 30. See also Sobel, *Trabelin' On*, 101.

20. Simpson, *Black Religion*, 225.

21. Albanese, *America: Religions and Religion*, 119–23. Sobel, *Trabelin' On*, 45.

22. Nash, *Forging Freedom*, 141; Johnson, *Black Savannah*, 17.

23. Lee, *Memoir of Pierre Toussaint*, 56.

24. Ibid., 51, 82.

25. Sherwood, *Oblates' Hundred and One Years*, 81.

26. Ibid., 88.

27. Cited in Du Bois, *The Negro Church*, 22.

28. Thurman, *Deep River and the Negro Spiritual*, 13. See also Genovese, *From Rebellion to Revolution*, 6.

29. Simpson, *Religious Cults of the Caribbean*, 306.

30. *Niles' Register* 2 (18 January 1817): 347.

31. *Niles' Register* 12 (22 March 1817): 58.

32. Cited in Métraux, *Voodoo in Haiti*, 50. See also St. John, *Hayti or the Black Republic*, 276–77.

33. St. John, *Hayti or the Black Republic*, 294.

34. Ibid., 286.

35. See Métraux, *Voodoo in Haiti*, 351–58.

36. St. John, *Hayti or the Black Republic*, 281.

37. Nicholls, *From Dessalines to Duvalier*, 118.

38. Cited in Pompilus, *Louis Joseph Janvier par lui-même*, 45.

39. Bird, *The Black Man or Haitian Independence*, 153.

40. Payne, *History of the African Methodist Episcopal Church*, 482.

41. Stanford to Steward, 20 March 1862, Dept. of State consular dispatches, Aux Cayes series.

42. George, *Segregated Sabbaths*, 118.

43. Holly, "Objects and Method," 300.

44. Cited in Charles Mossell, Introduction, *Toussaint L'Ouverture*.

45. Pressoir, *Le protestantisme haitien*, vol. 2, 23–24; Payne, *History of the A.M.E. Church*, 480.

46. Payne, *History of the A.M.E. Church*, 479.

47. Langston, *From the Virginia Plantation*, 394–95.

48. Holly to Denison, August 1855, James Theodore Holly Papers.

49. Ibid.

50. Holly, "Thoughts on Hayti," 187.

51. Holly, "Disabilities," 220.

52. Walker, "Appeal to the Colored Citizens of the World," 71.

53. Holly, "Disabilities," 220–221.

54. Holly, "Objects and Method," 299–300.

55. Holly to Hare, 30 May 1872, in *Haiti Papers*.

56. Dean, *Defender of the Race,* 44–47.

57. Holly to Denison, 1 August 1868, *Haiti Papers.*

58. Annual Report of the Bishop of Haiti, 30 June 1879, in Holly, *Haiti Papers.*

59. Holly to Denison, 26 October 1868.

60. Holly to Denison, 13 April 1867.

61. Holly to Denison, 5 February 1868.

62. Holly to Denison, 13 April 1867.

63. Holly to Denison, 27 March 1876.

64. Martin, "Frederick Douglass," 70.

65. "Report of the Bishop of Haiti," October 1877, in Holly, *Haiti Papers.*

66. Holly, "For the Advance," *Haiti Papers.*

67. Tiffany, *A History of the Protestant Episcopal Church in the United States,* 516–17.

68. Archin to Holly, 27 April 1869.

69. Alonzo Potter Burgess Holly, *Religion and Public Charities in Haiti* (Port-au-Prince, n.d), 6.

70. Romain, *Le protestantisme dans la société haitienne,* 310 (my translation).

Chapter 4. Partners in Defending the Race, 1869–1915

1. Meinig, *The Shaping of America,* vol. 2, 191.

2. Cooper, *Twenty Modern Americans,* 144–47.

3. Miller, *Black Presence in American Foreign Affairs,* 7–9.

4. Williams, *History of the Negro Race in America,* 423–24. See also Foner and Walker, *Black National and State Conventions,* 71.

5. Franklin, *From Slavery to Freedom,* 431.

6. Sydney Tobin, "Don Carlos Ebenezer Bassett," in *Dictionary of American Negro Biography,* 32.

7. Heinl, "America's First Black Diplomat," 20.

8. Paquin, *Les haitiens,* 47–52.

9. Langston, *From the Virginia Plantation,* 360.

10. Ibid., 384.

11. Ibid., 385.

12. Ibid., 400.

13. Brown, *A Black Diplomat in Haiti,* vol. 1, 43.

14. Holland, *Frederick Douglass,* 389.

15. *Philadelphia Enquirer,* 1 December 1889.

16. Brown, *A Black Diplomat in Haiti,* 43.

17. A. P. Holly, "What Hayti Has Done," *New York Age,* 27 July 1889, in the *Frederick Douglass Papers.*

18. Brown, *A Black Diplomat in Haiti,* vol. 1, 45.

19. Brantley, "Black Diplomacy and Frederick Douglass," 205.

20. *Academic American Encyclopedia,* vol. 13, 117.

21. Douglass, "Haiti and the United States," 340.

22. Martin Sears, "Frederick Douglass and the Mission to Haiti," 223. See also

Plummer, *Haiti and the Great Powers*, 27.

23. Brown, *A Black Diplomat in Haiti*, vol. 2, 11.

24. Bellegarde, "Sunrise Memorial Service," in *Papers of the NAACP*, part 11, reel 8.

25. Holland, *Frederick Douglass*, 390.

26. Ibid., 395.

27. Douglass, "Lecture on Haiti," in the *Frederick Douglass Papers*.

28. Mossell, *Toussaint Louverture*, 477–78.

29. Ibid., 478.

30. Holland, *Frederick Douglass*, 387. Bontemps, *Free at Last*, 296–97.

31. Douglass, "Lecture on Haiti," in *Frederick Douglass Papers*.

32. Advertisements, *Voice of the Negro*, March 1904.

33. *Voice of the Negro*, April 1904, 140.

34. Fishel and Quarles, *The Negro American*, 91.

35. Cited in Karier, *Shaping the American Educational State*, 134

36. Ibid., 131–32.

37. Plummer, *Haiti and the Great Powers*, 71.

38. St. John, *Hayti or the Black Republic*, xi.

39. Irvine, *The Rise of the Colored Races*, 156–72.

40. Nicholls, *From Dessalines to Duvalier*, 128. See also Hazzard-Gordon, "Afrocentrism in a Multicultural Democracy," 21.

41. Firmin, *De l'égalité des races humaines*, vi-xviii.

42. Steward, *Roosevelt and Haiti*, 434.

43. Firmin to Magloire, 2 December 1907, in *Lettres de Saint-Thomas*, 393.

44. See Lenoir, *Le biographe* in *Papers of Frederick Douglass*, reel 11 (my translation).

45. Pompilus, *Louis Joseph Janvier par lui-même*, 20 (my translation).

46. Janvier, *L'égalité des races*, 19–20.

47. Ibid., 22–26.

48. Price, *De la rehabilitation de la race noire*, iii (my translation).

49. Ibid., iii–iv (my translation).

50. Brown, *The Black Man*, 1.

51. Ibid., 1–2.

52. Ibid., 56.

53. Ibid., 131.

54. Ibid., 105.

55. Du Bois, "The Conservation of Races," in *A Reader*, 22.

56. Du Bois, "Races," *Crisis*, 2 August 1911, 157.

57. Du Bois, "The Negro American at Paris," in *Writings in Periodicals*, 88.

58. Sydney Tobin, "Carlos Delarge," in *Dictionary of American Negro Biography*, 172; Christopher, *Black Americans in Congress*, 97–100.

59. Tobin, *Dictionary of American Negro Biography*, 512; Christopher, *Black Americans in Congress*, 100–103.

60. *Congressional Record*, 43rd Cong., 2nd Sess., vol. 2, 4782.

61. Ibid., 4786.

62. Desdunes, *Our People and Our History,* 142–43.

63. Logan and Winston, *Dictionary of American Negro Biography,* 497–98.

64. *Afro-American Encyclopedia,* vol. 7, 2044.

65. *African American Encyclopedia,* 1160–61.

66. "The Niagara Movement," in *Du Bois: A Reader,* 367.

67. *African American Encyclopedia,* vol. 5, 1140–42.

68. Martin, *Pan-African Connection,* 203.

69. Ibid., 208.

70. Sherwood, *Oblates' Hundred and One Years,* 135.

71. Ibid., 147–48.

72. Ibid., 239.

73. Meier, *Negro Thought in America,* 87.

74. Harlan, "A Sunday Evening Talk," 480–81.

75. Ibid., 481.

76. Harlan, *The Booker T. Washington Papers,* vol. 5, 180–81.

77. Magloire, *Etude sur le temperament haitien,* 7 (my translation).

78. Ibid., 10–11 (my translation).

79. Féquière, *L'éducation haitienne,* 118 (my translation).

80. Price-Mars, *Ainsi parla l'oncle,* 19–20.

81. Firmin, *Les lettres de Saint-Thomas,* 285.

82. Cited in Magloire, *Etude sur le temperament haitien,* 196.

83. Bellegarde, *Pour une Haiti heureuse,* vol. 1, 86.

84. Meier, *Negro Thought in America,* 168.

85. Du Bois, *Souls of Black Folks,* 246.

86. Ibid., 283–284.

87. Du Bois, "The Present Leadership of American Negroes," in *A Reader,* 354.

88. Firmin, *Les lettres de Saint-Thomas,* 212 (my translation).

89. Du Bois to Patterson, 6 January 1947, in Aptheker, *Correspondence,* 132.

90. Du Bois, *Souls of Black Folks,* 240.

Chapter 5. The Struggle Against a Racist Occupation, 1915–34

1. Holly, "Thoughts on Hayti," 187.

2. Bassett, "Should Haiti Be Annexed to the United States," *Voice of the Negro,* 191–98. See also Firmin, *M. Roosevelt et la république d'Haiti,* 472.

3. U.S. Senate, *Hearings before a Select Committee on Haiti and Santo Domingo,* 322.

4. Ibid., 309.

5. *Crisis* 20 (May 1920): 34.

6. Plummer, "The Afro-American Response," 125. See also Levy, *James Weldon Johnson,* 202.

7. Du Bois, *Correspondence 1905–1920,* vol. 1, 263. See also Du Bois, *The Autobiography,* 65–70.

8. *Crisis* 10 (October 1915): 291.

9. Du Bois, *Correspondence*, 211–12.

10. Washington, "Dr. Booker T. Washington on the American Occupation of Haiti," *New York Age*, 18 October 1915.

11. *Outlook*, 17 November 1915, 681. See also *Independent*, 13 March 1916, 369.

12. Jackson to Wilson, 12 July 1915, Records of the Dept. of State, file 838.52/4.

13. Perry to Wilson, 10 July 1915, Records of the Dept. of State, file 838.55/3.

14. Villard to Lansing, 3 September 1915, Records of the Dept. of State, file 838.007/1364.

15. Fanon, *Black Skin, White Masks*, 157.

16. Records of the Dept. of State, 7 September 1915, file 838.55.

17. Records of the Dept. of State, 10 December 1915, file 838.55/2.

18. "Restoring a Republic," *World's Work* 30, no. 623 (15 October 1915): 633.

19. Marvin, "Healthy Haiti," 40–43.

20. Schmidt, *United States Occupation of Haiti*, 102.

21. U.S. Senate, *Hearings*, 1749–50.

22. Craige, *Black Bagdad*, 240–41.

23. U.S. Senate, *Hearings*, 1472.

24. Price-Mars, *La vocation de l'élite*, 52 (my translation).

25. Danache, *Le président Dartiguenave et les américains*, 68 (my translation).

26. Pressoir, *L'enseignement de l'histoire en Haiti*, 50 (my translation).

27. Johnson, *Along This Way*, 3–4.

28. Johnson, *Self-Determining Haiti*, 19.

29. Johnson to Villard, 28 October 1920, in *Papers of the NAACP*, part 11, reel 8.

30. Johnson, "The Truth about Haiti," 224.

31. Price-Mars to Johnson, 18 October 1920, in *Papers of the NAACP*, part 11, reel 8.

32. Légitime to Johnson, 17 May 1921, in *Papers of the NAACP*, part 11, reel 8.

33. De Reid, *The Negro Immigrant*, 97.

34. Adam to Johnson, 29 September 1920, in *Papers of the NAACP*, part 11, reel 8.

35. Villard to Lansing, 3 September 1915, in *Papers of the NAACP*, part 11, reel 8.

36. Scott to McCormick, 23 June 1922, in *Papers of the NAACP*, part 11, reel 9.

37. Hurst to Johnson, 4 November 1920, in *Papers of the NAACP*, part 11, reel 8.

38. Hurst to Scott, n.d., in *Papers of the NAACP*, part 11, reel 9.

39. Cobb to Johnson, 16 October 1920, in *Papers of the NAACP*, part 11, reel 8.

40. Moseley to Johnson, 11 November 1920, in *Papers of the NAACP*, part 11, reel 8.

41. Abbot to Johnson, 3 December 1920, in *Papers of the NAACP*, part 11, reel 8.

42. Russell to Knapp, 4 December 1920, Records of the Dept. of State, file 838.00/1738.

43. Johnson to Einstein, 29 October 1920, in *Papers of the NAACP*, part 11, reel 8.

44. Johnson, *Along This Way*, 359.

45. *New York Times,* 18 September 1920, 14.

46. "Says Haitians Approve Our Action," *New York Times,* 6 October 1920, 2.

47. Johnson to Harding, 21 September 1920, in *Papers of the NAACP,* part 11, ' reel 8.

48. Ovington to Harding, 14 October 1920, in *Papers of the NAACP,* part 11, reel 8

49. *New York Times,* 25 October 1920, 12.

50. *New York Times,* 17 October 1929.

51. "Pitiless Publicity for Haiti," *Nation* 111, no. 2885 (6 October 1920): 367.

52. Medill McCormick, "Our Failure in Haiti," *Nation* 111, no. 2891 (1 December 1920): 615.

53. Adam to Johnson, 24 September 1920, in *Papers of the NAACP,* part 11, reel 8.

54. Adam to Johnson, 7 December 1920, in *Papers of the NAACP,* part 11, reel 8.

55. White to Wilson and other editors, 22 September 1920, in *Papers of the NAACP,* part 11, reel 8.

56. White to NAACP branch officers, 28 July 1920 in *Papers of the NAACP,* part 11, reel 8.

57. White to NAACP branch officers, 20 October 1920 in *Papers of the NAACP,* part 11, reel 8.

58. Danache, *Le président Dartiguenave et les américains,* 98.

59. Johnson, *Along This Way,* 347–48.

60. Price-Mars to Johnson, December 1920, in *Papers of the NAACP,* part 11, reel 8.

61. *Eleventh Annual Report of NAACP,* January 1921, 12. See also Sylvain, *Dix années de lutte,* vol. 1, 79.

62. Sylvain, *Dix années de lutte,* vol. 1, 84 (my translation).

63. Pauléus Sannon et al., "Memoir," *Nation* 112, no. 2916 (25 May 1921): 754.

64. *Nation* 112, no. 2916 (25 May 1921): 759.

65. Mirault to Johnson, 12 November 1923; Johnson to Mirault, 11 December 1923; Mirault to Johnson, 27 December 1923, in *Papers of the NAACP,* part 11, reel 8.

66. Sylvain, *Dix années de lutte,* vol. 1, 109 (my translation).

67. U.S. Senate, *Hearings,* 784.

68. *Crisis* 22, no. 6 (October 1921): 247.

69. U.S. Senate, *Hearings,* 152.

70. Sylvain, *Dix années de lutte,* vol. 1, 125 (my translation).

71. Ibid., 14.

72. Schmidt, *United States Occupation of Haiti,* 122.

73. Hughes to Harding, 22 August 1922, Records of the Dept. of State, file 838.4237/17.

74. Russell to Harding, 10 October 1922, Records of the Dept. of State, file 838.42/4237/20.

75. Hughes to Coolidge, 5 October 1922, Records of the Dept. of State, file 838.4237/33.

76. Harding to Hughes, 5 October 1922, Records of the Dept. of State, file 838.4237/33.

77. Munro to White, 7 December 1923, Records of the Dept. of State, file 838.61/58.

78. Hughes to Coolidge, 14 December 1923, Records of the Dept. of State, 838.61/63a

79. Jolibois to Johnson, 20 March 1922, in *Papers of the NAACP,* part 11, reel 9.

80. Johnson to Roosevelt, 16 May 1923, in *Papers of the NAACP,* part 11, reel 9.

81. Du Bois, *Writings in Periodicals Edited by Others,* vol. 2, 156.

82. White to Hurst, 16 December 1929, in *Papers of the NAACP,* part 11, reel 9.

83. NAACP press release, 11 December 1929, in *Papers of the NAACP,* part 11, reel 9.

84. Ibid.

85. White to NAACP branch officers, 12 December 1929, in *Papers of the NAACP,* part 11, reel 9.

86. Records of the Dept. of State, file 838.42–Moton Commission.

87. Johnson to Moton, 12 February 1930, in *Papers of the NAACP,* part 11, reel 9.

88. Records of the Dept. of State, file 838.42–Moton Commission 24.

89. White to Vincent, 19 November 1930, in *Papers of the NAACP,* part 11, reel 9.

90. Press Service of the NAACP, February 1931, in *Papers of the NAACP,* part 11, reel 10.

91. White, "The Present Situation in Haiti," 231–32.

92. Bellegarde, *Appréciations sur un haitien,* 147.

93. *Crisis* 21, no. 6 (April 1926): 295–96.

94. Bellegarde to White, 22 February 1931, in *Papers of the NAACP,* part 11, reel 10 (my translation).

95. Bellegarde to Du Bois, 22 February 1931, in *Papers of the NAACP,* part 11, reel 10 (my translation).

96. Bellegarde to White, 15 August 1931, in *Papers of the NAACP,* part 11, reel 10 (my translation).

97. White et al. to Hoover, 6 October 1931, in *Papers of the NAACP,* part 11, reel 10.

98. White to Bellegarde, 10 September 1932, in *Papers of the NAACP,* part 11, reel 10.

99. Bellegarde to White, 9 September 1932, in *Papers of the NAACP,* part 11, reel 11 (my translation).

100. White to Vincent, 9 October 1933, in *Papers of the NAACP,* part 11, reel 11.

101. Record of White long-distance telephone conversation with Bellegarde, 19 October 1933, in *Papers of the NAACP,* part 11, reel 11.

102. Ibid.

103. White to Vincent, 28 September 1932, in *Papers of the NAACP,* part 11, reel 11.

104. Bellegarde to White, 21 November 1933, in *Papers of the NAACP,* part 11, reel 11 (my translation).

105. *Twenty-fifth NAACP Annual Report* (1934): 39.

106. Letter to Roy Wilkins, *Crisis* 41 (October 1934): 292.

107. *Papers of the NAACP,* part 1, 1909–1950.

Chapter 6. The Rise of Black Consciousness, 1920–40

1. Bracey, Meier, and Rudwick, *Black Nationalism in America,* xliv.

2. Price, *De la rehabilitation de la race noire,* vii.

3. DuBois, in Bracey, Meier, and Rudwick, *Black Nationalism in America,* 261.

4. Locke, *The New Negro,* 3–4.

5. Meier, *Negro Thought in America,* 277.

6. Garvey, "Talk with Afro-West Indians," in *Papers,* vol. 1, 57. See also Franklin, *From Slavery to Freedom,* 489–92; *Negro Almanac,* 292–93.

7. Garvey, *Papers,* vol. 2, 90.

8. Garvey, *Papers,* vol. 2, 496.

9. *Les annales capoises,* 30 October 1924.

10. Russell to Scott, 4 December 1924, Records of the Dept. of State, file 838.00/2060.

11. Du Bois, "Marcus Garvey and the NAACP," in *A Reader,* 343–44.

12. Bronz, *Roots of Negro Racial Consciousness,* 72.

13. McKay, *Home to Harlem,* 132.

14. *New York Herald Tribune,* 1 January 1934.

15. Bearden and Henderson, *Six Black Masters of American Art,* 107–9.

16. Hughes, *I Wonder as I Wander,* 16.

17. Ibid., 21.

18. Ibid., 27.

19. Hughes, *Emperor of Haiti,* 19 and 48.

20. Bontemps and Hughes, *Popo and Fifina,* 44.

21. Hurston, *Tell My Horse,* 113.

22. Ibid., 114.

23. Ibid., 147–51.

24. Ibid., 145.

25. Simpson and Cinéas, "Folk Tales of Haitian Heroes," 176–85. Additional folk tales include Suzanne Comhaire-Sylvain, "Creole Tales from Haiti" (July–September 1937): 207–95.

26. *Negro History Bulletin* 8 (November 1944): 36.

27. Hoffmann, "Francophilia and Cultural Nationalism," 64.

28. Price-Mars, *Ainsi parla l'oncle,* 43–47 (my translation).

29. Ibid., 43–47 (my translation).

30. Ibid., 256–57 (my translation).

31. Garrett, *Renaissance of Haitian Poetry,* 79–80 (my translation).

32. Piquion, *Langston Hughes,* 30.

33. See Roger Galliard's article on Hughes, Roumain, and Guillen in *Le Nouvelliste,* 2 and 25 December 1989.

34. Piquion, *Manuel de négritude,* x.

35. Coulthard, "The French West Indian Background of Negritude," 128–36.

36. Bellegarde to Baldwin, August 1932, in *Papers of the NAACP,* part 11, reel 10.

37. Hurston, *Tell My Horse,* 73.

38. Ibid., 74.

39. Ibid., 76–77.

40. Franklin, *From Slavery to Freedom,* 496.

41. Cobb, *Harlem, Haiti, and Havana,* 74.

42. Hughes, *I Wonder as I Wander,* 28.

43. Hughes, "People Without Shoes," *New Masses* (October 1931).

44. Hughes, *I Wonder as I Wander,* 25.

45. Du Bois, "As the Crow Flies," *Amsterdam News,* 22 June 1940.

46. Cobbs, "Concepts of Blackness," 262.

47. Kesteloot, *Anthologie negro-africaine,* 7 (my translation).

48. Berry, *Langston Hughes,* 210.

49. Roumain, *Masters of the Dew,* 47–48.

50. Cobb, *Harlem, Haiti, and Havana,* 102.

51. Cook, "Trends in Recent Haitian Literature," 230. See also Garrett, *Renaissance of Haitian Poetry,* 84–85.

52. Collins, *Black Poets in French,* 63–67.

53. Yeargan to Roosevelt, 9 December 1937, in *Papers of the NAACP,* part 14, reel 8.

54. Welles to White, 31 December 1937, in *Papers of the NAACP,* part 14, reel 8.

55. Crump to White, 16 December 1941, in *Papers of the NAACP,* part 11, reel 7.

56. Press release of the NAACP, 3 October 1941, in *Papers of the NAACP,* part 11, reel 7.

57. Du Bois to Walter White, 12 August 1944 in *Correspondence of W. E. B. Du Bois,* vol. 2, 417.

58. Aptheker, *Newspaper Columns by W. E. B. DuBois,* 608.

59. Aptheker, *Writing by W. E. B. Du Bois,* vol. 1.3, 201 (my translation).

60. Aptheker, *Newspaper Columns,* 304.

61. Ibid.

62. Locke, *Le rôle du nègre dans la culture des Amériques,* 23–24 (my translation).

63. Locke, *Le rôle,* 71.

64. Cited in Bellegarde, *Appréciations sur un haitien,* 19 (my translation).

Chapter 7. Promoting Human Rights and Economic Development, 1940–56

1. White to Magloire, 18 May 1950, in *Papers of the NAACP,* part 14, reel 8.

2. White to Magloire, 9 June 1950, in *Papers of the NAACP,* part 14, reel 18.

3. Trouillot, *Haiti: State Against Nation,* 133; Paquin, *Les haitiens,* 86.

4. Rayford Logan, "Haiti Revolt Traditional," *Pittsburgh Courier,* 19 January 1946.

5. Raymond Pace Alexander, "Haiti Wants to Be a Good Neighbor of United States," *Pittsburgh Courier,* 4 May 1946.

6. *Pittsburgh Courier* (national edition), 6 April 1946.

7. *Pittsburgh Courier*, 24 August 1946.

8. White to Charles regarding "Public Relations Campaign for Haiti," December 1947, in *Papers of the NAACP*, part 11, reel 7.

9. Ibid.

10. Ibid.

11. Charles to White, 17 December 1947, in *Papers of the NAACP*, part 11, reel 7.

12. White to Truman, 5 February 1947, in *Papers of the NAACP*, part 14, reel 7.

13. Ibid.

14. Charles to White, 10 February 1947, in *Papers of the NAACP*, part 14, reel 7 (my translation).

15. Haitian senate to White, 7 March 1947, in *Papers of the NAACP*, part 14, reel 7.

16. Marshall to Hughes, 22 March 1924, National Archives Decimal file 838.40/ orig.

17. René Piquion and Jean F. Brierre, *Marian Anderson* (Port-au-Prince: Henri Deschamps, n.d.), 12.

18. Ku, *A Comprehensive Handbook of the United Nations*, vol. 2, 705.

19. *Color* (April 1951): 19.

20. White to Magloire, 10 May 1950, in *Papers of the NAACP*, part 14, reel 8.

21. Magloire to White, 12 June 1950, in *Papers of the NAACP*, part 14, reel 8.

22. *Papers of the NAACP*, part 14, reel 8.

23. Bouchereau to White, 10 October 1950, in *Papers of the NAACP*, part 14, reel 8.

24. Baldwin to White, 16 October 1951, in *Papers of the NAACP*, part 14, reel 8.

25. Fouché to White, 3 November 1951, in *Papers of the NAACP*, part 14, reel 8.

26. White to Curtis, 19 July 1951, in *Papers of the NAACP*, part 14, reel 8.

27. Chauvet to White, 20 July 1951, in *Papers of the NAACP*, part 14, reel 8.

28. White to Curtis, 13 July 1951, in *Papers of the NAACP*, part 14, reel 8.

29. Chauvet to White, 16 July 1951, in *Papers of the NAACP*, part 14, reel 8.

30. White to Chauvet, 18 July 1951, in *Papers of the NAACP*, part 14, reel 8.

31. Chauvet to White, 20 July 1951, in *Papers of the NAACP*, part 14, reel 8.

32. King, *Stride Toward Freedom*, 456.

33. Ibid., 483.

34. White to Acheson, 25 August 1951, in *Papers of the NAACP*, part 14, reel 8.

35. NAACP press release of 21 November 1951, in *Papers of the NAACP*, part 14, reel 8.

36. Cannon to Fouché, 6 September 1951, in *Papers of the NAACP*, part 14, reel 7.

37. Hepburn, "President Magloire: Can He Pull Haiti Out of Trouble?" 17–18.

38. White to Davis, 10 April 1953, in *Papers of the NAACP*, part 14, reel 8.

39. NAACP press release, 8 September 1952, in *Papers of the NAACP*, part 14, reel 7.

40. Baldwin to Magloire, 4 February 1953, in *Papers of the NAACP*, part 14, reel 8.

41. White to Baldwin, 10 February 1953, in *Papers of the NAACP,* part 14, reel 8.

42. White to Magloire, June 1953, in *Papers of the NAACP,* part 14, reel 8.

43. Magloire to White, 28 September 1951, in *Papers of the NAACP,* part 14, reel 8.

44. White to Acheson, 25 August 1951, in *Papers of the NAACP,* part 14, reel 8.

45. White to Murrow, 4 May 1953, in *Papers of the NAACP,* part 14, reel 8.

46. White to Fouché, 20 February 1952, in *Papers of the NAACP,* part 14, reel 8.

47. White to Dulles, 26 April 1953, in *Papers of the NAACP,* part 14, reel 8.

48. White to Magloire, 1 January 1955, in *Papers of the NAACP,* part 14, reel 8.

49. Magloire to White, 26 February 1955, in *Papers of the NAACP,* part 14, reel 8 (my translation).

50. White to Zephirin, 20 March 1953, in *Papers of the NAACP,* part 14, reel 8.

51. "The Negro's Oldest Government Celebrates 150th Anniversary," in *Color,* April 1954, 54–57.

52. White to Gorman, 24 December 1953, in *Papers of the NAACP,* part 14, reel 8.

53. "World's Greatest Negro Monuments," in *Color* (April 1954): 54.

54. White and Tobias to Magloire, 12 December 1953, in *Papers of the NAACP,* part 14, reel 8.

55. Trouillot, *Haiti: State Against Nation,* 148.

Chapter 8. Managing the Haitian Political Quagmire, 1957–2000

1. Walter Fauntroy, "Demonstration Remarks."

2. Anglade, *Espace et liberté en Haiti,* 43 (my translation).

3. Eural, "Haiti's Challenge to America," 30.

4. *New York Age,* 10 January 1959.

5. *New York Age,* 31 January 1959.

6. Rotberg, *Haiti: The Politics of Squalor,* 204.

7. Laguerre, *Voodoo and Politics,* 100; Diederich and Burt, *Papa Doc et les Tontons Macoutes,* 339–344.

8. Romualdi, "Haiti: Forgotten Dictatorship," 15.

9. Greene, "Nightmare Republic," 19.

10. *Afro-American Baltimore,* 12 October 1957.

11. *Afro-American Baltimore,* 17 May 1958.

12. David Smithers, "Bogeymen and Blackmail," *New York Amsterdam,* 18 August 1962.

13. *New York Age,* 31 January 1959.

14. *Pittsburgh Courier* (New York edition), 10 December 1960.

15. *Pittsburgh Courier* (New York edition), 31 December 1960.

16. *New York Age,* 7 March 1959.

17. *New York Age,* 2 May 1959.

18. *New York Age,* 21 March 1959.

19. David Smithers, "Cursed by Race Hatred," *New York Amsterdam,* 25 April 1962.

20. Smithers, *New York Amsterdam*, 25 August 1962.

21. *New York Age*, 7 March 1959.

22. See editorial "Terrorism in Haiti," in *Afro-American Baltimore*, 17 May 1958.

23. King, *Stride Toward Freedom*, 160.

24. *Pittsburgh Courier*, 8 October 1960.

25. Ibid, 3.

26. Abbott, *Haiti: The Duvaliers and Their Legacy*, 195.

27. Chisholm, "Statement of Freedom."

28. John M. Goshko, "Young Warns Haiti on Human Rights," *Washington Post*, August 16, 1977.

29. *New York Amsterdam*, 6 December 1980.

30. Fauntroy, "United States' Impact." See also "Fauntroy Cautions Haitian Human Rights Violations Will Lead to Halt in Aid," *Jet*, 6 June 1984, 14.

31. Brown, "Memo to Jean-Claude Duvalier," 18.

32. *National Journal*, 1 January 1994.

33. Brooks, "Conditions of Drought in Haiti," 11212.

34. Lawyers' Committee for International Human Rights, "Violations of Human Rights in Haiti," February 1981, 4; Plummer, "Haitian Migrants and Backyard Imperialism," 36–43.

35. Fascell, "Haiti's Participation."

36. Rotberg, *Haiti: The Politics of Squalor*, 243–49.

37. Eilberg, "Haitian Asylum Seekers."

38. *New York Times*, 23 July 1978.

39. Walsh, "The Boat People of South Florida," 420.

40. Gaines-Carter, "Boat People Come Ashore," 21.

41. General Accounting Office, "Detention Policies Affecting Haitian Nationals," 2.

42. Colbert, "Haitian Aliens," 237.

43. Department of State *Bulletin*, August 1980.

44. Brutus to Isham in *Congressional Record-House* 123, pt. 9 (19 April 1977): 11133.

45. Department of State *Bulletin*, August 1980, 78.

46. Jay Ross, "Haitians Win Round on U.S. Asylum," *Washington Post*, 3 July 1980.

47. Colbert, "Haitien Aliens," 238.

48. Fauntroy, "*Statement on Refugee Policy*."

49. Letter to U.S. Immigration and Naturalization Service from "Unhappy Refugees of Enclave VI," quoted in Alex Stepick, *Haitian Refugees Minority Report*, no 52, 4.

50. General Accounting Office, "Detention Policies," 2.

51. Chisholm, "Haitian Refugees."

52. Leland, "Haitian Refugee Problem."

53. Chisholm, "Haitian Refugee Problem."

54. Fauntroy, "Statement on Refugee Policy."

55. William French Smith, "The Reagan Administration Proposal," testimony before Joint Session of House and Senate Immigration Subcommittee, 30 July 1981.

56. "Coast Guard Intercepts Boat Bearing Haitians," *Washington Post*, 26 October 1981.

57. Chisholm, "Statement of Freedom," 30733–36.

58. Miller, *Plight of Haitian Refugees*, 96.

59. "Resolution Adopted by the NAACP Board of Directors, 14 April 1980," *Crisis*, August–September 1980, 233.

60. *Crisis*, December 1981, 504.

61. *Congressional Record*, 14 December 1981: 31287.

62. *Washington Post*, 20 April 1980.

63. Johnson, "Bound for Atlanta," 23.

64. Farmer, *AIDS and Accusation: Haiti and the Geography of Blame* 2; *Jet*, 5 September 1983, 8; *Black Enterprise*, December 1983, 24.

65. "Haitians Say Tourism Off Because of AIDS Scare," *Jet*, 5 September 1983, 8.

66. Cinéas, "Letter to the Editor," 668.

67. *Black Enterprise*, 24; Cinéas, "Letter to the Editor," 668–69.

68. "Haiti: An Impossible Democracy," *Institute For European–Latin American Relations*, May 1992.

69. "Haiti: The Human Rights Tragedy—Human Rights Violations Since the Coup," in *Congressional Record-Extension Remarks*, Microfiche, 138, pt. 6: S1114.

70. *Institute For European–Latin American Relations*, 35.

71. "Jackson, Rangel Visit Haitian Refugees at U.S. Naval Base and Request Asylum for Them," in *Jet*, 23 December 1991, 6–8.

72. Thompson, "The Disturbing Turmoil in Haiti," 23.

73. Wheat, "*Haitian Refugees*," E823.

74. *Congressional Record-House* 138, pt. 3 (26 February 1992): 3495–96.

75. Hooks, publisher's foreword, 3.

76. "Dance Legend Katherine Dunham Ended Her Hunger Strike for the People of Haiti," in *Congressional Record-Extensions of Remarks* (27 March 1992): E847–48; Wilson, "The *Crisis* 1992 Woman of Courage Katherine Dunham," 26–28.

77. *Jet*, 2 May 1994, 5–6; "Churches Keep Pressure on U.S. Haiti Policy," *Christian Century*, 18–25 May 1994, 521–22.

78. *Haiti: An Impossible Democracy*, 14–15.

79. Fauriol, *Haitian Frustrations*, 207–8.

80. *Congressional Record-House* 139, pt. 9 (14 June 1993): H3505.

81. *U.S. News and World Report*, 9 May 1994; Lowry, "The Robinson Hoods," 22–24.

82. William Gray's interview with *Daily News* as reprinted in *Haiti Observateur*, 25 July 1994.

83. Fauntroy to Clinton, *Congressional Record-Extension of Remarks* 140, pt. 18. (29 September 1994): E1987.

84. "General Colin Powell Plays Key Role in Solving Impasse in Haiti," *Jet* 3 October 1994, 4–5.

85. Fauntroy to Clinton, 19 September 1994, 141.

86. Danticat, "Let My People Go," 124.

Epilogue: The Ongoing Struggle

1. Lundahl, "Roots of Haitian Underdevelopment," 181–82.

2. *World Almanac* (1997), 377. Williamson, *New People*, 187.

3. Smedley, *Race in North America*, 8–9.

4. Zéphir, *Haitian Immigrants in Black America*, 44–67. Laguerre, *Diasporic Citizenship*, 112–41.

5. Zéphir, *Haitians in Black America*, 91.

6. Dunham, *Island Possessed*, 6.

7. Williamson, *New People*, 24.

8. Quoted in *Public Interest*, summer 1992.

9. Ridgeway, *The Haiti Files*, 27.

10. Ako, "Leslie Pinckeney Hill's Toussaint L'Ouverture," 190–95.

11. Cook, "Review," 390.

12. Barrett, *Soul-Force*, 2.

13. King, *Strength to Love*, 89.

Bibliography

Primary Sources

Black Abolitionist Papers. Edited by George E. Carter and C. Peter Ripley. Sanford, N.C.: Microfilming Corporation of America, 1981.

Brooks, Edward (Mass.). "Conditions of Drought in Haiti." *Congressional Record—Senate*. 19 April 1977. Vol. 123, pt. 9: 11212. 95th Cong., 1st sess.

Chisholm, Shirley (N.Y.). "The Haitian Refugee Problem." *Congressional Record—House*. 20 December 1979. Vol. 125, pt. 28: 37262–66. 96th Cong. 1st sess.

———. "Haitian Refugees." *Congressional Record—House*. 25 October 1979. Vol. 125, pt. 23: 29703. 96th Cong., 1st sess.

———. "Statement of Freedom for the International Human Rights Day." *Congressional Record—House*. 10 December 1981. Vol. 127, pt. 23: 30733–36. 97th Cong., 1st sess.

Department of State. *Diplomatic Instructions of the Department of State, 1801–1906*. Haiti and Santo Domingo Microform (18 July 1862–9 August 1906). Washington, D.C.: National Archives and Records Service, General Services Administration, 1946.

———. *Diplomatic Instructions of the Department of State, 1820–1825*. Wilmington, Del.: Scholarly Resources, n.d.

———. *Dispatches from United States Consuls in Aux Cayes, 1797–1869*. Washington, D.C.: National Archives and Records Service, General Services Administration, 1959.

———. *Dispatches from United States Consuls in Cap Haitien, 1797–1906*. Washington, D.C.: National Archives and Records Service, General Services Administration, 1942–61.

———. *Dispatches from United States Consuls in Port-au-Prince, 1835–1906*. Washington, D.C.: National Archives and Records Service, General Services Administration, 1960–62.

———. *Notes to Foreign Legations in the United States from the Department of State, 1834–1906*. Haiti and the Dominican Republic Microform (18 September 1866–13 July 1906). Washington, D.C.: National Archives and Records Service, General Services Administration, 1963.

———. *Records of the Department of State relating to political relations between the United States and Haiti, 1910–29.* Washington, D.C.: National Archives and Records Service, General Services Administration, 1965.

———. *Records of the State Department relating to internal affairs of Haiti, 1910–1929.* Washington, D.C.: National Archives and Records Service, General Services Administration, 1970.

———. *Records of the U.S. Department of State relating to political relations between the United States and Latin America and the Caribbean States.* Wilmington, Del.: Scholarly Resources, 1988.

———. *Records of the U.S. Department of State relating to political relations of Latin America and the Caribbean States, 1930–1944.* Wilmington, Del.: Scholarly Resources, 1988.

Douglass, Frederick. Papers. Library of Congress, Photoduplication Service, Washington, D.C., 1974.

Douglass, Frederick. Papers, 1841–1846. Vol. 1. Edited by John W. Blassingame. New Haven, Conn.: Yale University Press, 1979.

Eilberg, Joshua (Pa.). "Haitian Asylum Seekers." *Congressional Record*—House. 8 August 1979. Vol. 124, pt. 18:24925. 96th Cong., 1st sess.

Fascell, Dante (Fla.). "Haiti's Participation in the American Revolution." *Congressional Record*—House. 20 July 1976. Vol. 122, pt. 18:22930. 94th Cong., 2nd sess.

Fauntroy, Walter (D.C.). "Demonstration Remarks." *Congressional Record*—House. 14 December 1981. Vol. 127, pt. 24:31238. 97th Cong., 1st sess.

———. "Statement on Refugee Policy: The Situation of Haitian Refugees." *Congressional Record*—House. 4 June 1980. Vol. 126, pt. 10:13255–6. 96th Cong., 2nd sess.

———. "The United States Impact on Haiti and the Haitian Refugees." *Congressional Record*—House. 24 June 1980. Vol. 126, pt. 13:16630. 96th Cong., 2nd sess.

Holly, James Theodore. Haiti Papers. Archives of the Episcopal Church, Austin, Tex.

Inter-American Commission on Human Rights. *Reports on the Haitian Situation.* Washington, D.C.: Pan American Union, 1963.

———. *Reports on the Situation Regarding Human Rights in Haiti.* Washington, D.C.: Pan American Union, 1963.

Lawyers Committee for International Human Rights. *Violations of Human Rights in Haiti: A Report to the United Nations Commission on Human Rights.* New York, 1981.

Leland, Mickey (Tex.). "The Haitian Refugee Problem." *Congressional Record*—House. 20 December 1979. Vol. 125, pt. 28:37262. 96th Cong., 1st sess.

Marcus Garvey and the Universal Negro Improvement Association Papers. Vol. 2. Edited by Robert A. Hill. Berkeley: University of California Press, 1983.

Organization of American States. *Reports on the Situation of Human Rights in Haiti.* Washington, D.C.: General Secretariat, Organization of American States, 1990.

Papers of Booker T. Washington. Edited by Louis R. Harlan. Urbana: University of Illinois Press, 1972.

Papers of the NAACP. Parts 1, 11, and 14. Edited by John H. Bracey Jr. and August Meier. Frederick, Md.: University Publications of America, 1982.

President's Commission for the Study and Review of Conditions in the Republic of Haiti. *Report.* Washington, D.C., 1930.

U.S. Commission on Education in Haiti, 1 October 1930. *Report.* Washington, D.C., 1930.

U.S. General Accounting Office. *Detention Policies Affecting Haitian Nationals.* Washington, D.C., 1983.

U.S. Senate. *Hearings before a Select Committee on Haiti and Santo Domingo.* Washington, D.C., 1922.

Wheat, Alan (Mo.). "Haitian Refugees." *Congressional Record*—House—Extensions of Remarks. 25 March 1992. Vol. 138, pt. 5:6906. 102nd Cong., 2nd sess.

Secondary Sources

Ako, Edward. "Leslie Pinckeney Hill's Toussaint L'Ouverture." *Phylon* (Fall 1987): 190–95.

Albanese, Catherine L. *America: Religions and Religion.* Belmont, Calif.: Wadsworth, 1992.

Anglade, Georges. *Espace et liberté en Haiti.* Montreal: Centre de recherches caraibes de l'université de Montréal, 1982.

Aptheker, Herbert. *American Negro Slave Revolts.* New York: International Publishers, 1952.

————. *A Documentary History of the Negro People in the United States.* New York: Citadel Press, 1969.

————. *Writings by W. E. B. Du Bois in 1883–1944.* Milwood, N.Y.: Krauss-Thompson, 1986.

Asante, Molefi Kete. *Afrocentricity.* Trenton, N.J.: Africa World Press, 1991.

Aurora, Vermont. "Haitien Independence." *Genius of Universal Emancipation* and *Baltimore Courier,* 1 September 1825, 20.

Baldwin, James. *Notes of a Native Son.* New York: Bantam, 1955.

Barrett, Leonard. *Soul-Force: African Heritage in Afro-American Religion.* New York: Doubleday, 1974.

Barskett, James. *History of the Island of St. Domingo.* Westport, Conn.: Negro Universities Press, 1971.

Basset, E. D. "Should Haiti Be Annexed to the United States?" *Voice of the Negro* 1 (May 1904): 191–98.

Bauer, J. E. "International Repercussions of the Haitian Revolution." *The Americas* (April 1970): 394–418.

Beard, John Relly. *Toussaint Louverture: A Biography and Autobiography.* 1863. Reprint, Freeport, N.Y.: Books for Libraries Press, 1971.

Bearden, Romare, and Harry Henderson. *Six Black Masters of American Art.* New York: Zenith Books, 1972.

Bell, Howard. *Black Separatism and the Caribbean, 1860.* Ann Arbor: University of Michigan Press, 1970.

————, ed. *Minutes of the Proceedings of the National Negro Conventions, 1830–1864,* New York: Arno Press, 1969.

Bellegarde, Dantès. *Appréciations sur un haitien.* Port-au-Prince: Imprimerie Théodore, 1962.

————. *La nation haitienne.* Paris: J. de Gigord, 1938.

Berlin, Ira, ed. "After Nat Turner: A Letter from the North." *Journal of Negro History* 55 (1970): 394–418.

————. "The Structure of the Free Negro Caste in the Antebellum United States." *Journal of Social History* 9, no. 3 (May 1976): 297–318.

Berry, Faith. *Langston Hughes: Before and Beyond Harlem.* Westport, Conn.: Lawrence Hill and Co., 1983.

Bird, M. B. *The Black Man or Haytian Independence.* 1886. Reprint, Freeport, N.Y.: Books for Libraries Press, 1971.

Bodin, Ron. *Voodoo Past and Present.* Lafayette, La.: University of Southwestern Louisiana, 1990.

Bontemps, Arna. *Free at Last: The Life of Frederick Douglass.* New York: Dodd, Mead & Co., 1971.

Bontemps, Arna, and Langston Hughes. *Popo and Fifina.* 1932. Reprint, New York/Oxford: Oxford University Press, 1993.

Bowers, John C. "How Can It Be Abolished." *Weekly Anglo-African,* 20 April 1861 in *Black Abolitionist Papers,* reel 13.

Bracey, John H., Jr., August Meier, and Elliott Rudwick, eds. *Black Nationalism in America.* Indianapolis and New York: Bobbs-Merrill Company, 1970.

————. *Free Blacks in America, 1800–1860.* Belmont, Calif.: Wadsworth, 1971.

Brantley, Daniel. "Black Diplomacy and Frederick Douglass' Caribbean Experiences, 1871 and 1889–1891: The Untold Story." *Phylon* 45, no. 3 (September 1984): 197–209.

Brasseaux, C. A., and C. Glenn. *The Road to Louisiana: The St. Domingue Refugees, 1792–1809.* Lafayette, La.: Center for Louisiana Studies, University of Southwestern Louisiana, 1992.

Bronz, Stephen H. *Roots of Negro Racial Consciousness, the 1920s: Three Harlem Renaissance Authors.* New York: Libra Publishers, 1964.

Brown, Jonathan. *The History and Present Condition of St. Domingo.* 1837. Reprint, London: Frank Cass and Company, 1972.

Brown, Norma, ed. *A Black Diplomat in Haiti: The Diplomatic Correspondence of U.S. Minister Frederick Douglass from Haiti, 1889–1891.* Vol. 1. Salisbury, N.C.: Documentary Publications, 1977.

Brown, Ronald H. "Memo to Jean-Claude Duvalier." *Harper's,* February 1994, 18.

Brown, William Wells. *The Black Man: His Antecedents, His Genius, and His Achievements.* 1863. Reprint, New York: Kraus Reprint Co., 1969.

——. *The Rising Son; or the Antecedents and Advancement of the Colored Race.* 1874. Reprint, Miami, Fla.: Mnemosyne Publishing, 1969.

Carroll, Joseph C. *Slave Insurrections in the United States, 1800–1865.* New York: Negro Universities Press, 1968.

Chace, William M., and Peter Collier, eds. *Justice Denied.* New York: Harcourt, Brace and World, 1970.

Childs, Frances Sargent. *French Refugee Life in the United States, 1790–1800.* Baltimore, Md.: Johns Hopkins University Press, 1940.

Christopher, Maurine. *Black Americans in Congress.* New York: Thomas Y. Crowell Company, 1976.

Cinéas, Fritz. Letter to the Editor, *New England Journal of Medicine* (15 September 1983): 668–69.

Cobb, Martha. "Concepts of Blackness in the Poetry of Nicolas Guillen, Jacques Roumain and Langston Hughes." *CLA Journal* 18 (December 1974): 262–72.

——. *Harlem, Haiti and Havana.* Washington, D.C.: Three Continents, 1979.

Colbert, Lois. "Haitian Aliens—A People in Limbo." *The Crisis,* August–September 1980, 235–38.

Cole, Hubert. *Henri Christophe, King of Haiti.* New York: Viking Press, 1967.

Collier's Encyclopedia. Vol. 3. New York: Collier's, 1995.

Collins, Marie. *Black Poets in French.* New York: Charles Scribner's Sons, 1972.

Cook, Mercer. "Books and Race." *Phylon* 1 (4th qtr., 1940): 390–91.

——. "Trends in Recent Haitian Literature." *Journal of Negro History* 32, no. 2 (April 1947): 225–31.

Cooke, Jacob E. *Frederic Bancroft, Historian.* Norman: University of Oklahoma Press, 1957.

Cooper, Cecilia. *Twenty Modern Americans.* New York: Harcourt, Brace and Company, 1942.

Coradin, Jean D. *Histoire diplomatique d'Haiti, 1804–1843.* Port-au-Prince: Editions des Antilles, 1988.

Coulthard, G. R. "The French West Indian Background of Negritude." *Caribbean Quarterly* 7, no. 8 (1961): 128–36.

Crummell, Alexander. "Hope for Haiti." *Black Abolitionist Papers,* reel 8.

Danache, B. *Le président Dartiguenave et les américains.* Port-au-Prince: Les Editions Fardin, 1984.

Daniels, Ron. "Embracing the Struggle for Haiti's Self-Determination." *New Pittsburgh Courier,* 23 January 1999.

Danticat, Edwidge. "Let My People Go." *Essence,* July 1994, 124.

Dean, David M. *Defender of the Race: James Theodore Holly, Black Nationalist Bishop.* Boston, Mass.: Lambeth Press, 1979.

Debien, Gabriel. "The Saint-Domingue Refugees in Cuba, 1793–1815." In *Road to*

Louisiana: The Saint-Domingue Refugees, 1792–1809, edited by Carl Brasseaux and Glenn R. Conrad. Lafayette, La.: Center for Louisiana Studies, University of Southwestern Louisiana, 1992.

Delany, Martin Robinson. *The Condition, Elevation, Emigration and Destiny of the Colored People of the United States.* 1852. Reprint, New York: Arno Press and the New York Times, 1968.

Delatour, Leslie. Interview with Howard W. French. "When Neighbors Aren't Friends." *Haiti-Observateur,* 13–20 juillet 1994.

De Reid, Ira. *The Negro Immigrant, 1899–1937.* New York: Columbia University Press, 1939.

Desdunes, L. *Our People and Our History.* Baton Rouge, La.: Louisiana State University Press, 1973.

Desmangles, Leslie G. *The Faces of the Gods: Vodou and Roman Catholicism in Haiti.* Chapel Hill and London: University of North Carolina Press, 1992.

Dewey, Loring D. *Correspondence Relative to Emigration to Haiti of the Free People of Color in the United States Together with Instructions to the Agent Sent Out by President Boyer.* New York: Mahlon Day, 1824.

———. "Independence of Hayti." *Genius of Universal Emancipation* 4 (August 1825): 175.

Diederich, Bernard, and Al Burt. *Papa Doc et les Tontons Macoutes.* Port-au-Prince: Editions Henri Deschamps, 1969.

Douglass, Frederick. "Haiti and the United States." *North American Review* 153, no. 418 (1891): 340.

———. *Narrative of the Life of Frederick Douglass, an American Slave.* New York: Signet Books, 1968.

Du Bois, W. E. B. *Correspondence 1905–1920.* Edited by H. Aptheker. Amherst: University of Massachusetts Press, 1983.

———. *The Negro Church.* Atlanta: Atlanta University Press, 1903.

———. *The Souls of Black Folks.* In *Three Negro Classics.* New York: Avon Books, 1965.

———. *Writings in Periodicals.* Milwood, N.Y.: Krauss-Thompson, 1983.

Ducas, George, ed. *Great Documents of American History.* New York: Praeger Publishers, 1970.

Dunbar-Nelson, Alice. "People of Color in Louisiana." *Journal of Negro History* 1 (October 1916): 361–76.

Dunham, Katherine. *Island Possessed.* Garden City, N.Y.: Doubleday and Company, 1969.

Dupuy, Alex. *Haiti in the World Economy: Class, Race, and Underdevelopment Since 1700.* Boulder, Colo., and London: Westview Press, 1989.

Egerton, Douglass R. *Gabriel Rebellion: The Virginia Slave Conspiracies of 1800 and 1802.* Chapel Hill: University of North Carolina Press, 1993.

Féquière, Fleury. *L'éducation haitienne.* Port-au-Prince: Imprimerie de l'Abeille, 1906.

Firmin, Anténor. *De l'égalité des races humaines.* 1885. Reprint, Port-au-Prince: Editions Panorama, 1968.

———. *M. Roosevelt et la république d'Haiti.* Paris: F. Pichon et Durand-Augias, 1905.

Fishel, Leslie H. Jr., and Benjamin Quarles, eds. *The Negro American: A Documentary History.* Glenview, Ill.: Scott, Foresman and Co., 1967.

Fleury, Féquière. *L'éducation haitienne.* Port-au-Prince: Imprimerie de l'Abeille, 1906.

Foner, Philip S. "John Browne Russwurn: A Document." *Journal of Negro History* 54, no. 4 (October 1969): 393–97.

Foner, Philip S., and George E. Walker, eds. *Proceedings of the Black National and State Conventions, 1865–1900.* Philadelphia: Temple University Press, 1968.

———. *Proceedings of the Black National and State Conventions, 1840–1965.* Philadelphia: Temple University Press, 1979.

Fordham, Monroe. "Nineteenth Century Black Thought in the United States: Some Influences of the Santo Domingo Revolution." *Journal of Black Studies* 6 (December 1975): 115–25.

Franklin, John Hope. *From Slavery to Freedom: A History of Negro Americans.* New York: Vintage Books, 1969.

Frazier, Franklin E. *Black Bourgeoisie.* New York: Free Press, 1965.

Gaines-Carter, Patrice. "Black People Come Ashore." *Black Enterprise,* November 1979, 21–2.

Garnet, Henry Highland. "The Past, Present Condition, and Destiny of the Colored Race." In *The Black Abolitionist Papers,* edited by George E. Carter and Peter Ripley. Reel 4. Microfilm Corporation of America, 1981.

Garrett, Naomi. *The Renaissance of Haitian Poetry.* Paris: Présence Africaine, n.d.

Garrison, William Lloyd. *Thoughts on African Colonization,* edited by W. L. Katz. New York: Arno Press and the New York Times, 1968.

Genovese, Eugene D. *From Rebellion to Revolution: Afro-American Slave Revolts in the Making of the Modern World.* Baton Rouge and London: Louisiana State University Press, 1979.

George, Carol V. R. *Segregated Sabbaths: Richard Allen and the Emergence of Independent Black Churches, 1760–1840.* New York: Oxford University Press, 1973.

Granville, Jonathas. *Biographie: Par son fils Jonathas Granville.* Paris: E. Briere, 1873.

Greene, Graham. "Nightmare Republic." *New Republic,* 16 November 1963, 8–20.

Griggs, Earl Leslie, and Clifford H. Prator, eds. *Henri Christophe and Thomas Clarkson: A Correspondence.* Berkeley and Los Angeles: University of California Press, 1952.

Harvey, William Woodis. *Sketches of Haiti from the Expulsion of the French to the Death of Christophe.* 1827. Reprint, Westport, Conn.: Negro Universities Press, 1971.

Hazzard-Gordon, Katrina. "Afrocentrism in a Multicultural Democracy." *American Visions* 6 (24 August 1991): 21.

Heinl, Nancy. "America's First Black Diplomat." *Foreign Service Journal* 50, no. 8 (August 1973): 20.

Hepburn, David. "President Magloire: Can He Pull Haiti Out of Trouble?" *Our World* 8 (March 1953): 17–18.

Herrin, M. H. *The Creole Aristocracy*. New York: Exposition Press, 1952.

Hirsch, Arnold R., and Joseph Logsdon, eds. *Creole New Orleans*. Baton Rouge: Louisiana State University Press, 1992.

Hoffmann, Leo-François. "Francophilia and Cultural Nationalism." In *Haiti—Today and Tomorrow: An Interdisciplinary Study*, edited by Charles R. Foster and Albert Valdman. Lanham, Md., and London: University Press of America, 1984.

Holland, Frederic May. *Frederick Douglass: The Colored Orator*. 1891. Reprint, New York: Haskell House Publishers, 1969.

Holly, James Theodore. "The Disabilities Under Which That Country Labors." *Anglo-African Magazine* 1 (1859): 218–21.

———. "Emigration as a Means of Removing the National Disabilities of the Haytian People." *Anglo-African Magazine* 1 (1859): 241–43.

———. "The Objects and Method Necessary to a Successful Emigration of the Colored of the United States to Hayti." *Anglo-African Magazine* 1 (1859): 298–300.

———. "Thoughts on Hayti: The Important Position That This Nationality Holds in Relation to the Future Destiny of the Negro Race." *Anglo-African Magazine* 1 (1859): 185–87.

———. "A Vindication of the Capacity of the Negro Race for Self-Government and Civilized Progress as Demonstrated by the Historical Events of the Haytian Revolution." In *Black Separatism and the Caribbean*, edited by Howard Bell. Ann Arbor: University of Michigan Press, 1970.

———. Wrong Conceptions and False Expectations to be Guarded Against by Emigrants to Hayti. *Anglo-African Magazine* 1 (1859): 327–29.

Hooks, Benjamin L. Publisher's foreword, *The Crisis*, March 1992, 3.

Hughes, Langston. *Emperor of Haiti*. In *Black Heroes*, edited by Erroll Hill. New York: Applause Theatre Book Publishers, 1989.

———. *I Wonder as I Wander: An Autobiographical Journey*. New York: Rinehart and Company, 1956.

Hunt, Alfred N. *Haiti's Influence on Antebellum America: Slumbering Volcano in the Caribbean*. Baton Rouge: Louisiana State University Press, 1988.

Hunt, Benjamin S. *Remarks on Hayti as a Place of Settlement for Afric-Americans; and on the Mulatto as a Race for the Tropics*. Philadelphia: T. B. Pugh, 1860.

Hurston, Zora Neale. *Tell My Horse: Voodoo and Life in Haiti and Jamaica*. New York: Harper and Row, 1990.

Irvine, Keith. *The Rise of the Colored Races*. New York: W. W. Norton and Co., 1970.

Jackson, Eural Grant. "Haiti's Challenge to America." *Negro History Bulletin* (October 1957): 22–23, and (November 1957): 30–31.

Jackson, James O'Dell, III. *The Origins of Pan-African Nationalism: Afro-American and Haitian Relations, 1800–1863*. Ann Arbor, Mich.: University Microfilms International, 1976.

James, C. L. R. *Black Jacobins*. New York: Vintage Books, 1963.

———. *Negro Revolt*. London: Race Today Publications, 1985.

Janvier, Louis Joseph. *L'égalité des races*. Paris: Imprimerie G. Rougier et cie., 1884.

Johnson, James Weldon. *Along This Way*. New York: Viking Press, 1935.

———. *Self-Determining Haiti*. New York: The Nation, 1920.

Johnson, Julie Williams. "Bound for Atlanta." *Black Enterprise*, April 1984, 23.

Johnson, W. B. *Black Savannah, 1788–1864*. Fayetteville: University of Arkansas Press, 1996.

Karier, Clarence J. *Shaping the American Educational State, 1900 to the Present*. New York: Free Press, 1975.

Kesteloot, Lilyan. *Les écrivains noirs de langue française: Renaissance d'une littérature*. Brussels: Les Editions de l'Université de Bruxelles, n.d.

King, Martin Luther, Jr. *Stride Toward Freedom*. In *A Testament of Hope*, edited by James M. Washington. New York: HarperCollins Publishers, 1991.

Korngold, Ralph. *Citizen Toussaint*. 1944. Reprint, New York: Hill and Wang, 1965.

Ku, Chin-Chuan. *A Comprehensive Handbook of the United Nations*. Vol. 2. New York: Monarch Press, 1979.

Lachance, Paul. "The 1809 Immigration of Saint-Domingue Refugees in New Orleans: Reception, Integration and Impact." *Louisiana History* 29 (1988): 109–41.

Laguerre, Michel S. *American Odyssey: Haitians in New York City*. Ithaca, N.Y.: Cornell University Press, 1984.

———. *Diasporic Citizenship: Haitian Americans in Transnational America*. New York: St. Martin's Press, 1998.

———. *Voodoo and Politics in Haiti*. London: Macmillan, 1989.

Langston, John Mercer. *From the Virginia Plantation to the National Capitol*. 1884. Reprint, New York: Kraus Reprint, 1969.

———. *The World's Anti-Slavery Movement: Its Heroes, Its Triumphs*. Oberlin, Ohio: Shankland and Harmm, 1858.

Lee, Hannah Farnham. *Memoir of Pierre Toussaint: Born a Slave in St. Domingo*. 1854. Reprint, Westport, Conn.: Negro Universities Press, 1970.

Léon, Rulx. *Propos d'histoire d'Haiti*. Port-au-Prince: Imprimerie de l'Etat, 1945.

Levine, Barry B., ed. *The Caribbean Exodus*. New York: Praeger, 1987.

Levy, Eugene. *James Weldon Johnson: Black Leader, Black Voice*. Chicago and London: University of Chicago Press, 1973.

Lewis, David Levering. *W. E. B. Du Bois: A Reader*. New York: Holt and Co., 1995.

Locke, Alain. *The New Negro*. New York: Arno Press and the New York Times, 1968.

———. *Le rôle du nègre dans la culture des Amériques.* Port-au-Prince: Imprimerie de l'Etat, n.d.

Logan, Rayford W. *The Diplomatic Relations of the United States with Haiti.* New York: Kraus Reprint Co., 1969.

———. "Education in Haiti." *Journal of Negro History* 15 (October 1930): 401–60.

Logan, Rayford W., and Michael R. Winston. *Dictionary of the American Negro Biography.* New York: Norton, 1982.

Lowry, Rich. "The Robinson Hoods." *National Review,* 29 August 1994, 22–23.

Lundahl, Mats. "The Roots of Haitian Underdevelopment." In *Haiti—Today and Tomorrow: An Interdisciplinary Study.* Edited by Charles R. Foster and Albert Valdman. Lanham, Md.: University Press of America, 1984.

Lundy, Benjamin. "Address to the Public." *Genius of Universal Emancipation,* 7th month, 1821, 1.

Mackenzie, Charles. *Notes on Haiti.* 2 vols. 1830. Reprint, London: H. Colbern and R. Bentley, 1971.

Martin, Tony. *Pan-African Connection: From Slavery to Garvey and Beyond.* Dover, Mass.: Majority Press, 1984.

Martin, Waldo E. "Frederick Douglass: Humanist as Race Leader." In *Black Leaders of the Nineteenth Century,* edited by August Meier and Leon Litwack. Urbana and Chicago: University of Illinois Press, 1988.

Marvin, George. "Healthy Haiti: The Changes Accomplished During a Year and a Half of American Administration." *World's Work* 34, no. 1 (May 1917): 40–43.

Matthewson, Tim. "Abraham Bishop, the Rights of Black Men and the American Reaction to the Haitian Revolution." *Journal of Negro History* 67, no. 2 (summer 1982): 151.

Mbiti, John S. *African Religions and Philosophy.* New York: Anchor Books, 1969.

———. *Introduction of African Religion.* New York: Praeger, 1975.

McAdoo, Bill. *Pre-Civil War Black Nationalism.* New York: D. Walker Press, 1983.

McConnell, Roland C. *Negro Troops of Antebellum Louisiana.* Baton Rouge: Louisiana State University Press, 1968.

McKay, Claude. *Home to Harlem.* New York: Pocket Books, 1965.

McKissack, Patricia, and Frederick McKissack. *W. E. B. Du Bois.* New York: Franklin Watts, 1990.

Meinig, D. W. *The Shaping of America: A Geographical Perspective on 500 Years of History.* Vol. 1, *Atlantic America, 1492–1800.* New Haven and London: Yale University Press, 1986.

———. *The Shaping of America: A Geographical Perspective on 500 Years of History.* Vol. 2, *Continental America 1800–1867.* New Haven and London: Yale University Press, 1993.

Métraux, Alfred. *Haiti: Black Peasants and Their Religion.* London: George G. Harrap and Co., 1960.

———. *Voodoo in Haiti.* New York: Oxford University Press, 1959.

Miller, Floyd J. *The Search for a Black Nationality.* Urbana: University of Illinois Press, 1975.

Miller, Jake C. *The Black Presence in American Foreign Affairs.* Washington, D.C.: University Press of America, 1978.

———. *The Plight of Haitian Refugees.* New York: Praeger, 1984.

Montague, Ludwell Lee. *Haiti and the United States.* New York: Russell and Russell, 1961.

Mossell, C. W. *Toussaint Louverture: The Hero of Saint-Domingo or Hayti's Struggle.* Lockfort, N.Y.: Ward and Cobb, 1896.

Nash, G. B. *Forging Freedom: The Formation of Philadelphia's Black Community, 1720–1840.* Cambridge: Harvard University Press, 1988.

Nicholls, David. *From Dessalines to Duvalier.* Cambridge: Cambridge University Press, 1979.

Ott, Thomas. *The Haitian Revolution.* Knoxville: The University Press of Tennessee, 1973.

Padget, James A. "Diplomats to Haiti and Their Diplomacy." *Journal of Negro History* 25 (July 1940): 265–330.

Paquin, Lyonel. *Les haitiens: Politique de classe et de couleur.* Port-au-Prince: Imprimerie Le Natal, 1988.

Payne, Daniel A. *History of the African Methodist Episcopal Church.* 1898. Reprint, New York: Johnson Reprint Corporation, 1968.

Phillips, Wendell. "Eulogy of Toussaint Louverture." *Negro History Bulletin* 4 (January 1941): 74.

Piquion, René. *Langston Hughes: Un chant nouveau.* Port-au-Prince: Imprimerie de l'Etat, n.d.

———. *Manuel de négritude.* Port-au-Prince: H. Deschamps, 1966.

Plummer, Brenda Gayle. "The Afro-American Response to the Occupation of Haiti, 1915–1934." *Phylon* 43 (June 1982): 125–43.

———. *Haiti and the Great Powers, 1902–1915.* Baton Rouge and London: Louisiana State University Press, 1988.

———. *Haiti and the United States: The Psychological Moment.* Athens and London: University of Georgia Press, 1992.

———. "Haitian Migrants and Backyard Imperialism." *Race and Class* 26, no. 4 (May 1985): 35–43.

Pompilus, Pradel. *Louis Joseph Janvier par lui-même.* Port-au-Prince: Imprimerie des Antilles, 1976.

Porter, Dorothy B., ed. *Early Negro Writings, 1760–1837.* Boston: Beacon Press, 1971.

Pressoir, Catts. *L'enseignement de l'histoire en Haiti.* Mexico, D.F.: Instituto Panamericano de Geographia, n.d.

———. *Le protestantisme haitien.* 2 vols. Port-au-Prince: Imprimerie Adventiste, 1976.

Price, Hannibal. *De la réhabilitation de la race noire par la république d'Haiti.* Port-au-Prince: Imprimerie T. Verrollot, 1900.

Price, Richard, ed. *Maroon Societies: Rebel Slave Communities in the Americas.* Garden City, N.Y. : Anchor Books, 1973.

Price-Mars, Jean. *Ainsi parla l'oncle.* 1928. Reprint, Ottawa: Lemeac, Collections Caraibes, 1973.

———. *La vocation de l'élite.* Port-au-Prince: Imprimerie Edmond Chenet, 1919.

Redpath, James. *A Guide to Hayti.* 1861. Reprint, Westport, Conn.: Negro Universities Press, 1970.

Ridgeway, James. *The Haiti Files: Decoding the Crisis.* Washington, D.C.: Essential Books, 1994.

Ripley, C. Peter, ed. *The Black Abolitionist Papers.* Vol. 2. Chapel Hill: University of North Carolina Press, 1986.

Rollin, Frank L. *Life and Public Service of Martin R. Delany.* 1868. Reprint, New York: Kraus Reprint Co., 1969.

Romain, Charles-Poisset. *Le protestantisme dans la société haitienne.* Port-au-Prince: Imprimerie Henri Deschamps, 1986.

Romualdi, Serafino. "Haiti: Forgotten Dictatorship." *New Leader,* 18 July 1960, 15–16.

Rotberg, Robert I. *Haiti: the Politics of Squalor.* Boston: Houghton Mifflin Co., 1971.

Roumain, Jacques. *Masters of the Dew.* Translated by Langston Hughes and Mercer Cook. Oxford and Portsmouth, N.H.: Heinemann Educational Publishers, 1978.

Schmidt, Hans. *The United States Occupation of Haiti, 1915–1934.* New Brunswick, N.J.: Rutgers University Press, 1971.

Schoelcher, Victor. *Vie de Toussaint Louverture.* Paris: Editions Karthala, 1982.

Sears, Louis Martin. "Frederick Douglass and the Mission to Haiti, 1889–1891." *Hispanic Historical Review* 21 (May 1941): 222–38.

Seraille, William. "Afro-American Emigration to Haiti During the Civil War." *The Americas* 35 (October 1978): 192–93.

Sherwood, Grace H. *The Oblates' Hundred and One Years.* New York: Macmillan, 1931.

Simpson, George Eaton. *Black Religion in the New World.* New York: Columbia University Press, 1978.

———. *Religious Cults of the Caribbean: Trinidad, Jamaica and Haiti.* Rio Piedras: Institute of Caribbean Studies, University of Puerto Rico, 1980.

Simpson, George, and J. B. Cinéas. "Folk Tales of Haitian Heroes." *Journal of American Folklore* 54 (January–June 1941): 176–85.

Smedley, Audrey. *Race in North America: Origin and Evolution of a Worldview.* Boulder, Colo.: Westview Press, 1993.

Smith, Edward D. *Climbing Jacob's Ladder.* Washington, D.C.: Smithsonian Institution Press, 1988.

Smith, James McCune. *A Lecture on the Haytien Revolutions; with a Sketch of the Character of Toussaint L'Ouverture.* New York: Daniel Fanshaw, 1841.

Smith, Patrick Bellegarde. *Haiti: The Breached Citadel.* Boulder, Colo.: Westview Press, 1990.

——. *In the Shadows of Powers.* Atlantic Highland, N.J.: Humanities Press International, 1985.

Sobel, Mechal. *Trabelin' On: The Slave Journey to an Afro-Baptist Faith.* Princeton, N.J.: Princeton University Press, 1979.

Starobin, Robert S., ed. *Denmark Vesey: The Slave Conspiracy of 1822.* Englewood Cliffs, N.J.: Prentice-Hall, 1970.

Staudenvaus, P. J. *The African Colonization Movement.* New York: Columbia University Press, 1961.

Stepick, Alex. *Haitian Refugees in the United States.* London: Minority Rights Group, 1982.

Sterling, Dorothy. *The Making of an Afro-American: Martin Robinson Delany.* Garden City, N.Y.: Doubleday and Company, 1971.

Steward, Frank Rudolph. "Roosevelt and Haiti." *Voices of the Negro* (June 1906): 434.

Steward, T. G. *The Haitian Revolution.* New York: Thomas Crowell Company Publishers, 1914.

Stewart, Jeffrey C. *The Critical Temper of Alain Locke.* New York: Garland Publishing, 1983.

St. John, Spencer. *Hayti or the Black Republic.* 1884. Reprint, London: Frank Cass and Co., 1971.

St. Méry, Moreau de. *Description de la partie française de St-Domingue.* 1789. Reprint, Paris: Société de l'Histoire des Colonies Françaises, 1958.

Sylvain, George. *Dix années de lutte pour la liberté.* Port-au-Prince: Editions Henri Deschamps, 1950.

Tallant, Robert. *Voodoo in New Orleans.* Gretna, La.: Pelican Publishing Company, 1974.

Thompson, Garland L. "The Disturbing Turmoil in Haiti: What to Do?" *The Crisis,* December 1993, 23.

Thurman, Howard. *Deep River and the Negro Spiritual Speaks of Life and Death.* Richmond, Ind.: Friends United Press, 1975.

Tiffany, Charles C. *A History of the Protestant Episcopal Church in the United States.* New York: Christian Literature Co., 1895.

Trouillot, Hénock. *La guerre de l'independence d'Haiti.* Sobretiro de Revista de historia de America, no. 72 (July–December 1971).

Trouillot, Michel-Rolph. *Haiti, State Against Nation: The Origins and Legacy of Duvalierism.* New York: Monthly Review Press, 1990.

Tyson, George, Jr., ed. *Toussaint L'Ouverture: Great Lives Observed.* Englewood Cliffs, N.J.: Prentice-Hall, 1973.

Walker, David. "Appeal to the Colored Citizens of the World." In *Great Documents in Black American History,* edited by George Ducas. New York: Praeger Publishers, 1970.

Walsh, Bryian O. "The Boat People of South Florida." *America* (May 17, 1980): 420.

Washington, H. A. *The Writings of Thomas Jefferson.* Vol. 4. Washington, D.C.: Taylor and Maury, 1854.

Watkins, William, Jr. "Address." *Genius of Universal Emancipation* 4 (August 1825): 170–71.

White, A. O. "Prince Saunders: An Instance of Social Mobility Among Antebellum New England Blacks." *Journal of Negro History* 60 (October 1975): 526–35.

Williams, Eric. *From Columbus to Castro: The History of the Caribbean.* New York: Vintage Books, 1984.

Williams, George. *History of the Negro Race in America from 1619 to 1880.* 1883. Reprint, New York: Arno Press and the New York Times, 1968.

Williams, Michael W. *The African American Encyclopedia, vol. 6.* New York: Marshall Cavendish Co., 1993.

Williams, Peter. "Discourse in St. Phillip's Church for the Benefit of the Coloured Community of Wilberforce in Upper Canada on Fourth of July 1830." In *Black Abolitionist Papers,* edited by George E. Carter and C. Peter Ripley. Reel 1. Microfilming Corporation of America.

Williamson, Joel. *New People: Miscegenation and Mulattoes in the United States.* Baton Rouge: Louisiana State University Press, 1995.

Wilson, Erasmus. *History of Pittsburgh.* Chicago: H. R. Cornell and Co., 1878.

Wilson, Gloria Dulan. "The *Crisis* 1992 Woman of Courage Katherine Dunham: High Priestess of Protest." *The Crisis,* October 1992, 26–28.

Winch, Julie. *American Free Blacks and Emigration to Haiti.* San German, P.R.: Centro de Investigaciones del Caribe y America Latina, Universidad Interamericana de Puerto Rico, 1988.

———. *Philadelphia's Black Elite: Activism, Accommodation, and the Struggle for Autonomy, 1787–1848.* Philadelphia: Temple University Press, 1988.

Woodson, Carter Godwin. *The Education of the Negro prior to 1861.* New York: Arno Press, 1968.

———. *The History of the Negro Church.* Washington, D.C.: Associated Publishers, 1972.

Zéphir, Flore. *Haitian Immigrants in Black America: A Sociological and Sociolinguistic Portrait.* Westview, Conn.: Bergin and Garvey, 1996.

Index

Leon D. Pamphile is the founder and executive director of the Functional Literary Ministry, providing reading materials and instruction in Haiti. He is the author of *La croix et le glaive: L'église catholique sous l'occupation américaine* (1991), winner of the prize for best book of 1990 from the Historical and Geographical Society of Haiti; and "The NAACP and the American Occupation of Haiti" (1986).